SYSTEMS DEVELOPMENT USING STRUCTURED TECHNIQUES

SYSTEMS DEVELOPMENT USING STRUCTURED TECHNIQUES

Malcolm Bull

London   New York

Chapman and Hall

First published in 1989 by
Chapman and Hall Ltd
11 New Fetter Lane, London EC4P 4EE
Published in the USA by
Chapman and Hall
29 West 35th Street, New York NY 10001

© 1989 Malcolm Bull

Typeset in 10/12 Photina by Thomson Press (India) Limited, New Delhi

Printed in Great Britain by St. Edmunsbury Press,
Bury St. Edmunds, Suffolk

ISBN 0 412 31010 4   (hardback)
     0 412 31020 1   (paperback)

British Library Cataloguing in Publication Data

Bull, Malcolm, 1941-
Systems development using structured techniques.
1. Computer systems. Structured systems analysis
I. Title
004.2'1

ISBN 0-412-31010-4

Library of Congress Cataloging in Publication Data

Bull, Malcolm, 1941-
Systems development using structured techniques / Malcolm Bull.
    p. cm.
Includes index.
ISBN 0-412-31010-4.—ISBN 0-412-31020-1 (pbk.)
1. System design. 2. Electronic data processing—Structured
techniques. I. Title.
QA76.9.S88B85   1989
004.2'1—dc20   89-15883
                                                CIP

72572

Contents

Acknowledgements

A number of people have contributed directly or indirectly to the conception, content and final presentation of this book.

Those who have attended my training courses on any of a number of subjects – systems analysis, systems design, file design, programming or project management – will recognize much of my arguments and lecture material here. Teaching is never a one-way flow, and I must thank all my students, past and present, for their questions and their questioning. Their needs led to the conception of the book.

Special thanks are due to my editor, Elizabeth Johnston of Chapman and Hall, for the unfailing encouragement with which she spurred me on to produce the book you see here. Her ideas and suggestions were helpful throughout and her, albeit daunting, list of changes, and her persistence in implementing them, reduced my original manuscript from a wordy tome on system design theory down to the manageable and, let us hope, practical form which you see here.

My thanks also to Kay Birtles of McDonnell Douglas for her help with PRO IV in the section on fourth generation languages.

Finally, I should like to thank Paul Anstee for his tireless reading, re-reading and proof-reading of the text in its various manifestations.

If, after all this support, there are any omissions or any errors remaining in the book, then the responsibility and blame for these can only be laid at my own door.

Malcolm Bull
Lusaka

Preface

The principle aim of this book is to introduce and illustrate the structured techniques which are available for use during the development of a computer system.

When the book was conceived, it was the author's intention to direct the discussion at those readers who are experienced project leaders, systems analysts and programmers and who, being familiar with traditional methods, now wish to move on to more structured techniques. However, discussion with potential readers – and especially those who have come into systems development via other disciplines – suggested that this scope be widened. As a result, the principles of systems investigation are also considered. The book is suitable for anyone who may be new to systems analysis, including programmers who are making the transition to analysis. It is especially suitable for end-users who are increasingly having to work with systems anaysts practising structured techniques, and who, with the growth in application-oriented tools, and the increasing accessibility of computer systems, now need to play a greater role in the design and development of the computer systems.

Structured techniques were developed for use in the commercial environment, and the book is particularly appropriate in such areas, whether it be used for private study or as a part of a formal training course. It is also suitable for use in the academic setting as supplementary reading for students following Computer Studies and Computer Science courses at schools and colleges, and for those studying first year Information Technology and other computer subjects at university. It will adequately prepare anyone leaving such a course for a career in the commercial computing environment.

Since structured techniques were introduced, the choice of available techniques and methodologies has widened. The present book does not aim to increase this range. Instead, we have tried to strip off much of the jargon and cant which may be encountered, revealing the reasons and the reasoning behind the methodologies. This produces a systems development approach which is valid as an independent methodology and which will also prepare the reader for any more detailed methodology which may be implemented in his or her own working environment.

The book is divided into eight chapters with two interludes:

Chapter 1 introduces the concepts of structured techniques.

Chapter 2 looks at the techniques involved during the preliminary stages of systems investigation.

Chapter 3 looks at the tools and techniques which are available for systems analysis.

Interlude 1 considers the intermediate stage before the systems design phase.

Chapter 4 looks at the tools and techniques which are available for the data analysis stage of the systems design phase.

Chapter 5 looks at the tools and techniques which are available for the functional analysis stage of the systems design phase.

Chapter 6 discusses structured programming and modular programming, and looks at the ways in which these interact with the systems design phase.

Interlude 2 discusses the final stages and we consider the future life of a computer system.

Chapter 7 looks at some of the ways in which systems development is supported by automated tools and techniques. Within this chapter, the reader will find an introduction to a number of the newer aspects of data processing, such as prototyping, database management systems, query languages and fourth generation languages.

Chapter 8 comprises a number of practical projects. The first one is worked and illustrates the points discussed in the main text. The remaining case studies are provided to allow the readers to develop their own solutions.

Finally, there are appendices comprising a short bibliography and a glossary of some of the terms that the reader may encounter in the present book and in the literature of the subject.

Within the audience mentioned above, it is anticipated that:

- project managers will find all sections of interest
- trainee systems analysts and trainee programmers will find all sections of interest
- systems analysts could probably omit Chapter 2 and Interlude 2, but those who are unfamiliar with structured techniques may find the remaining sections of interest
- programmers will find Chapters 4, 5 and 6 of interest
- experienced programmers may wish to omit Chapter 6
- end-users will find all sections of interest if they omit the practical work and the detailed examples, and if they skim those areas which they feel are too technical for them.

For each of the major elements of the analysis and design phases, there is a separate section with a title such as:

Producing the data flow diagram

These sections provide a summary of the guidelines for the preparation of the various tools. Examples of all the documents which are covered in these sections can found in Chapter 8 where we produce the solution to our Case Study.

The book is intended to be practical, and for this reason, many of the arguments for and against the use of structured techniques have been left to more critical authors. With this same intention, the various topics are illustrated by their application to a simple case study. The reader should bear in mind that there is no definitive answer – no right or wrong solution – to systems development problems. In offering a worked case study, we are not implying that ours are the best possible answers – for in data processing, there are only solutions and better solutions and only our fictitious user could arbitrate here. But if we can stimulate the reader to find a better solution, then we have achieved our objective – that of getting the analyst and programmer to use the structured techniques.

Malcolm Bull

List of acronyms

CAD	Computed Aided Design
CAP	Computer Aided Programming
CASA	Computer Aided Systems Analysis
CASD	Computer Aided Systems Design
DBA	Database Administrator
DBMS	Database Management System
DBTG	Data Base Task Group
DDL	Data Description Language
DFD	Data Flow Diagram
DML	Data Manipulation Language
DocFD	Document Flow Diagram
DocFM	Document Flow Matrix
DSD	Data Structure Diagram
1GL	First Generation Language
2GL	Second Generation Language
3GL	Third Generation Language
4GL	Fourth Generation Language
5GL	Fifth Generation Language
1NF	First Normal Form (also FNF)
2NF	Second Normal Form (also SNF)
3NF	Third Normal Form (also TNF)
SSA	Structured Systems Analysis

1
Introduction to structured techniques

General systems theory (GST) applies scientific principles and methods to the study of systems of all kinds, and is able to predict and determine the short-term and the long-term behaviour of systems. The scope of this behaviour includes its day-to-day and its year-to-year operation, its reactions to the outside world and to other systems, and the ways in which it changes, dies and grows. We can define a system as follows:

System: an organized collection of parts, the **sub-systems**, which are linked together so as to function as a unit with a common purpose or objective.

In the present context, we are concerned with business systems, management information systems and computer systems. These, like any other, comprise a number of smaller sub-systems, each of which performs a specific purpose. The operation of the system as a whole is determined and affected by the interaction, the inter-relation, the co-ordination and the co-operation of these various sub-systems. If we take a steel manufacturing company as an example, then systems theory concerns itself with the company's short-term and long-term behaviour, and addresses questions such as:

1. How does the company utilize its resources and how does it react to the outside world – what happens when the world price of steel falls or when the national economy goes up or down?
2. How does its own sub-systems interact – how is the production affected by a shortage of workers, and how is the price affected by the production?

All systems – and sub-systems – are based upon five fundamental activities: input, storage, processing, control and output. Within a system, the output from one sub-system will often be the input to another. The amount of its resources which a system expends on reacting to internal and external stimuli depends upon the particular system. A **closed system** may interact little with the outside world, if at all, so there will be minimal input and output in such a case. This may be because the system is self-sufficient, such as a large country which is able to support itself completely and independently of all other nations.

A business system interacts with the social, commercial and technical facets of its environment and is said to be an **open system**.

It is the systems analyst's task to study a business system or sub-system. The result of the study will be a model, a representation of the current system – with all its good and bad features. This model will then be used as a basis for the design of a new system. This new system may well be implemented as a computer system, and for the purposes of the present book, we shall assume that this is so.

1.1   SYSTEMS DEVELOPMENT

For many years, systems analysis, systems design and programming have been taught in what we might call the traditional manner, with the trainee learning the principles and skills required to perform the various tasks in the development of a computer project. Fig. 1.1 shows the traditional stages of systems development.

In the real world of computers and data processing, it has long been apparent that being able to perform this sequence of operations was not sufficient. The process was not flexible enough. If the users change their minds during the investigation and analysis stages, then the analyst can accommodate these, alterations fairly easily. However, when a project is just beginning, the business ideas are new to the analyst and the computer ideas are new to the user. The future system is quite likely to be based upon the ideas established at this primitive stage, and for this reason these ideas will not be as grand or as comprehensive as they might be.

Furthermore, the existing methods of systems analysis were proving to be too slow, and the time-scales involved meant that, whilst the analyst was producing and correcting the system specification, the users were quite likely to have changed their minds about what they wanted from the system. This may have come about as a result of incomplete understanding about what the system could have done for them, or there may have been organizational and other changes which must be reflected in the computer system.

Frequently, this came about as a result of information and possibilities which the user discovered during his discussions with the analyst, or as a result of pursuing topics raised during such discussions. How many times will the analyst hear the user's cry:

'I didn't know that you could do that.'
'You didn't tell me that I could have had that in my system.'
'Smith-Watsons have got a nice facility . . . and I wondered if . . .'

The user was then faced with the dilemma of either not having the new system do what was really required, or of expending still more money and time in order for the system design to be modified and the changes to be implemented.

It has been estimated that if users change their mind whilst the systems analyst is carrying out the investigation and it costs £1 to make that change, then the same change will cost £10 if it is made when the systems analysis is being performed, £100 if it is made when the systems design phase is being carried out, and so on, rising to a cost of £100 000 to make exactly the same change after the

THE TRADITIONAL PATH OF SYSTEMS DEVELOPMENT

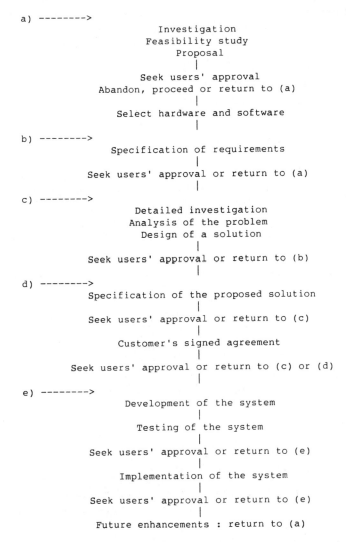

```
a)  -------->
                    Investigation
                  Feasibility study
                      Proposal
                         |
                  Seek users' approval
          Abandon, proceed or return to (a)
                         |
            Select hardware and software
                         |
b)  -------->
              Specification of requirements
                         |
          Seek users' approval or return to (a)
                         |
c)  -------->
                Detailed investigation
                Analysis of the problem
                 Design of a solution
                         |
          Seek users' approval or return to (b)
                         |
d)  -------->
            Specification of the proposed solution
                         |
          Seek users' approval or return to (c)
                         |
              Customer's signed agreement
                         |
        Seek users' approval or return to (c) or (d)
                         |
e)  -------->
                Development of the system
                         |
                 Testing of the system
                         |
          Seek users' approval or return to (e)
                         |
              Implementation of the system
                         |
          Seek users' approval or return to (e)
                         |
          Future enhancements : return to (a)
```

Figure 1.1 The traditional path of systems development.

system has been finally implemented. Obviously, such figures are very approximate, but they do emphasize the escalating costs of making a change later – rather than earlier – in the development cycle.

Even if it is designed and implemented with few modifications, almost every system will be subject to some changes after implementation. We have seen that changes are expensive, and they also have the disadvantage that the associated documentation must be changed to incorporate these changes: the analyst must change the specifications, the programmer must amend the programs, the user documentation must be corrected, and the users may have to be re-trained. In practice, these were not always done adequately.

What was needed was a methodology – a way of analysing, designing and producing systems – a methodology which:

1. would be more responsive to the users' needs
2. would enable systems to be developed more quickly

and if that methodology would also enable systems to be developed more cheaply, and ease the task of system and program maintenance and be easy to learn and apply, then so much the better.

The solutions to some of the problems came in the guise of **structured techniques**. The techniques include **structured systems analysis** and **design** for the analyst, and **structured programming** for the programmer. In this book, we shall present these topics and show how they achieve the goals of modern systems analysis and design. We shall also see what impact these and other techniques have upon the programmer.

The interest in structured techniques is such that several methods and styles have been produced, each with its own advantages and disadvantages. The trainee analyst will meet, amongst others, those of: Codd, DeMarco, Dijkstra, Jackson, Parnas, Warnier and Orr, and Wirth. There are also a large number of acronyms, e.g.:

- HIPO – Hierarchy plus Input Processing and Output
- SASD – Yourdon's Structured Analysis and Structured Design
- SMDM – Systems Modelling Development Method
- SSADM – the structured systems analysis and design methodology which is recommended for use on administrative computer projects undertaken by the British Government
- STRADIS – Structured Analysis, Design and Implementation of Information Systems, a McDonnell Douglas product developed with Gane and Sarson.

The concepts of **software engineering** and **information engineering** have emerged. These are concerned with the application of structured techniques to the production of reliable and maintainable software. A very close parallel can be recognized with the principles which we shall consider here and the processes of design, development, prototyping, production, quality assurance and maintenance which are practised in the field of mechanical engineering.

A number of software packages and computer aided software engineering (CASE) tools will be encountered, such as the PROKIT software and STRADIS/DRAW, the McDonnell Douglas Information Systems graphics software for the Gane and Sarson STRADIS methodology, and the DATAMATE, AUTOMATE, AUTOMATE PLUS and SUPER-MATE software from Learmonth and Burchett Management Systems plc (LBMS).

1.2 OVERVIEW OF STRUCTURED SYSTEMS ANALYSIS

The techniques of systems analysis and design break the analyst's work down into a number of discrete phases. The first phase – systems analysis – requires us to look at the existing system which is to be replaced or modified, or to derive the requirements for a completely new system. A number of tools are available for this:

1. **Document flow diagrams** – these depict the key documents which are associated with the existing system, their source and destination, the flow and the information which they carry;
2. **Data flow diagrams** – these depict the flow of data around the system, the sources and destination of data, the places in which data are stored, and the processes which handle those data;
3. **Data structure diagrams** – these depict the entities about which data are to be held and processed, and show the relationship between these entities;
4. **Problems and requirement list** – this records the shortcomings of the present system, including problems recognized by the user and the analyst and requirements stated by the user. The ultimate solution should endeavour to address all these.

These documents will represent a model of the features of the existing system, whether it be a manual system or a computer-based system.

Like the other documents which we shall produce, these are quite suitable for presentation to the users and allow the results of the analysis to be continually reviewed to ensure that they reflect the true situation.

1.3 OVERVIEW OF STRUCTURED SYSTEMS DESIGN

Before proceeding to the systems design phase, the analyst must stand back and appraise the current system. The first step is to identify the ways in which the existing system could be reorganized so as to achieve some, or all, of the goals established in the problems and requirements list. Up to this point, no decision has been made as to the nature of the future system – indeed, it may not be necessary to implement a computer solution at all if we can reorganize the current working methods and practices.

The analyst will then identify a number of possible solutions which may be provided to achieve the required system. These are presented to the user in a manner which will emphasize the cost effectiveness and the benefits to be gained by the proposed solutions.

If a decision is made to go ahead with a computer-based solution, then the user will choose one – or a combination – of the possible solutions, and the analyst will proceed to design the proposed system around these solutions.

The tools which are available for the systems design phase will describe the features of the proposed system.

1. **Data flow diagrams** – for the proposed system
2. **Data normalization** – this enables the analyst to determine the nature and contents of the data and the physical files which will be used by the system, such that they serve the system efficiently
3. **Data structure diagrams** – for the proposed system based upon the results of the data normalization task
4. **Entity descriptions** – these list the data items contained within each entity or physical file
5. **Entity/function matrix** – this is a chart in which each function in the data flow diagram is cross-referenced to each entity on the data structure diagram, to produce an entity/function matrix. In this way, the analyst can ensure the complete integrity of the data and the processing
6. **Function catalogue** – this accompanies the data flow diagrams and provides a free text description of the processing requirements
7. **Function descriptions** – these specify the detail of the processing requirements of the system and ultimately they will serve as the program specifications
8. **Function maps** – these depict the routes by which the users will access the functions of the system
9. **Module catalogue** – this combines and summarizes the various low-level routines which are shared and used by the functions of the system
10. **Module descriptions** – these give a detailed description of the processing which each module performs
11. **Module maps** – these depict the modules and the functions which use them.

These documents will represent a model of the proposed system. As before, the documents can be reviewed with the user to confirm that they reflect the required situation.

1.4   OVERVIEW OF STRUCTURED PROGRAMMING

It is in the field of programming that structured techniques have had most popular impact. Most programmers will be familiar with the concepts of **structured programming** and **modular programming**. For this reason, we shall only touch lightly upon these topics in the book in order to see how they interact with the products of the systems design phase.

We shall also look at the concept of **prototyping** as this, too, may affect the programmer.

1.5   THE TOP-DOWN APPROACH

One of the valuable features of a structured methodology is the **top-down** approach. This begins by taking a top-level view of a system. When this has been comprehended, the picture can be expanded to get a second-level, more detailed view. The new information at this level is then studied and assimilated. This

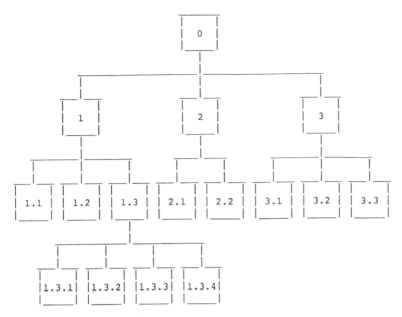

Figure 1.2 A Jackson diagram.

process of refinement is repeated until the complete system has been broken down and the view represents all the details of the system.

A useful device for depicting this process is the tree structure, or Jackson Diagram, shown in Fig. 1.2. Box 0 represents the broad picture of the system with hardly any detail, and might be the detail which you would give if your grandmother were to ask what the system does:

'Oh, it's a computer system to calculate the wages for the people at the carpet factory.'

We might then expand this to a more detailed level – Boxes 1, 2 and 3 – such as you might explain to a fellow analyst:

'They want the system to read in the clock cards, calculate the pay and make up the wages packets.'

Going down to an even-lower level – Boxes 1.1, 1.2 and so on – we go into the detail which would be needed for a programmer who is going to have to write the programs which perform the processing:

'You read in the clock card and calculate the number of hours worked that week. Then you get the personnel number from the card and read the staff record from the Staff file. Then...'

Some of the more complex parts of this – as with Box 1.3, in this illustration – may have to be expanded into even more detail.

We can represent the information in other ways: a Warnier – Orr Diagram would depict it as shown in Fig. 1.3.

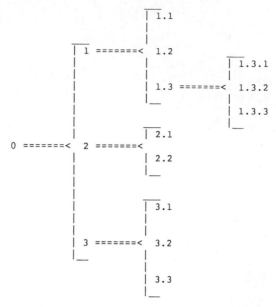

Figure 1.3 A Warnier–Orr diagram.

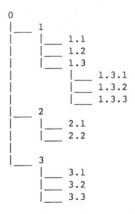

Figure 1.4 A structured list.

A third method, and one which is preferred by the author, is the structured list. This has the advantage that it is does not make too many demands on graphical facilities, and it allows space for annotating, as shown by the examples in Figs 1.4 and 1.5.

Whenever we are faced with a problem – be it analysing a commercial operation, or even writing a book – if we approach the task in such a top-down

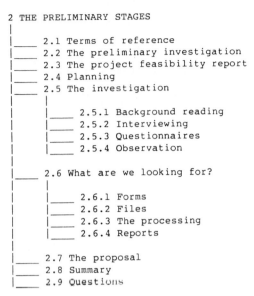

Figure 1.5 A structured list in use.

manner, we reduce it to a series of manageable steps. This makes the work psychologically less daunting, and it makes the whole job much more manageable. By using diagrams such as those shown here, we are also capable of setting the picture down on paper. Fig. 1.5 illustrates this diagramming technique used to develop the contents of Chapter 2.

This renders the structure suitable for appraisal – we can see where we are – and it also enables us to show other people where we are.

When we discuss top-down programming, we shall also mention the reverse, **bottom-up** programming. Fig. 1.6 contrasts the two approaches. A bottom-up approach takes the refined design for a program, such as might be represented by the one of the diagrams above, and concentrates on each low-level step, coding each module, one by one, until the entire program is assembled and complete.

The final systems testing and the implementation may also be accomplished by the bottom-up approach. If we were to consider a system represented by the design shown in Fig. 1.6, bottom-up testing would first look at the low-level modules, N, O, P and Q, individually. When these are correct, they would be integrated and module H would then be tested. This would be repeated until all the lowest-level modules are complete. Testing would then be carried out on the next level up, and so on until the entire system has been tested. By contrast, top-down testing would first test module A, using dummy stub modules to simulate the action of the lower-level modules B, C, D and E. Testing would then be carried out on the next level down, and so on until the entire system has been tested.

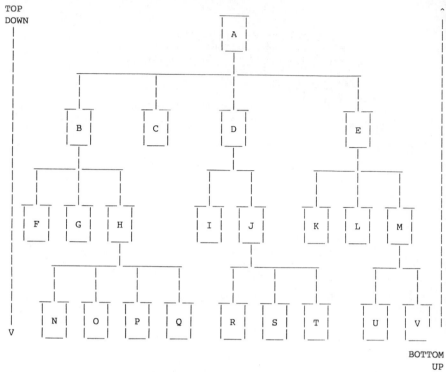

Figure 1.6 Top-down and bottom-up approaches.

1.6   WHY USE A STRUCTURED METHODOLOGY?

Commercial systems analysis and design has been proceeding very well for over thirty years using essentially the same techniques. So what is this new methodology and why do we need a new methodology now? The following points may answer these questions:

- The fundamental top-down approach means that the analyst can readily get an overall grasp of the system – both the processes and the information which is handled. The analyst may then break this picture down into more and more detailed parts as the investigation and analysis proceed. This further means that the analyst need only ask detailed questions during the later stages, at which time the questions become meaningful and the answers become necessary to the analysis. This makes more productive use of time spent with the users.
- Structured techniques avoid the duplication of effort and wasted resources. Only a minimum of paperwork need be produced and this becomes an essential, integral and permanent part of the system documentation. The same documentation can serve as a non-technical representation for users for

review purposes, and also as a detailed technical description for analysts and programmers for development purposes, and as a specification of requirements between the analysts and the data administration personnel during implementation.

- The reduced volume of work means that the overall system development activity is speeded up, and this, in turn, means that the systems become less expensive.

- Structured techniques afford a medium of communication between the users and the data processing staff. Much of the documentation is in the form of diagrams and charts. These are much more intelligible to the non-technical user than are carefully worded system specifications and descriptions, although they still meet the needs of the analysts and programmers.

- By breaking down the tasks – analysis, design and programming – into smaller units, structured techniques allow the analyst or programmer to concentrate on one particular task at a time. This allows the work to be dispersed more easily, encourages clear thinking and results in a simplicity of design and tidiness in the work done, rather than by the production of a single, vast, controlled unit.

- Structured techniques afford a standard method for producing computer systems. A new team member who is familiar with the methods can quickly assimilate and work on any computer system which has been designed and documented using a standard methodology.

- With structured techniques, system maintenance becomes less hazardous. The reduced quantities of documentation are easier to maintain, but more importantly, the standard design and coding approach means that programs themselves are less difficult to understand, amend and maintain.

- Structured methods provide techniques and tools which the analyst and programmer will recognize as useful and practical. They are not doctrinarian sets of inflexible rules, and are quick and easy to learn and apply.

- These tools may be used and applied as necessary in each specific situation. This means that, whilst a large system may use all the tools, a small system may only need to apply one or two of them.

- The tools force the analyst to ask questions of the users – and of himself – and this minimizes the implementation of wrong assumptions during the design stage.

- Structured techniques require the analyst to approach the same problem from several different directions, thus offering a cross-check on the results derived by the various methods.

- Project control is less hazardous. The Project Manager knows the steps which are to be taken and, in the light of experience and the results obtained at each stage, he can refine his time and cost estimates for a project.

- With current facilities for word-processing and computer-aided design, most parts of the analysis and design task can be developed, maintained and held on a computer system. This eases the work of producing the documentation, it ensures that all those involved – users, analysts, programmers and

administrators – have access to the most up-to-date version of that documentation, and it permits a hard-copy of that documentation to be produced as
required.
• The principles of structured techniques are more compatible with modern
systems and requirements, and fit in much more neatly with the current third
and fourth generation languages, and with recent techniques such as
prototyping. They are also much more suited to a business world in which the
end-user is familiar with computing methods and needs a responsive solution.
This was not true in the days when the traditional systems analysis and design
principles originated.

In conclusion, it should be stressed that, when we are presenting a
methodology such as that discussed here – whether it be for small system users or
for those in any other operating environment – we are not constraining the
analyst or the programmer, nor are we imposing unrealistic disciplines upon
them. We are merely providing a framework within which they can work, and we
are offering a set of development tools which they can use as they feel appropriate
to their own particular circumstances.

1.7 STRUCTURED METHODOLOGY FOR SMALL SYSTEMS

In recent years, the accessibility of computers and computing systems has become
much greater. These are frequently small systems: micros, PCs or terminals
offering easy access to a larger machine.

The reader may ask whether we need a special methodology when we are
developing systems for the smaller computer, and why. The answer can only be:

'We do not need a **special** methodology when we are developing systems for a small
system...but, as with any other computer environment, it is necessary to have **some**
methodology if such systems are to be developed with any degree of efficiency.'

If we compare such users with those who are working on larger computer
systems, we find that they are in an unusual position:

1. The systems are developed for on-line use.
   A good database design is essential if files are to be processed effciently and
   quickly. Process design, menu organization and program construction must
   be properly considered and at the right time.
2. The systems themselves are developed on-line.
   Many of the advantages of the formal design procedure are lost if the
   programmer simply sits down at the terminal and begins to type the programs
   in live as the statements come into his or her head. If this happens, the
   requirements for flexibility, adaptability and maintainability are also lost.
3. Small systems invariably grow larger.
   Many small systems are written as one-off programs, but as their usefulness is
   realized, they grow. New bits are added here and there; they are borrowed and
   extended by other users; they are linked in to other systems. Unless the
   program – or programs – have been developed systematically, there will be

endless problems in moving them around and modifying them.
4. Typical users have had no formal systems analysis and design training. Many of today's analysts and programmers – or the people who are performing the tasks of systems analysis and programming – have graduated from end-users. Greater access to computers has attracted people with a specialist knowledge in areas such as finance, accountancy, engineering, administration, design, and many other disciplines, and placed them in a position where they are eager, willing and required to produce computer systems for themselves. Such users need to be shown that formal analysis and design is not as daunting a task as they may have feared.

1.8 SUMMARY

A structured methodology offers us a way of performing the systems analysis, the systems design and the programming tasks of system development. By taking a top-down approach and using diagrams to avoid much of the volume of paperwork and documentation which have long been a part of the systems development task, a structured approach allows us to investigate and analyse the requirements more quickly and to react more quickly to the users' changing requirements. They also lead us to produce systems which are more appropriate to the users' needs, systems whose design can be repeatedly reviewed with the users, systems which are more intelligible to the users, and systems which are easier to maintain in the future.

We would remind the reader that the structured techniques described in the present book are not applied in the following are as:

1. For producing the initial feasibility study, although the top-down approach can be used during the investigation. Structured systems analysis and design *begin* with the assumption that a decision has already been made to proceed with a project.
2. For program or system testing – although the structured techniques do facilitate program testing.
3. For systems conversion.
4. For implementing the new system.
5. For training the users – although the systems documentation is more intelligible to the user and the prototyping techniques encourage the user to participate in the development of the system.
6. For documenting the system – although much of the traditional technical documentation is superseded by the documents and tools which are used in the structured methodology.

For these stages in the conception and realization of the computer project, we continue to use the tried and tested methods.

Structured systems analysis, structured systems design and structured programming methodologies and other techniques provide a number of tools for the systems analyst and the programmer. Those which we shall consider are listed in Fig. 1.7.

```
-----------------------------------------------

            Structured tools
-----------------------------------------------

     1.  Document flow diagram
     2.  Problem and requirements list
     3.  Data flow diagram
     4.  Data structure diagram
     5.  Normalization
     6.  Entity / function matrix
     7.  Entity description
     8.  Function catalogue
     9.  Function description
    10.  Structured English
    11.  Function map
    12.  Module catalogue
    13.  Module description
    14.  Module map
    15.  Structured and modular programming
    16.  Prototyping

-----------------------------------------------
```

Figure 1.7 Structured tools.

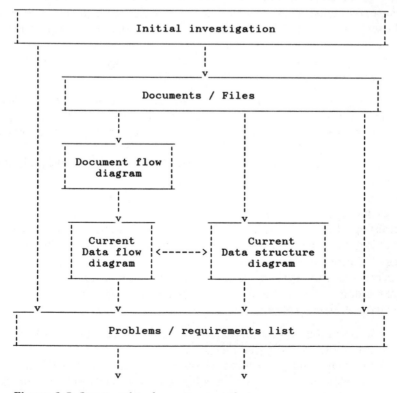

Figure 1.8 Structured tools – systems analysis.

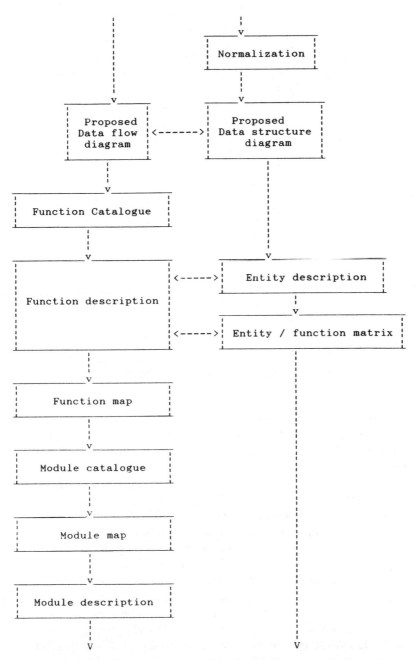

Figure 1.9 Structured tools – systems design.

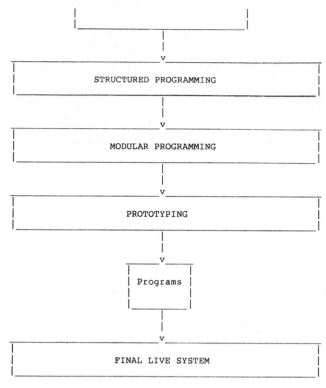

Figure 1.10 Structured techniques – programming.

Many of the tools are used in parallel, one moulding and cross-checking – challenging or corroborating – the results of the other. The general sequence in which they are used and the ways in which they interact are shown in the following diagrams: Fig. 1.8 shows the tools which can be used during the systems analysis phase; Fig. 1.9 shows those for the systems design phase; Fig. 1.10 shows those for the programming phase.

It should be said that, since many of the tools and documents take the form of charts and diagrams, and many of these may have to be revised and re-drawn several times, the use of automated techniques and graphics packages is a great advantage. We shall make frequent reference to on-line techniques.

In conclusion, we repeat that a structured methodology is not a dogma, nor is it a doctrinarian set of rules which are to be followed blindly. We are dealing with a set of guidelines which direct you – even though you may be the rawest trainee – along a path to successful systems analysis and systems design. Moreover, the approach is not a replacement for intelligent thought. You must still make assessments and judgements and decisions, and you must still think. A structured methodology merely gives a stimulus to such thinking and allows you to benefit from it.

2

The preliminary stages

Structured systems analysis and design methodologies are applied when it has been decided to proceed with a computer project. They do not, therefore, include the preliminary stages – the **terms of reference**, the **feasibility study**, the **systems investigation**, or the **statement of requirements** – within their scope. However, many readers may be new to any form of systems analysis – structured or otherwise. It is for them that this chapter is presented.

Readers who have some experience of systems investigation and systems analysis may omit this chapter.

2.1 TERMS OF REFERENCE

It is essential that a firm basis for the investigation is established before the analyst starts to pursue the project. The terms of reference form this basis and are produced so that the user can decide whether or not he wants to proceed with the project. The terms of reference take the form of a document specifying:

1. the title of the project
2. the subject of the study
3. the objectives and scope of the study
4. the department/section involved
5. the personnel involved
6. the timescales, for the initial survey and for the final implementation of any subsequent system
7. the budget which is available for the initial survey and also for the final project
8. the resources available to the analyst
9. the constraints within which the analyst must work

When the analyst has received these terms of reference, he will be in a position to perform the preliminary investigation and to produce a project feasibility report.

2.2 THE PRELIMINARY INVESTIGATION

The preliminary investigation is based upon the terms of reference, and is a smaller version of the full systems study which may have to be performed later – if it is decided to pursue the project. The aim at this stage is to obtain a broad picture of the work which the new system is to do. The main product of this preliminary investigation will be the project feasibility report.

If, in the light of the feasibility report, the management decision is that the project shall proceed, then the analyst will have to carry out a full systems study, duplicating much of the work done in the earlier investigation. On the other hand, it may be that the decision will be to abort the project – for example, it may be too expensive, or it may take too long to implement – in which case any work which has already been done and any money which has been spent will be written off. For these reasons, the preliminary study should be of sufficient depth to produce a valid feasibility report, but not so deep that the costs of producing the report will incur any substantial loss in the event of cancellation.

2.3   THE PROJECT FEASIBILITY REPORT

The feasibility report will present the following information:

1. The terms of reference under which the study was made;
2. A description of the current system: this may describe a manual system or an existing computer system which is to be replaced, and will include the problems or shortcomings realized by the users of the current system, together with the costs for the system;
3. A description of the hardware and software of the proposed system;
4. A description of the functions of the proposed system: this will be a summary describing the input, processing and output which will be involved in the new system;
5. A discussion of the reliability of the proposed system, its flexibility and ability to respond to the organization's changing needs in the future. The security, integrity and confidentiality of the information which is to be held will also be addressed;
6. A development plan: this will show the resources and time-scales which will be required for the development, implementation and transition to the new system;
7. The social and other impacts of the proposed system, considering its effect within the organization – employees and management – and also outside the organization – the customers and the suppliers;
8. Costs: the development and the operational costs should be indicated;
9. Recommendation and justification: out of the several possibilities and options which are presented and contrasted, you, as analyst, will draw your own conclusions and make your own recommendations about which course of action should be followed. These will be described in this report, and must always be presented as benefits to the user. Some benefits will be tangible and quantifiable – a 15% increase in the number of invoices processed each day or a 4% increase in turnover – whereas others will be intangible – greater job satisfaction for the staff, better service to the clients, or better use of the resources available. Wherever possible, the benefits should be quantified in terms of reduced costs or increased income.

The feasibility report will be circulated to all interested parties: the user department, the data processing department, the finance department, and possibly union representatives and the board of management. Based upon their reactions, a decision will be made as to whether or not the organization will proceed with the project. Once an affirmative decision has been made, then the analyst will be able to begin his systems investigation.

Under exceptional circumstances, you may come to the conclusion that the current system is perfectly adequate, and that any really effective improvement in the system could only be achieved by spending a disproportionate amount of money, or that only a new manual system is required – without any need for computerization. In such cases, you should state these conclusions in your report. You should always strive to be fair in your proposal, even though a large number of data processing departments and computer service organizations will – in order to justify their very existence – always propose a computer solution.

2.4 PLANNING

The feasibility report will include an estimate of the time and costs for the various stages in the life of the project – from the systems analysis, and systems design through to programming, testing and the final implementation. For small- to medium-scale projects, it is customary to present this as a bar-chart, showing the duration of each activity in days, as illustrated in Fig. 2.1. As with most projects, it is possible to perform many of the activities concurrently, if the number of staff permits. The chart will show this.

The chart can also carry some indication of the number of people to be involved at each stage. This will enable a reasonable estimate to be made of the cost of the project. Thus, we may depict the Programming activities as shown in Fig. 2.2 indicating that a total of 80 man-days are required for the coding of the programs, and 35 man-days for the testing.

Such a bar-chart does not show how the various tasks depend upon each other. Some tasks cannot start until others have been completed: we cannot start to test a program until it has been written. We cannot start to write a program until the specification has been produced. An **activity network** such as that shown in Fig. 2.3 is able to show such dependencies.

The chart shows the start (S) and the finish (F) of the whole project. The separate activities, or tasks, which must be completed are shown, T1, T2 and so on, with the time (in weeks) taken to complete each task shown in square brackets. The **nodes** or **events** are numbered (1), (2) etc., and indicate the termination of one task and the start of another task. For example, if we look at task T9, the [5] tells us that this task takes five weeks to complete.

If we look at node (4), we see that we can reach this node along two paths; T6 and T4, or T9 and T7. Therefore, task T5, which starts at node (4), only starts when both tasks T4 **and** T7 have been completed. It takes nine weeks to reach node (4) via T9 and T7, and three weeks via T6 and T4. This implies that there is six weeks' leeway available in completing tasks T6 and T4. This leeway is known

```
                    CUSTOMER BILLING SYSTEM

                   Week1 Week2 Week3 Week4 Week5 Week6 Week7 Week8 Wee

Systems Design:

  Data analysis    XXXXX XXXXX XXXXX

  File design            XXXXX XXXXX XXXX

  Forms design           XXXXX

  Report design          XXXXX XXXXX

  Screen design                XXXXX XXXXX

  Functional          XXX XXXXX XXXXX XXXXX
  analysis

Programming:

  Coding                       XXXXX XXXXX XXXXX XXXXX

  Testing                            XXXXX XXXXX XXXXX XXXXX

User training            X     X     X     X     XXXXX XXXXX XXX

Data conversion                                  XXXXX XXXXX       XXX

Implementation                                         XXXXX  XXX XXX

Documentation          XXXXX       XXXXX XXXXX XXXXX       XXXXX
```

Figure 2.1 A planning chart.

```
PROGRAMMING:

  CODING      |____|____|44444|44444|44444|44444|____|____|____

  TESTING     |____|____|____|11111|22222|22222|22222|____|____
```

Figure 2.2 A planning chart – programming activities.

as the **float time**, and implies that these two tasks may be delayed by a total of up to six weeks without affecting the entire project.

Assuming that all the tasks are completed within the estimated time, then the duration of the project can be determined from the longest time path through the network from start to finish. In this example, this is sixteen weeks, and is represented by the path (S)–(6)–(4)–(5)–(F). This longest path is called the **critical path** because the entire project will be affected if a delay occurs in completing any of the tasks T9, T7, T5 or T8. This technique is sometimes known

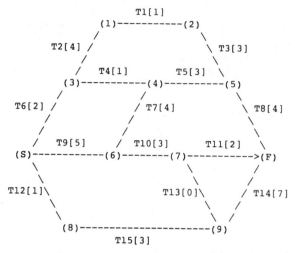

Figure 2.3 An activity network.

as **critical path analysis**, and the **Programme Evaluation and Review Technique**
(**PERT**); computer packages are available to control and monitor the progress of
large projects by means of these techniques.

2.5 THE INVESTIGATION

The main differences between the preliminary investigation – to produce the
project feasibility study – and the full systems study – on which the final project
will be based – is the depth to which you will go in your investigation. They are
both fact-finding exercises and you will start by asking questions:

How ... ?
What ... ?
When ... ?
Where ... ?
Who ... ?
Why ... ?

Some of the questions which you might ask are shown in Fig. 2.4.

At some stage during your investigation, you will also ask further
questions – directly or indirectly. Some of these are shown in Fig. 2.5.

You will already have found the answers to some of these questions when you
were producing the feasibility report, but now you must go deeper.

2.5.1 Background reading

Before you start your investigation proper, you should be thoroughly familiar
with the environment in which you are working. If you are employed by, say, a

---

```
Who are the people who are involved with the system?
What does the system achieve - or attempt to achieve?
How successful is it?
What data are being handled?
Who provides the input information?
What do they think of the system?
Where do the data come from?
When are the data processed?
How do the data get into the system?
What data are being stored?
How and where are the data held?
What work is done on the data?
Who does the work?
What do they think of the system?
What is the structure of the department concerned?
Who are the managers?
What do they think of the system?
What results are produced by the system?
When are the results produced?
Where do the results go to?
What reports are produced?
What do the reports look like?
How are the reports presented?
When are the reports produced?
Who receives the reports and the output results?
What do they think of the system?
What happens to the reports?
How much does it cost to run the present system?
What problems are there within the system?
What additional features should be incorporated into the system?
What more would the users like the system to do?
```

Figure 2.4 Investigation questions – 1.

```
Why are these various jobs carried out?
What is the point of producing such a report?
What other ways are there to achieve the required results?
How could the work be reorganized to solve the current
     problems and any further requirements?
How could the system be modified without any loss of
     efficiency?
```

Figure 2.5 Investigation questions – 2.

carpet manufacturing company, then you presumably know something about the company's business and about carpet-making. However, if you are an independent consultant or if you work for a software house, then you may be required to work for a company whose business is unfamiliar to you. In this case you must do some background reading.

2.5.2 Interviewing

Your informants will be those who are in any way concerned with the system in its present form, or who will be involved with the proposed system. These will include:

1. people who supply the input data
2. people who process the data
3. the people who receive the results

Before you talk to your informants try to look at:

1. the relevant organization chart to see:
   (a) where your informant fits within the company;
   (b) whom the informant reports to – his or her boss;
   (c) who reports to the informant – his or her staff
2. the job description for the informant
3. any procedure manuals which the informant uses
4. the forms and files which the informant uses.

2.5.3 Questionnaires

In some situations, it may not be possible – or it may be too expensive – to interview all your informants face-to-face. Reasons for this may be that there are too many people involved, or it may be that they are situated too far away from the organization's main area of activity. These difficulties may be overcome by the use of a questionnaire.

2.5.4 Observation

No matter what questions you ask and no matter whom you interview, you will get varying responses to what is essentially the same question. For example:

What does your senior wages clerk do?
What do you, as senior wage clerk, do?
What does your boss, the senior wages clerk, do?
What does the job description for the senior wages clerk say that he does?

The best solution to this and similar problems is to watch the senior wages clerk perform his or her job. You may even find that you get a fifth and different answer!

2.6 WHAT ARE WE LOOKING FOR?

The main goal of our work is to identify the various fundamental activities of the system – input, storage, processing, control and output – so that we can equip ourselves to construct a model of the current system. In fact, we shall build **two** models of the system: a **data model**, representing the data which the system handles, and a **process model**, representing the operational functions of the system. From these models we shall be able to design a computer system which will perform all the functions of the present system. To do this, we need to know everything – or as much as we can determine – about:

1. the input data
2. the processing
3. the control of this processing
4. the output results
5. the stored results.

Our methodology will concentrate primarily upon the data model, taking a **data-driven approach** to the work. We do this because the ways in which an organization works – the process model – will change with time. Indeed, the whole reason for our work is to look at ways of making such changes. But behind these changes in the processing, there lies a firm and relatively unchanging mass of data, facts and information upon which the organization's business is based – the data model.

So let us first see how we can find out about the data which is processed.

2.6.1 Forms

By collecting all the forms which are handled by the informant, you have access to the greatest proportion of the informant's raw materials. You should try to obtain samples of the blank forms and also the completed forms.

2.6.2 Files

Most administrative operations use a large number of files. These may be simple manila folders where the clerk stores invoices as they arrive, they may be card indexes recording the names and addresses of the staff, or they may be ledgers and ledger cards holding account details. You should endeavour to obtain samples – preferably copies of real examples – of the information which is held in the files.

We have now collected enough information to enable us to lay the foundations for our data model. Let us move on to the process model.

2.6.3 The processing

The part of the activity which seems hardest to capture is what the clerk actually does. You can record this information in a variety of ways: as a piece of narrative text, as a chart, as a decision table, or as a formula.

Let us imagine that you are working with a clerk – Amy – who is responsible for checking sales orders which come into the office from the post room. A narrative description of what Amy does might look like that shown in Fig. 2.6.

Such a **process narrative** is a perfectly acceptable way of recording Amy's work. It can, however, be imprecise and open to ambiguities. This is particularly true when there are lots of **ifs** and **ands** and **ors**. A more formal method can be found in

She checks that the details of the order - particularly the
stock code - are correct.   If not, then she returns the
order with a covering letter to the client.

She then checks that sufficient products are in stock.   If
she cannot complete the entire order, then the order form is
placed in the pending file.   If the order can be filled,
then the clerk amends the stock record, initials the order
and sends it through to the stores.

Figure 2.6 A process narrative.

PROCESS FLOW

PROCESS: VALID ORDERS

N U M B E R	DETAILS	R E C E I V E	P R O C E S S	D E L A Y	C H E C K	F I L E	P A S S O N	COMMENTS
1	Orders from Post room	*						
2	Check order details		*					
3	Check stock details		*					
4	Pass on to the stores						*	

Figure 2.7 A process flow matrix.

the Process Flowcharts, such as those shown here. Fig. 2.7 records the processing
of a valid order, and Fig. 2.8 records the processing of an order which is rejected
because it was completed incorrectly. Each task which Amy performs is written
on the chart, and an asterisk is put beneath the appropriate column: Receive the
document, perform some Process, Delay until some other activity is complete,
Check a previous operation, File the document, or Pass on the document.

Alternatively, you may care to use a **clerical procedures flowchart** to record the
actions, as shown in Fig. 2.9.

PROCESS FLOW

PROCESS: INVALID ORDERS - INVALID ORDER FORM

N U M B E R	DETAILS	R E C E I V E	P R O C E S S	D E L A Y	C H E C K	F I L E	P A S S O N	COMMENTS
1	Orders from Post room	*						
2	Check order details		*					Looking for errors on the form
3	Prepare covering letter		*					
4	Return order and letter to client						*	

Figure 2.8 A process flow matrix – invalid orders.

The flowchart is a clear representation of the activities which are involved in the clerical process. It also shows more information – the nature of the files, for example – than does the text description. It is, however, difficult to amend and may demand considerable time if omissions and corrections are to be made.

A third method is the **decision table**. If we chose this method, our order processing setting might look like Fig. 2.10.

The table comprises four parts: the condition stub, the condition entry, the action stub and the action entry. The condition stub shows the questions which we are asking, or the decisions which we are taking:

CODES CORRECT
PRODUCT STILL SOLD
SUFFICIENT STOCK

The condition entry shows the possible outcomes of these decisions: Y for yes, N for no.

Underneath, we see the action entry shows the actions which can be taken:

REFER TO SUPERVISOR
WRITE TO CUSTOMER
PUT IN PENDING FILE
INITIAL AND PASS TO STORES

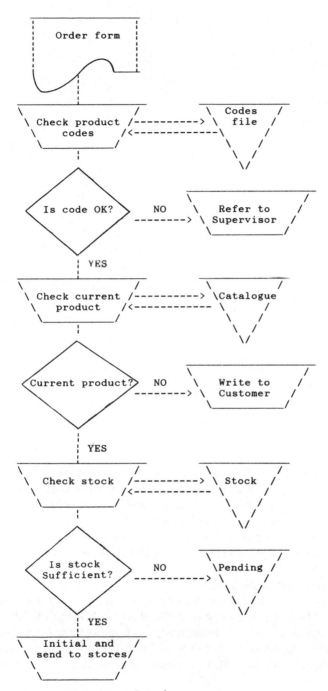

Figure 2.9 A process flow chart.

Condition:				
Codes correct	Y	N	Y	Y
Product still sold	Y		N	Y
Sufficient stock	Y			N
Action:				
Refer to supervisor		X		
Write to customer			X	
Put in pending file				X
Initial and pass to stores	X			

Figure 2.10 A decision table – 1.

Condition:								
Codes correct	Y	Y	Y	Y	N	N	N	N
Product still sold	Y	Y	N	N	Y	Y	N	N
Sufficient stock	Y	N	Y	N	Y	N	Y	N
Action:								
Refer to supervisor					X	X	X	X
Write to customer				X	X			
Put in pending file			X					
Initial and pass to stores	X							

Figure 2.11 A decision table – 2.

The appropriate action is linked to the outcome – Y or N – of the various decisions by putting an X in the corresponding position of the action stub.

You will see that this particular decision table is logically incomplete. We have not represented every possible combination of the three conditions. Each of the three conditions has two possible outcomes; therefore, there are eight ($2 \times 2 \times 2$) possible combinations of Y and N. We should perhaps construct the decision table as shown in Fig. 2.11. You will notice the (binary) pattern of Y and N in the condition entry part of the table.

For example, if you look at the third column – this shows what happens if the **CODES ARE CORRECT** and there is **SUFFICIENT STOCK** but **PRODUCT IS NOT STILL SOLD**. This may be the situation when a product has been withdrawn, but there are still a few left in the warehouse. Can we be sure that we have assumed correctly that Amy would write to the customer rejecting the order, as we have indicated?

When you are expanding your decision table in this manner, you must be sure that you are putting in the correct information. If you are in any doubt, then you must go back to Amy, and ask her. She might even say something like:

'Oh, no. If we have any items left in the stores, even if it's been withdrawn from the catalogue, then we supply it.'

This is a useful process in that it forces you to ask questions to which you must know the answer.

So far we have seen devices to record simple processing and fairly complex decisions. How do we record calculations or complex processing? The narrative text can be used.

We could record the calculations using formulae, or we could even incorporate these into a stylized narrative form – known as **structured English**. When we consider structured English later, we shall see how it has the advantage that it is intelligible to the end-user who has to check it to ensure the accuracy, and it also leads quite naturally into the final programming phase.

2.6.4 Reports

We have looked at the data which the system uses: we have seen the source of those data and we have looked at the ways in which they are processed. Now we need to see the results of processing those data. The main products of any computer system include the printed reports, and these can appear in a variety of shapes and sizes:

invoices
accounts
ledger sheets
statistics
bank statements
wage slips
cheques
driving licences
examination certificates
departmental analyses

You will collect samples of all those which are the concern of your system. These will contribute to the data analysis activity.

2.7 THE PROPOSAL

Your preliminary investigation has provided you with facts and information to enable you to build a model of the current system. You can now make some suggestions about what is wanted from and what is required of any new system.

In some environments, a proposal will be produced after the feasibility report and before the final approval is given for a project to proceed. This is based upon the systems analyst's work and may be delivered either after the initial investigation, before further expense is incurred by the detailed systems analysis phase, or, after a partial appraisal of the situation.

As the name implies, the document proposes a solution – or possibly several possible solutions – to the specific problems addressed in the terms of reference. It is essentially concerned with selling its solution to the user, and for this reason is frequently encountered in the work of software houses, systems houses and others who provide data processing solutions as a service.

For each proposed solution, the proposal will give details of:

1. what is to be done – this may be based upon the statement of requirements, or upon a functional specification provided by the user
2. how it will be achieved
3. how much it will cost
4. how long it will take
5. the benefits to be gained by adopting the solution.

Following acceptance of the proposal, there will be an agreement drawn up showing the obligations and responsibilities of all parties and any penalties and bonuses falling to the supplier on completion of the project.

2.8   SUMMARY

When an organization is considering the implementation of a new computer system – or the modification of an existing system – the systems analyst will be given the terms of reference under which to conduct a preliminary investigation in order to produce the project feasibility report. Whilst preparing this report, the investigation looks at the information which the system uses, the processing which is carried out, and the reports and results which are produced.

If, as a result of the project feasibility report, a decision is made to proceed with the project, then the analyst will begin work on the systems analysis phase.

2.9   QUESTIONS

2.1.   A small coach company has decided to adopt a computerized seat reservation system. Will this be feasible? Give your reasons.

2.2.   A small airline company has decided to adopt a computerized seat reservation system. Will this be feasible? Give your reasons.

2.3.   I use a computer terminal to test programs which I have written as part of my Open University assignment. I must carry out the following tasks:

   (a) test the program
   (b) send off my homework to the tutor

(c) read the question specifying the work to be done
(d) write the program
(e) code the program
(f) go along to the computer terminal
(g) design some test data
(h) read and understand the textbook
(i) dial the computer's telephone number
(j) design the program
(k) telephone the university to book a terminal session

Put them in the correct sequence.

2.4. Suggest some preliminary background reading and other research which might be carried out by an analyst who has been called in to investigate each of the following systems:

(a) a book ordering and cataloguing system for a large chain of bookshops
(b) a patients recording system for a small optician
(c) a purchase order system for a market gardening company

2.5. The Acme Jobs Galore recruitment agency currently uses a manual system for recording job vacancies and applicant details for a recruitment agency. Consideration is being given to computerizing the system. What sources do you think the analyst could look to for background reading before starting the investigation? We shall look at other aspects of this system below.

2.6. The owner of the Acme Garage wants to transfer his spare part re-ordering system on to a computer. Whom would you interview during your investigations of the current system?

2.7. Make a list of the sort of people the analyst might wish to interview in connection with the investigation which you are carrying out for the Acme Jobs Galore recruitment agency.

2.8. You are going to interview a clerk at the Acme Jobs Galore agency. The clerk's responsibility is to answer telephone queries about suitable job vacancies. Draft a questionnaire which you might use to ask the clerk about his/her work.

2.9. What types of form and document would you collect during your investigation into the Acme Jobs Galore Agency system?

2.10. What data are the Acme Jobs Galore Agency likely to use?

2.11. What sort of files would you expect the analyst to find there?

2.12. Write down some notes on the processing which you would expect a clerk at the Acme Jobs Galore agency to carry out when:

(a) someone goes in to the office to ask if there are any suitable vacancies for a shorthand typist with clerical experience who is living in and wants to work in central Devchester

(b) a manager telephones the office to say that his company is looking for a receptionist.

2.13. What reports do you think the Acme Jobs Galore Agency would use?

3
Structured systems analysis

We have made some progress with our investigation: we have some ideas about what the current system does; we know something about the data which it uses and the results which it produces. We must now analyse our findings and ensure that they present a true picture of the current state of affairs within the organization.

We shall take a **data-driven** approach to systems analysis, looking first at the data which flow through the system. We do this because, in general, the **nature** of the data which an organization handles will stay the same. A car manufacturing company, for example, always handles data relating to cars: the stock of cars; the sales of cars; the delivery of cars to showrooms and to customers. Whilst the range of cars, the number of customers and the prices may change, the nature of the data remains fairly static. A Payroll Department always handles information relating to people: their money; their taxes; their pensions and their payments. The number of people on the payroll may change, income tax codes and allowances may change, but the general pattern of the data is fairly constant.

In contrast, the **ways** in which the data are handled may be subject to considerable change: it may be decided to pay the employees by bank transfer instead of cash; the Board of Directors may want more information about wage rates; a new bonus scheme may be introduced; new statistical analyses may be called for. Indeed, the very fact that the current processing system is to be modified may imply that the data are to be handled differently. A firmer foundation on which to build our initial investigations may be laid by first looking at the data and assembling our analysis around that.

3.1 DOCUMENT FLOW DIAGRAM

The most tangible form in which the data are encountered is the **document**. The document flow diagram (DocFD) is a chart which depicts the key documents and the physical resources – such as materials and goods – which are associated with the existing system. It shows the flow of these between the functional areas within the organization – such as the Accounts Department or the Warehouse – and the external entities – such as the Clients or the Suppliers. These functional areas and external entities will be the sources and/or the recipients of the documents.

As the worked examples in Fig. 8.5 and Fig. 8.6 show, a DocFD depicts:

1. the documents and physical resources, such as goods and materials, which flow within the system
2. the sources and the recipients of the document or the physical resource
3. the flow of the document or physical resource.

In a simple ordering system, we might encounter a number of documents – Orders, Invoices, Payment notifications, and Delivery notes – and a number of physical resources – Goods, Returned goods, Money, cash and cheques.

The sources and recipients of these documents and the physical resources fall into two main groups: the **internal functional areas** – within the organization – and the **external entities** – outside the organization. Typical internal functional areas might be the Accounts Department, the Sales Department or the Warehouse. It is not necessary to be precise in the grouping of the functional areas at this stage. If you have considered several departments under one heading, then these may well emerge as individual functional areas later in the analysis and design phases. The reverse is also true: one analyst may have recognized several distinct functional areas within the Accounts Department, e.g. New Accounts, Debt collecting, Account Queries, Account transactions, whilst another may have grouped all these under the single functional area Accounts.

Typical external entities might be the Clients, the Suppliers, the Bank, and Management. The organization's own Management – its managers, the directors and the auditors – may be considered as an external entity and outside the main processing part of the organization. This is because they represent recipients of information and are not involved in the provision or the processing of that information. Their only **contribution** to the system may be the submission of enquiries and questions.

The sources and recipients are represented by named boxes. The documents and the flow of the documents are represented by named arrows.

Note that storage areas, such as library shelves, depots, ledgers, warehouses, filing cabinets and files, do not appear on the document flow diagram.

We combine these various elements to produce a simple DocFD showing the flow of the documents. A simple diagram might look like that shown in Fig. 3.1.

The diagram does not attempt to show the sequence in which the operations take place, but simply illustrates the nature of the documents and the direction in which they move. Thus, the documents passing between the **CUSTOMER** and **ACCOUNTS** boxes could have been represented as in Fig. 3.2.

When you have drawn your DocFD, you should check it with the users to confirm that you have represented all the documents and resources which are involved.

In some cases, the diagram may signal omissions – yours or those of the system. If you can see any entities which have only one document linking them into the other entities, this may imply that a document is spontaneously submitted by a source, or that a document is received with no further action being taken. You must check that these are valid situations, or investigate further and amend the diagram as necessary.

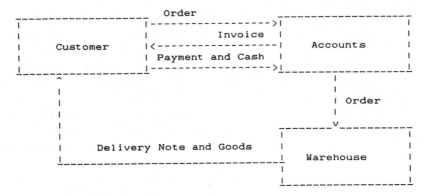

```
 _____      Order        _____
I                     I  I-------------->I                          I
I                     I  I      Invoice  I                          I
I     Customer        I  I<--------------I     Accounts             I
I                     I  I  Payment and Cash I                      I
I_____I  I------------------>I_____I
        ^                I                          I
        I                I                          I
        I                I                          I Order
        I                I                          I
        I                I                    _____v_____
        I                I                   I                   I
        I    Delivery Note and Goods         I                   I
        I_____I     Warehouse     I
                                             I                   I
                                             I_____I
```

Figure 3.1 A document flow diagram.


```
 _____      Payment      _____
I                     I  I-------------->I                          I
I                     I  I      Invoice  I                          I
I     Customer        I  I<--------------I     Accounts             I
I                     I  I  Order        I                          I
I_____I  I-------------->I_____I
```

Figure 3.2 A document flow diagram.

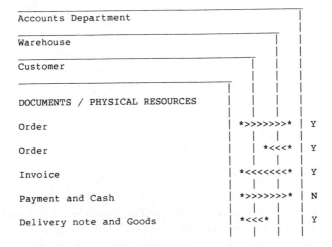

DOCUMENT FLOW MATRIX

ENTITIES / FUNCTIONAL AREAS

```
Accounts Department                      I
_____ I   I
Warehouse                              I I   I
_____ I I   I
Customer                             I I I   I
_____ I I I   I
DOCUMENTS / PHYSICAL RESOURCES        I I I   I

Order                                 I *>>>>>>* I  Y
                                      I   I  I   I
Order                                 I   I *<<<* I  Y
                                      I   I  I   I
Invoice                               I *<<<<<<<* I  Y
                                      I   I  I   I
Payment and Cash                      I *>>>>>>* I  N
                                      I   I  I   I
Delivery note and Goods               I *<<<* I   I  Y
                                      I   I  I   I
```

Figure 3.3 A document flow matrix,

As a preliminary to producing the DocFD, you may produce a document flow matrix, as shown in Fig. 3.3. Because the production and amendment of a document flow matrix is relatively simple, you may prefer to use it in place of the document flow diagram. A further advantage of the matrix is that, when you are reviewing it with the users, you can use it to indicate those areas which are to be the subject of your detailed investigation and those which are not; for example, we imagine that the client does not wish us to look at the Payment and cash receipts area. This can be done by writing a Y or N to the right of the line, as illustrated in Fig. 3.3. The document flow matrix can also be used to show the sequence in which the documents flow.

The DocFD will be used to provide a framework for the data flow diagram which is produced later. Indeed, some analysts regard the **document** flow diagram as a high level **data** flow diagram.

3.1.1   Producing the document flow diagram

Examples of the document flow matrix, the DocFD – and indeed all the documents which we shall introduce in the text – are to be found in Chapter 8 where we produce a solution to our Case Study.

The following points should be borne in mind when producing the document flow diagram:

1. The forms and other documents which are encountered within the system are used to provide the information. You will have identified these documents and collected samples during your preliminary investigation.
2. Make a list of the internal functional areas or internal entities, the offices and people within the organization – such as Accounts, New customer accounts, Personnel or Wages – which send or receive information, documents or physical resources.
3. Make a list of the external entities – such as Clients, Suppliers or Management – which send or receive information, documents or physical resources.
4. Make a list of the documents and physical resources – such as materials and goods – which flow within the system. If telephone calls or verbal orders or enquiries represent a substantial feature of the system, then these too should be included in this list.
5. Draw up a document flow matrix to show what documents and physical resources pass between which external entities and functional areas.
6. The DocFD may be drawn from this matrix, or it may be drawn directly without the use of the matrix.
7. The DocFD represents the various external entities and functional areas linked by flow lines. These flow lines bear the name of the document or physical resource which passes between the two entities, and have a single arrow-head showing the direction in which the document is flowing.
8. Storage areas and files do not appear on the DocFD.

9. Review the DocFD with your users to ensure that you have not missed anything important.
10. If you are using manual methods – that is, pencil and paper – to produce the DocFD, and not an on-line documentation package, then remember that your first attempts will certainly be changed as your thoughts and the users comments feed back. So make sure that the diagrams are clear and accurate, but do not spend too much time and effort embellishing them. It is also a good idea to start the first draft near the centre of a large sheet of paper. Otherwise, you may find yourself falling off the edge of the sheet!

The resulting DocFD will subsequently be used to derive the data flow diagram (DFD) for the current system.

3.2 PROBLEMS AND REQUIREMENTS LIST

As you proceed with the analysis, you will gradually build up a list of the shortcomings of the present system. These will include problems which you and the users have recognized, together with additional requirements which the users have said they would like.

There will be a number of problems and grievances with the existing system. Many of the problems fall into recognizable areas:

1. the users are currently expecting too much of their system
2. the original requirements have changed
3. there is an increasing volume of work
4. the system cannot respond quickly enough to the users' needs
5. the security and confidentiality of the system are inadequate
6. there are inadequate audit checks and controls
7. the system makes too many demands on the users.

The additional requirements are those areas which the user prefaces by a statement such as:

'It would be nice if...'
'Could I have a report showing...'
'The present system doesn't let us...'
'Would it be possible for the new system to...?'

Such problems and requirements should be recorded as detailed points on a problems and requirements list. If possible, some criteria or yardstick should be given whereby it will – subsequently – be possible to assess whether the difficulty has been resolved. For example, if the users say that the system does not handle their work quickly enough, get them to quantify this by indicating that they would like '... all their new invoices ready for dispatch with 24 h'. By having this information, you know that if your system will produce the invoices in 23 h, then the users will be satisfied, but that if it takes 25 h, they will not be satisfied.

The problems and requirements list will grow as your investigation proceeds. It will be helpful if you can also assess the impact which the problems – and the gaps implied by the requirements – are currently having on the company. This information will be of value when you and the users come to consider the potential benefits from adopting your suggested solution.

At this stage, you need not consider the action which your future system might take to overcome the difficulties. It may be that, when you review the list with your users, they do not wish you to take any action to remedy certain points on your list.

It is essential that you put the problems and requirements down in writing. It is useless to make a mental note and then hope to recall it later.

We shall see that the ultimate solution should endeavour to address most, if not all, of the problems and requirements. If you do not address the various problems and requirements which you and the users recognize, then your proposed system is destined to be no more than an electronic version of the present system . . . warts and all!

3.2.1   Producing the problems and requirements list

The following points should be borne in mind when producing the problems and requirements list:

1. the production of the problems and requirements list is a continuous process
2. you will identify further entries for the list throughout your investigation, analysis and design activities
3. look for problem areas: where forms might be lost, where information might go missing, where information is not provided, where processing gets left undone, or where the finances of the organization are jeopardized
4. recognize voiced – and unvoiced – requirements when the users say things like:
   'It would be nice if . . .'
   'At my previous company, we had a system to . . .'
5. quantify the requirements by giving figures for the volumes, speeds and turnaround times which would be acceptable to the users
6. assess the impact of the problems and requirements on the company's performance
7. at this stage, it is not essential to consider ways in which any future system might overcome the difficulties on your list.

The resulting problems and requirements list is used as a basis – and a check – for the design of your proposed system.

3.3   CURRENT DATA FLOW DIAGRAM

The DocFD shows the pieces of paper and other physical resources which move about the organization. Now we need to resolve this into the data and the processing which these document flows represent.

A data flow diagram (DFD) depicts the processes, the data stores, the data flows and the external entities which are associated with a system. It is based upon the information shown on the DocFD, the functional areas which appeared on the DocFD being replaced by the processes which they carry out. The main difference between the two is that the DocFD shows the flow of documents – the flow lines carry the name of a document – whereas the DFD shows the flow of data – the flow lines carry the name of the information which passes along them.

The DFD is used to:

1. identify the various processes that exist within the user's view of the current system; these are the processes which receive the documents and data which flow within the organization
2. show the main flows of data through the system
3. show the inputs and outputs from each process

and, above all, it represents the system in terms which are understandable to the user.

There are four components in a DFD:

1. Boxes indicating the processes which are carried out. There will be a separate process to handle each set of information which comes into the system. Data which flow out of the system are the by-products of a process, but a process can only be triggered by the arrival of information. Thus a process to **PRINT PAYMENT REMINDER** must be triggered by the receipt of information; typically, this will be a query or demand from the operator or from management.
2. Data stores indicating where data are held.
3. External entities indicating agencies which are outside the system concerned and which provide information to, or receive information from, the system.
4. Data flows – these are labelled single headed arrows indicating the data which flows between the processes, the data stores and the external entities.

You may encounter a variety of different shapes and conventions for the components of a data diagram. Some analysts use different colours to highlight the various components. We shall use the symbols shown below.

3.3.1   Process

Process boxes on the DFD are derived from the DocFD, and can be identified by looking for the different events or arrival of data, such as the receipt of a new sales order, the receipt of a management enquiry or the arrival of a customer's payment, which will trigger a process. We shall use the following definitions:

Event: the receipt of information. Often corresponding to the termination of one or more activities. An occurrence in the outside world which triggers a process.

Process: any operation which logically changes the contents of a data store

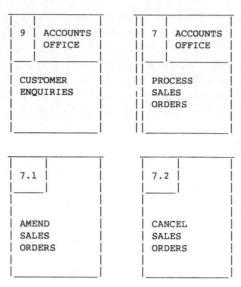

Figure 3.4 Processes.

or of a data flow, or which validates the contents of an input data flow. A process is triggered by an event.

There may be several levels of DFD, each one going into a little more detail than the previous one.

Each process box is uniquely identified by an arbitrary integer on the top-level DFD. The example in Fig. 3.4 shows DFD box number 7. As we proceed to lower levels, each process may be broken down into separate processes and each of these is given an identifier 7.1, 7.2 and so on, to indicate their refinement from process 7 at the previous level.

The process boxes on the top-level DFD may indicate the location where the process is carried out. For example, **ACCOUNTS OFFICE**, as in Fig. 3.4. If a process box is to be expanded on a lower-level diagram, then a double line may be drawn at the left of the box on the higher level diagram, as shown in Fig. 3.4.

The description of the process is written inside the box and should be an imperative statement of the action performed, such as **PROCESS SALES ORDER**, **PRINT PAYSLIPS**, and so on.

3.3.2 Data store

A data store is any place in which data are held. It is also the means whereby data are passed between processes. It is represented by an open rectangle on the DFD. We use the term data store because we are not yet thinking in terms of computer files.

Each data store is given an identifier consisting of a letter followed by an

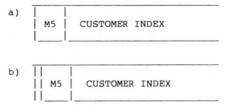

Figure 3.5 Data stores.

arbitrary integer to identify the data store uniquely, as shown in Fig. 3.5(a). The letter will be one of:

M if it is a manual data store: such as a card-index system, a ledger, an invoice which passes between departments, a filing cabinet or a wallchart;
D if it is a permanent computer file;
T If it is a temporary file.

To avoid too many interesecting data flow lines, it may be necessary to draw the same data store more than once on a large data flow diagram. In this case, a double line will be drawn at the left of the box, as shown in Fig. 3.5(b).

3.3.3 Entity

An external entity is represented by a box drawn outside the main framework of the DFD as Fig. 3.6 illustrates.

The entity is identified by a name inside the box, as illustrated in Fig. 3.6. If an external entity is repeated elsewhere on the same DFD, then a double line is drawn at the left of the box, as shown in Fig. 3.6(b).

Some analysts, and some software packages, use different colours, ellipses or perspective boxes to differentiate between the external entities and the internal functional areas, and between these and the process boxes.

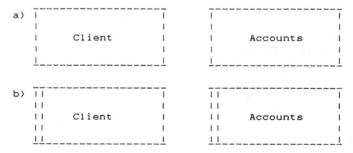

Figure 3.6 External entities.

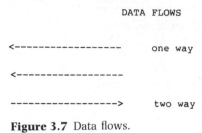

Figure 3.7 Data flows.

3.3.4   Data flow

A data flow is represented by a line with a single arrow-head and indicates the direction of flow of information, as illustrated in Fig. 3.7. It describes the information which passes between an entity and a process, or between a process and a data store. Any flow of information between one process and another is made via a data store.

Because the DFD shows the events – receipt of information – which trigger the process, the data flow should name the information which passes along the flow and not the document which carries that information. So, where the DocFD had:

INVOICE

you should declare the actual data which flows:

INVOICE NUMBER, LINES, TOTAL

There may not be sufficient space on the DFD for a long description of the data passing along a data flow. Consequently some analysts resolve this simply by writing:

INVOICE DETAILS

Others use this general description followed by the names of the key data items which are concerned:

INVOICE DETAILS: CUSTOMER NUMBER, DATE, TOTAL VALUE

and the key data may be underlined – or shown in a different colour – in order to highlight it. Fig. 3.8 shows some examples.

If a process deletes a record from a data store, then this could be shown by an annotation such as:

DELETE

or

DELETE: CUSTOMER NUMBER

on a data flow passing from the process to the data store.

Data flows in practice

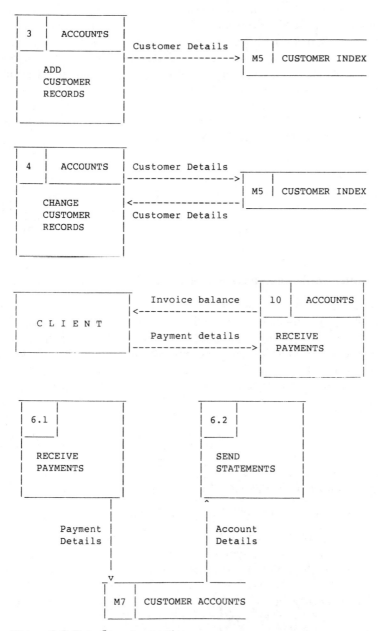

Figure 3.8 Data flows in practice.

3.3.5   Physical resources

It is best if the physical resources and materials – such as goods and money – are represented on the DFD by means of a data flow bearing the name of the information which accompanies that physical resource. In most cases, a physical resource will be accompanied by a covering letter, a delivery note or a deposit slip.

However, since we are depicting the current system, it may well be that goods and materials do wander about the factory – or even further afield – without any supporting documentation. If this is so, then these physical resources should be represented on a DFD by means of a broad arrow, with a description of the resource written within the arrow, as shown in Fig. 3.9.

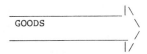

Figure 3.9 Physical resources.

3.3.6   Data flow diagram types and levels

On the first DFD, we do not indicate a process for every document which arrives, because this would make the picture too complex. Instead, we pursue our top-down approach, gradually expanding the functionality of each process box, producing a series of DFDs with various levels of detail. This is known as functional decomposition or process decomposition. For example, the process which is shown on one level as a single box and which the user knows as:

Order validation

may be represented by several processes:

Order input
Order errors processing
Orders requiring authorization

at a lower level. Three levels of DFD are usually sufficient. We might call these:

1. The top-level DFD: showing the overall effect of the system with each functional area, or sub-system, together with the major inputs and outputs.
2. The intermediate-level DFD: one such DFD for each process on the top-level DFD.
3. The low-level DFD: one such DFD for each process on the intermediate-level DFD.

It is not usual to go lower than the third such level, and – as a rule of thumb – each DFD should contain no more than 10 process boxes. This will allow us to handle up to 1000 processes in any one system – and this should be enough for even the most comprehensive processing. If you find that you need more than

10 boxes on any one DFD, then you are probably going into too much detail. A very simple process may only appear on the top-level DFD.

3.3.7 Producing the current data flow diagram

The following points should be borne in mind when producing the current DFD:

1. The DocFD is used to provide the necessary information for this DFD.
2. The DFD represents the processes, data stores, entities, data flows, and physical resources of the system.
3. The entities used on the DFD include the external entities and the internal functional areas of the organization. These are represented by boxes.
4. The data flows are represented by lines with a single arrow-head to indicate the direction in which the data flows.
5. The data flows show the nature of the data which they carry and not the names of the documents which they may represent.
6. Data flows are used to carry data between external entities and processes, or between processes and data stores.
7. The data stores show where data is held – be it permanently or temporarily. These are represented by open-ended boxes, each one having a unique identifier.
8. Data stores are used to pass data between processes.
9. To identify processes, think about the events – where information is received. Every event – the arrival of information – triggers a process. The production of information, such as the printing of a report, does not itself trigger a process. A process such a **PRINT SALES STATISTICS** must be triggered by the arrival of information – a request from the user or from management.
10. Ensure that the arrival of every document and physical resource shown on your DocFD triggers a process on your DFD.
11. Ensure that any process which produces information is triggered by the arrival of other information: this may simply be a user request, as mentioned in (9) above.
12. There may be up to three levels of DFD: the top-level, the intermediate-level and the low-level DFDs.
13. Each process box on the top-level DFD may be expanded into its own intermediate-level DFD, and each process box on the intermediate DFD may be expanded into its own low-level DFD.
14. If a top-level process box has a large number of data flows – for example, where a single event requires a large number of data stores to be involved – then you may prefer to produce a lower-level diagram so that the names of the data can be shown more clearly.
15. When you expand a process box at a lower level, make sure that the external entities and the data flows to the data stores are consistent with those at the higher level.

16. There should be no more than ten process boxes on any one DFD.

You will review and cross-check your data flow diagram as you produce your data structure diagram.

The resulting DFD will represent the processing which is carried out in the current system and will be used in conjunction with the problems and requirements list in order to derive a design for the proposed system.

3.4   CURRENT DATA STRUCTURE DIAGRAM

It is convenient to have a diagrammatic representation of the data used by the current system and the relationships between the various pieces of data. The chief components of such a diagram are the entities, and although the term may be interpreted as meaning record type, we shall use the definition:

Entity: an object or a concept which is meaningful to an organization and about which there is a need to record and hold data. The term is also used to denote the groups of data which are held about such objects or concepts. For this reason, an entity corresponds to a file at the physical level.

We can illustrate this by considering a customer invoicing system which might have entities such as customer, purchase order, product, invoice, storage depot and stock, or a personnel system may have entities such as manager, worker, department, and payroll. It should be noted that this use of the word 'entity' is quite different from that implied by the term external entity which we met earlier.

An entity does not exist in isolation, but is associated with other entities by means of a relationship. For example, one Product may be stocked at many Storage Depots; one Customer may submit several Purchase Orders; one Purchase Order may be submitted for several Products; one Department is controlled by one Manager; one Product may be ordered on several Purchase Orders.

A data structure diagram (DSD) represents the entities and the relationships which exist between these entities. The data structure diagram is also known as a data model or a logical model.

In a DSD, each entity is represented by a box with the name of the entity – a singular noun – written inside it, as illustrated in Fig. 3.10.

Some analysts use a hexagon instead of a box to represent the entity. Others use an ellipse, and for this reason their data structure diagrams are often called **bubble charts**.

Figure 3.10 Data entity.

One-to-one relationship

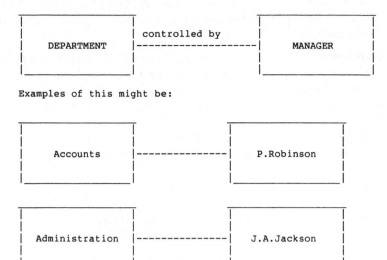

Figure 3.11 One-to-one relationship.

One-to-many relationship

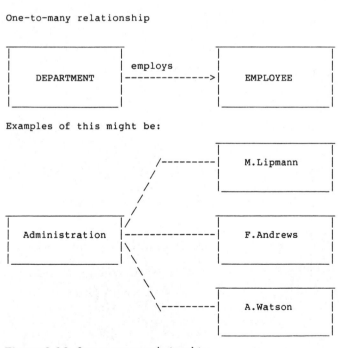

Figure 3.12 One-to-many relationship.

The relationships are represented by a line linking two entities with an arrowhead at one end, both ends or neither end. A description of the relationship is written above the line. If we consider the relationships logically, we see that there are four possible types:

1. One-to-one – one Department may be controlled by only one Manager, as shown in Fig. 3.11; this may be recorded in your notes as:
   Controlled by: Department 1:1 Manager
2. One-to-many – one Department may employ many Employees, as shown in Fig. 3.12.
   Employ: Department 1:many Employee
3. Many-to-one – many Employees may report to one Manager, as shown in Fig. 3.13.
   Report to: Employee many:1 Manager
4. Many-to-many – one Purchase Order may request many Products, and one Product may be ordered on many Purchase Orders, as shown in Fig. 3.14.
   Request: Purchase Order many:many Product: Ordered on

The contents of the relevant Purchase Orders are shown at the right of the diagram.

In practice, only two relationships need be used on DSDs: one-to-one and one-to-many. Many-to-one is really just another interpretation of one-to-many. A

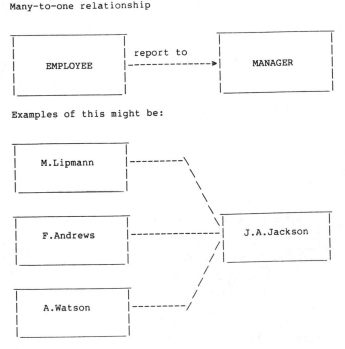

Figure 3.13 Many-to-one relationship.

Many-to-many relationship

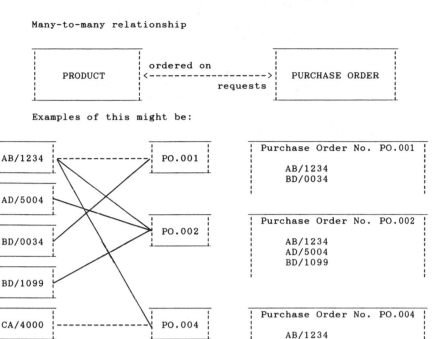

Figure 3.14 Many-to-many relationship.

many-to-many relationship can be resolved into two one-to-many relationships by means of a third entity. Thus, instead of the many-to-many relationship shown in Fig. 3.15(a) – which tells us that one Purchase order may order many Products, and one Product may be ordered on many Purchase orders – we would resolve this into two one-to-many relationships by the introduction of a third link entity Purchase order line, as shown in Fig. 3.15(b).

Some possible physical occurrences of such a structure are shown in Fig. 3.16. Compare this with the many-to-many examples shown in Fig. 3.14.

The ways in which the relationships are drawn may vary according to the conventions which are used. We shall use the following conventions, as illustrated in the examples:

1. A one-to-one relationship is represented by a simple line without arrow-heads:

   ———————————————

2. A one-to-many relationship is represented by a line with a single arrow-head at the many end:

   ————————————————————>

3. A many-to-many relationship (before it is resolved into two one-to-many relationships) is represented by a line with a single arrow-head at both ends:

   < ———————————————————— >

Other analysts use double arrow-heads and crows' feet!

a) Many-to-many relationship

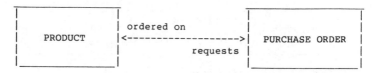

b) Two one-to-many relationships

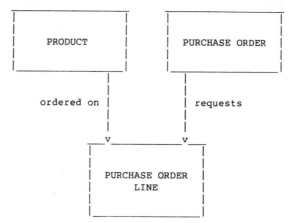

Figure 3.15 Resolving a many-to-many relationship.

Where possible, data structure diagrams usually show one-to-many relationships with the many end below that of the one end, as shown in Fig. 3.17.

In this example, the Customer is called the master entity, and the Purchase order is called the detail entity. As alternatives to master–detail, some analysts use the terms owner–member and parent–child.

The data structure diagram is derived intuitively from the investigations carried out previously, and is based upon the documents, files and records which are involved in the system. How does the analyst recognize entities and relationships? As a general rule, an entity is implied (1) whenever a **reference number** or a **code number** is encountered, e.g. Customer **reference**, Department **number**, Product **code**, Storage depot **i.d.**, or (2) when a **noun** is encountered, e.g. **order, Client, Depot, Employee**. A relationship is implied whenever a **transitive verb** is encountered, e.g.:

- a customer <u>sends in</u> an order
- an order <u>comprises</u> several order lines
- each student <u>attends</u> a course
- each employee <u>has</u> a manager

or when a **number** or a **repeating** idea is encountered, e.g.:

- a borrower may take out <u>up to three</u> books
- an order has <u>several</u> order lines

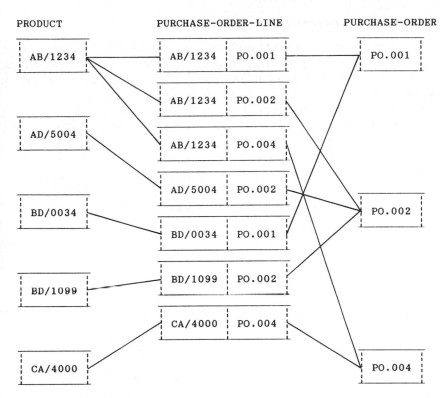

Figure 3.16 Link entity in practice.

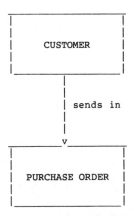

Figure 3.17 One-to-many relationship.

- a customer submits a number of orders
- an employee can have several job titles during his or her career
- we keep adding the details into the ledger.

3.4.1   Optional relationships

The '...-to-many' end of a relationship includes the three cases: none, one, or many. Thus, Fig. 3.17 implies that a Customer may send in no Purchase orders, one Purchase order, or several Purchase orders. Note that this implies that there may be Customers who do not send in any Purchase orders.

The ...-to-one or one-to-... end of a relationship includes only one case: there must be one and only one occurrence at the one end. Thus, Fig. 3.17 implies that any particular Purchase order is sent in by one Customer; there cannot be Purchase orders without an associated Customer.

In some situations, it may be possible for the detail entity to occur without the occurrence of an associated master entity. In the relationship shown in Fig. 3.18, each School may have none, one or many Persons attending it, and each Person may attend only one School.

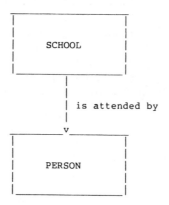

Figure 3.18 One-to-many relationship.

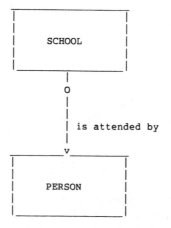

Figure 3.19 Optional relationships.

But there may be Persons – such as babies – who do not attend any School. In this case, the many-to-one detail–master relationship is said to be optional, and is drawn as in Fig. 3.19. The letter O along the relationship indicating that the Person–School relationship is optional.

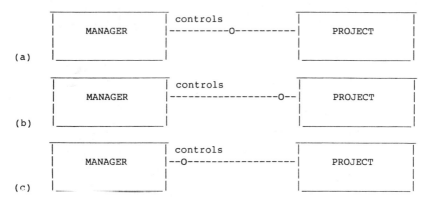

Figure 3.20 Examples of optional relationships.

We could also envisage a situation in which a one-to-one relationship had an optional entity, as illustrated in Fig. 3.20. For example, a Project may or may not be controlled by a Manager, and a Manager may or may not control a Project, Fig. 3.20(a). Fig. 3.20(b) shows the situation where a Project must be controlled by a Manager, but a Manager need not necessarily control a Project. Fig. 3.20(c) shows the situation where a Manager must control a Project, but a Project need not necessarily be controlled by a Manager.

3.4.2   Navigating through a diagram

In any DSD, it is possible to navigate from entity to entity by way of the relationships. By doing this, we shall be creating paths by which we – or our programs – can access the data and use these paths to answer enquiries about the data. Let us look at the DSD in Fig. 3.21 and see what sort of questions we are able to answer.

If we consider our diagram to be laid out as shown here, with the relationships going vertically downwards, then, in general, the questions require us to navigate:

1. **down** the relationship in the direction of the arrow – for a given relationship, find all the details for a specific master, and
2. **up** the relationship – for a given relationship, find the master of a specific detail.

The ease and elegance by which these access paths are traversed in the physical environment is a function of the database management system and the file handler which we use. We shall look at this again in Section 7.8.

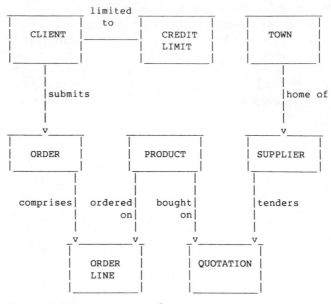

Figure 3.21 Data structure diagram.

We can only enter the diagram at a specific occurrence of any entity and from there we can navigate along any relationship in either direction. This means that we must know the key of the occurrence at which we wish to enter the diagram. Typical questions, among many others, which we might ask are:

1. What orders have been submitted by client number 1200?

    To answer this, we first obtain the information from **CLIENT** relating to client number 1200, and then follow the submits relationship to the **ORDER** entity to find all orders for that client.

2. What is the credit limit for the client who submitted order number S4000?

    We go the **ORDER** entity and obtain the information relating to order number S4000, and then follow the submits relationship to the **CLIENT** entity to find the number of the client who submitted that order. Then we follow the limited to relationship to the **CREDIT-LIMIT** entity to find that client's credit limit.

    We can extend this process indefinitely, and we leave the reader to trace the access paths for the remaining questions:

3. What orders are there for product number AM/12300?
4. Which clients have submitted orders for product AV/34?
5. Which suppliers have tendered quotations for product FD/054?
6. Several suppliers have submitted quotations for product GG/77. In which towns are they based?
7. Which suppliers live in Dublin?
8. In which town does supplier number 4560 live?
9. What products do we obtain from suppliers who live in Brighton?

10. What are the credit limits for the clients who have submitted orders for products which come from suppliers who are based in Halifax?

We could not, however, answer these questions if they were phrased as:

- What orders have been submitted by the client Arthur Johnson? We cannot do this because Arthur Johnson is not the key field for a client.
- What orders are there for Plastic Grommets?
- Which clients have submitted orders for Sandalwood Paint?
- Which suppliers have tendered quotations for Brilliant White Emulsion Paint?
- In which town is supplier Acme Industrial Supplies based?

None of these pieces of information is the key field which we need to be able to enter the DSD. If we want to access a DSD by means of an entry point such as:

... client Arthur Johnson

then we must establish an **operational entity** which uses the **client name** as the key, as the section of the DSD in Fig. 3.22 illustrates.

To highlight any such operational entities that have been added to our diagram for purely practical reasons, we write a letter O – for operational – in the top right-hand corner of the box.

An **inverted file** is a common physical example of an operational entity, allowing a file to be accessed via the contents of non-key data field on that file. For example, it would be possible to access a Client file, with records such as those shown in Fig. 3.23, by means of the inverted files which are organized on the Name and the Location of the Client.

When we need to make an equiry about Arthur Johnson, we can enter the DSD using the Name file to obtain the Client number for Arthur Johnson, and then use this value (1101) to obtain Arthur Johnson's record from the Client file. Similarly,

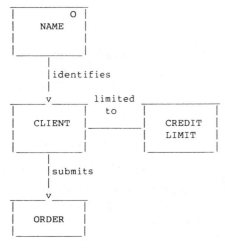

Figure 3.22 Operational entity using Client name as key.

NUMBER	NAME	LOCATION
1101	ARTHUR JOHNSON	MANCHESTER
2000	RITA COPLEY	LONDON
2003	JOHN DAVIES	LONDON
3455	ETHEL STEELE	MANCHESTER
4511	HARRY ANDREWS	MANCHESTER
6022	SHIRLEY MORRIS	LONDON

(a)

NAME	NUMBER
ARTHUR JOHNSON	1101
RITA COPLEY	2000
JOHN DAVIES	2003
ETHEL STEELE	3455
HARRY ANDREWS	4511
SHIRLEY MORRIS	6022

(b)

LOCATION	NUMBER
LONDON	2000 2003 6022
MANCHESTER	1101 3455 4511

(c)

Figure 3.23 Examples of a man data file (a); and inverted files (b), (c).

if we want to know the Clients who live in Manchester, then we can use the Location file to obtain the Client numbers for the Clients living in Manchester, and then use these values (1101, 3455, and 4511) to obtain the appropriate records from the Client file.

3.4.3   Producing the current data structure diagram

The following points should be borne in mind when producing the DSD:

1. The DSD is used at this stage to ensure that we have represented all the data used by the current system; it offers facilities to cross-check the information represented on the DFD;
2. The DSD shows the entities and their relationships with each other;
3. The DFD and the associated forms are used to identify the entities;

4. You will recognize an entity as something which is given a name or which is identified by a reference number;
5. You will recognize a relationship in the verbs which are used;
6. Remove any many-to-many relationships by introducing a third link entity to produce two one-to-many relationships.

The resulting DSD is used to verify other stages in the data analysis of the system, and will serve as a means of cross-checking and corroborating your DFD.

3.5 SUMMARY

A number of documents are used during the analysis of the current system:

- document flow matrix
- document flow diagrams
- problems and requirements list
- data flow diagrams
- data structure diagrams.

These are produced by the analyst in order to gain a picture of the current system. In deriving these documents, the analyst will be forced to ask questions, and in the light of the answers it will be possible to cross-check and modify the diagrams to be certain that they represent a consistent and accurate picture.

Although a sequence has been implied in the production and use of these documents, they are developed in parallel, with the results at one stage reinforcing or questioning those found at another. Moreover, their life is a continuous cycle of review and amendment.

3.6 QUESTIONS

3.1. Describe the purpose of a document flow diagram.

3.2. How does a document flow diagram differ from a data flow diagram?

3.3. What are the main components of a document flow diagram?

3.4. We have been asked to look at the member and retailing billing parts of a system which is concerned with the billing and payments for the Acme Credit Company. This is currently based upon outdated punched-card equipment. If they have a lot of membership applications at once, they have to turn customers – retailers and members – away because they can only just cope with their present business. This has led to delays in their processing. Briefly, the business is as follows:

The Acme Credit Company's business is to offer credit facilities to their members.
Members are recruited through advertisements in the press. A member

submits a completed application form and, assuming that this is in order, the member is issued with a card which authorizes him to make purchases at participating retail outlets.

When making the purchase, the member shows his card to the retailer who checks its authenticity and validity, then issues a sales voucher. The member signs the sales voucher and takes the goods. The member retains one copy of the sales voucher, the retailer retains a copy for his files, and one copy is sent to the credit company.

The retailer sends a copy of the sales voucher to the Retailer Accounts Section of the credit company, and receives a monthly statement showing the total value of the sales. The retailer is paid this amount less a 10% service charge. This copy of the sales voucher is then passed on to the Member Accounts Section. Sales vouchers sometimes get lost because of the volume of paperwork going around inside the company.

The Member Accounts Section send a monthly statement of account to the member, against which the member must pay 5% of the total, or, if this is less than £5, the full amount. The member may, if he wishes, pay the full outstanding amount. The payment must be sent to the credit company within 20 days of the date of the statement. If the full outstanding amount is not paid, then interest is charged on the full amount and the balance is carried forward to next month. If the member makes no payment, then a reminder letter is sent. This is followed by a legal letter if no payment is received in response to a second monthly statement. If a member has no outstanding balance then no statement is sent.

For brevity, we have given only a minimum of detail about this fictitious company, but, whilst the system mentioned here is much simpler than a real company might be, some of the external aspects envisaged here are similar to those of well-known credit companies, and some inferences can be drawn and assumptions made, based upon any experience which the reader may have of similar organizations.

We shall refer to the Acme Credit Company again below.

First, make a list of the external entities which send or receive information, documents or physical resources.

3.5.   For the Acme Credit Company, make a list of the internal functional areas, or internal entities which send or receive information, documents or physical resources.

3.6.   For the Acme Credit Company, make a list of the documents and physical resources – such a materials and goods – which flow within the system.

3.7.   For the Acme Credit Company, draw up a Document Flow Matrix to show what documents and physical resources pass between which external entities and functional areas.

3.8. Draw a document flow diagram using the document flow matrix produced for Question 3.7.

3.9. What are the main components of a data flow diagram? Describe and give an example of each.

3.10. What is the difference between a data store and a data flow?

3.11. A data flow diagram can show an outline of the system, or it may go into more detail. What are these various levels of data flow diagram called?

3.12. At the local lending library, a member may borrow books. Members' details are held on a file. If a book is out on loan, a member may complete a reservation form to reserve the book when it is returned. If a certain book is not available, a member may complete a suggestion form to suggest that the library purchases the book. Books are bought – one copy of each – from a number of suppliers. Each book is identified by its acquisition number. Each supplier and each member are identified by their respective names.

   Draw a data structure diagram for the entities and the relationships encountered in such a system.

   Modify your data structure diagram so that it is possible to enquire about the availability of a book by its title or by its author.

3.13. A stationery supply company has a number of goods depots located around the country. The company's products are promoted by a number of salesmen who visit the clients and prospective clients. The salesmen take orders from the clients and send these to the depot which is nearest to the client.

   Draw a data structure diagram for the entities and the relationships encountered in such a system.

3.14. At the Acme College of Further Education, there are 1700 students. Each student is following one or more of 70 different courses of study – for example, O-level Mathematics, A-level French, BSc. in Physics, and so on. A course of study is made up of several study modules – usually about eight modules per course. Each module is made up of about six lessons. Some of these lessons are common to more than one course – for example lesson L034 may be attended by A-level Computer Science students and also by first year business studies undergraduates. Each student takes an examination on completion of each module. The students' scores for each module are recorded.

   For administrative purposes, each student is allocated to one of 30 counsellors. The lessons are given by one of 78 teaching staff. Counsellors are drawn from the teaching staff.

Draw a data structure diagram for the entities and the relationships encountered in such a system.

3.15. A car hire company has 50 cars at its disposal. Each car is identified by its registration number. These cars are based at one of seven garages, each of which is known by its name: East Sussex, Gatwick, Heathrow, and so on. Any car can be serviced at one of three service centres. The service centres are at Gatwick, Brighton and Heathrow. Any of the company's clients may hire an available car for one or more hours, collecting the car from the garage and leaving it at any other garage.

Draw a data structure diagram for the entities and the relationships encountered in such a system.

3.16. What is meant by an optional relationship? Give some examples.

3.17. What is an operational entity? Why are they used? Give some examples of operational entities that might be required in the Acme Credit Company system mentioned above.

3.18. The records on a name and address file have the following format:

- 4-digit record-key
- alphabetic surname
- alphabetic initials
- alphanumeric street number
- alphanumeric street name
- alphabetic town name
- alphanumeric postcode

as shown in the table in Fig. 3.24.

The data are to be inverted. Show the format of the inverted lists – or records – relating to this file, and say what use could be made of each inverted list. How could you use the inverted lists to answer the questions:

'What are the names of the people who live in Main Street?'
'What are the initials of the people called Smith who live in Doncaster?'

3.19. What are the main components of a data structure diagram?

3.20. An entity is the same as a file. Is this true?

3001	SMITH	J	34	HIGH STREET	LINCOLN	LN1 2FG
4001	WILSON	A	96	MAIN ROAD	LINCOLN	LN7 7XC
5003	SMITH	P	34	MAIN AVENUE	DONCASTER	DO8 8XC
6003	WILSON	J	12	GREEN STREET	LINCOLN	LN1 2FG

Figure 3.24 Part of a database.

3.21. Why is it important to make a written list of the problems and requirements of the current system?

3.22. What use will be made of the problems and requirements list during the systems analysis phase? During the systems design phase? Will any use be made of the list after the final system has been implemented?

3.23. Look at the description of the current system at the Acme Credit Company given in Question 3.4, and produce a list of potential problems and any requirements suggested there.

Interlude 1

The intermediate stages

On the basis of your investigations and analysis, you have derived two models of the current system – the process model represented by the data flow diagrams – and the data model represented by the data structure diagram. You should now be in a position to say that you understand the business problems involved in the system.

It should be stressed that your knowledge may not be complete. The structured methodology will make you think more deeply about the system, and you will often be forced to return to your users to ask them specific questions – questions which you did not ask earlier, possibly questions which they had never needed to consider in the existing system. In the light of the users' answers to your questions, your findings must be revised and your documents and diagrams amended.

What happens next depends very much on the business environment in which you will be working. In some situations, you may be required to report to the users to describe what you and your proposed system could do and how much it would cost. This information will form a part of your argument when you seek approval before going on to design the system. In other situations, you may be able to proceed directly to the design stage. If yours is the latter case, then the activities described in this chapter will be incorporated with those of data analysis and functional analysis which we discuss in the following chapters.

You are now equipped to offer the user a number of possible ways in which the present system could be reorganized and extended to achieve at least some of the goals established in the problems and requirements list, whilst losing none of its present facilities, for example:

1. remove redundant processes: cease production of the weekly report which is not used
2. modify existing processes: allow orders to be made by telephone, or replace a printed report by an on-line enquiry
3. rearrange existing processes: produce the invoices in a batch run overnight, instead of producing each one as it is generated
4. combine existing processes: a membership application may be vetted by one department and then passed on to another department for addition to the files; the vetting and addition could be performed in a single process
5. add new processes: introduce an order vetting process to check the customer status and product availability before proceeding with the order
6. produce a new report: a customer credit report would allow management to make better decisions

... or change the existing resources:

7. employ new staff: an extra temporary clerk might solve a bottle-neck
8. reorganize existing staff: change the distribution of work amongst the staff
9. re-train existing staff: sending a secretary on a business management course might enable her to perform other duties
10. replace existing staff: a qualified accountant would be more expensive than two junior clerks but the savings might be recouped quickly
11. obtain new equipment: a word processor would speed up the acknowledgement of orders
12. replace existing equipment: a bar-code reader might be simpler than the current keyboard terminal when stock-taking.

When the user has considered and reacted to your suggestions, you can proceed to design the proposed system.

Int. 1.1   TECHNICAL SYSTEM

Up to this point, we have made no real assumptions that a computerized solution will be – or even need be – adopted. We have looked at the current system, and based upon our findings we have decided what is required logically of any new system, but another streamlined manual system, possibly incorporating some of the suggestions made in the previous section, may be perfectly suitable. For the purposes of the present book, however, we shall assume that a decision has been made to proceed with a computer-based system. It is now time, therefore, for you to offer the user a number of possible technical solutions to achieve your business system. In order to do this, you must become completely familiar with the current range of equipment which is available. When you have done this, you should check that it meets the requirements of your proposed system by asking:

1. Will it do what is needed?
2. Is it compatible with the other equipment which is already used, or which may be needed in the future?
3. What is the capacity of the device? Will it hold enough data for this application?
4. What is the speed of the device? Will the access times and the data transfer times be suitable for this application?
5. Will it be available in time?
6. Is the after-sales support adequate?
7. Is the price right?
8. Is any special training required for the users?
9. Can I talk to anyone who has used this equipment? Can I visit a working installation?

When you have found the answers to these questions, they will be presented to your users in a manner which will emphasize the cost effectiveness and other benefits to be gained by obtaining the equipment which you propose.

Int. 1.2 FUNCTIONAL SPECIFICATION

Traditional systems analysis produces a statement of requirements as a part of its formal documentation. This will be produced after the systems analysis and used as a basis for the design. It is a report covering the following areas:

1. introduction to the system, the terms of reference, the reasons for change, and the objectives
2. the functional requirements of the system: what it does for the user
3. the process model for the system: this is represented by the data flow diagrams
4. input data and documents, together with details of their source, preparation, format and volumes
5. file descriptions and record formats: there may be a preliminary data model for the system supported by the data structure diagrams
6. output results, data and reports, together with details of their distribution, format and volumes
7. description of the clerical and other procedures associated with the system
8. the hardware configuration which is required including the computer hardware and the supporting equipment; we discussed this in the previous section.

When such a document is presented as a functional specification, it will describe what the system is to do but not how it is to do it.

This statement of requirements can be used as basis for a decision as to whether or not the user will proceed with the system, or it may pre-suppose such a decision and represent the starting point for the more detailed systems design activity. In many commercial situations, the document represents a proposal for the solution which is to be provided, and the user will be asked to sign his acceptance of this specification, and all further development will be based upon the contents of the specification. In other environments, there is considerable overlap in the aims and objectives of the statement of requirements and the proposal.

Int. 1.2.1   Cost-effective solution

In order to demonstrate that any particular solution is cost-effective, the analyst must provide cost comparisons for the current system – if there is one – and for each alternative. Each comparison statement should be supported by information about costs: the capital cost of any equipment; the development costs of any software; the running costs; personnel and salaries; the overheads; the estimated life of the system.

These should be offset by figures for any measurable benefits of the proposals: increased income; savings on reduced stock-holdings; cash flow.

You should also indicate any non-measurable benefits: improved turnaround of orders; goodwill; public good, public standing and respect.

Int. 1.2.2   Benefits

Whenever you present any proposal for consideration, you must always stress the benefits to be gained by adopting your proposal.

The benefits of most commercial systems can be reduced to one essential factor: money – either an increase in income, or a reduction in costs and outgoings. If you are proposing – selling the idea of – a computerized invoicing system, your user may not be influenced by the simple facts that it is faster, that it gives more information on the invoices, or that it works on the same equipment that is being used at present. You must present the features as benefits to your user and in terms of what they mean to the user:

- It is faster, therefore it will speed up the billing process and improve the user's cash flow situation;
- It gives more detailed information on the invoices, therefore your user's clients will be more satisfied and possibly spend more money with the company;
- It runs on the current equipment, therefore your user need not go to the expense of buying new equipment or extending his present equipment.

You must remember these points at all times when you are preparing a proposal, making a presentation, motivating staff, and teaching your users.

Int. 1.3   SUMMARY

We have performed the analysis and derived an accurate picture of the current system. We have built up a list of problems which the users have experienced with the current system and further requirements which they may have of any future system. Using our business experience we are able to make recommendations to the users and suggest ways in which the current system could be modified to solve some of the problems and meet some of the requirements without affecting the results and without putting additional strain upon the existing resources.

We can also suggest commercial and technical possibilities about a proposed system, such as what new tasks it will perform and what equipment might be used. We shall use these suggestions – backed up by our investigations – to produce a document which proposes the future system. This will indicate the costs of the proposed system and the benefits which are to be gained.

When a decision is made to go ahead, the systems design phase will commence.

4

Structured systems design – data analysis

Having completed your investigation and analysis, and obtained approval to go ahead with the proposed system, you are now ready to proceed to the systems design phase. The design for the proposed system – both in terms of data and the processing – must address all of the areas of the current system and the modifications made to it in the light of the users' problems and requirements together with your own suggestions. The likely problem areas will include the following aspects of the new system:

1. Acceptability: the system must be accepted by all the users, management, auditors, financial controllers, customers, staff and unions.
2. Accuracy: the required accuracy must be afforded by the system.
3. Adaptability and flexibility: the system must be able to cope with anticipated demands, in terms of the volume of business and data which are handled, and it must also handle reasonable unexpected variations without degradation or loss of information. In the longer term, it must also be possible to modify and extend the system to accommodate any reasonable changes which are as yet unknown.
4. Availability: it must be available when promised, for example, where systems are required in the time for the new tax year. The system must also be available as required after implementation, and must not be tied up with routine housekeeping tasks when the users need it.
5. Confidentiality, privacy and security: the contents of the system must be protected from unauthorized access. This may be necessary for social and legislative reasons, as in the case of information held about individuals, and for commercial reasons in the case of information about the organization itself. You should ask yourself about the data within the system: Are they accessible? Are they readable? Are they transportable? Does this accessibility, readability and transportability apply to any unauthorized parties?
6. Control: the information offered and provided by the system must be presented in a timely and appropriate manner in order to enable the management to exercise the necessary control on the organization.
7. Cost: the prime objective of any computer system is to minimize the costs to the organization and to make the best possible use of the finances which are available.

8. Data integrity: the processes within the system must ensure that all items of data are mutually consistent.
9. Efficiency: the system must be efficient in terms of doing what the users want, and also in terms of the ways in which it utilizes the resources of the organization and those of the computer environment.
10. Integration: the system must integrate the numerous data resources which are used within the organization, ensuring that they are held in a manner which is consistent and accessible to all users.
11. Reliability: the system must be reliable in the face of breakdowns or disruptions of either the human elements or the mechanical elements.

Armed with the results of our initial investigation – the problems and requirements list, data flow diagrams and data structure diagrams – and with the above points at the back of our mind, we are now ready to start the design. The major elements of the design stage are known, perhaps a little confusingly, as data analysis and functional analysis.

We start with data analysis. Chapter 5 considers the functional analysis.

4.1   DATA ANALYSIS

When we were producing the data structure diagram, we considered the data of the system in an informal, almost intuitive, manner. We now need to perform a more rigorous analysis, using essentially the same sources, and use this to produce a data model of the proposed system. We shall use the following definition:

> **Data analysis:** the analysis and structuring of information in order to produce a global data model representing the information needs of an organization.

The first step on our way to producing the global data model is to produce a series of local data models. We do this by gathering information from the various functional areas, collecting samples of the data, the files, the forms and the documents which they use. These will include:

- record cards
- ledgers
- manual files
- reports
- input documents

and, if the data is already held on a computer system:

- computer file layouts
- screen formats
- report formats

The proposed system is certain to include new processes, new reports, new documents. So you will also include your draft reports and the intended documents which are to be concerned with the new processes. You will have drawn up these new documents and reports in conjunction with the users.

4.2 DATABASE

Most users, analysts and programmers are familiar with the term database. Some consider the term – at its most fashionable – to be synonymous with a collection of files. This is not necessarily true. Let us look at a set of files for a simple personnel system, such as we might find in a traditional commercial computing environment and see how they stand up against this definition.

Database: a collection of stored data which is organized in such a way that it satisfies all the data requirements of an organization. In general, there is only one copy of each data item within the databse.

Fig. 4.1 shows three files holding details of Employees, the Duty-list, and the Departments.

These files probably evolved as a result of the needs of three separate users or

EMPLOYEES

EMP	SURNAME	INIT	ADDRESS	PHONE
1001	SMYTHE	J.A	34 WALTER ST	466557
1003	WATKINS	R.P	123 HIGH ROAD	466166
1005	WATTS	A	3 ILFORD RD	466304
1006	DENTON	M	5 ATHERSTONE ST	466451

DEPARTMENTS

DEPT	EMP	NAME
LAB	1001	J.A.SMITH
LAB	1006	M.DENTON
ADMIN	1003	R.P.WATKINS
ADMIN	1005	A.WATTS

DUTY-LIST

NUMBER	NAME	PHONE	DATE
1001	SMITH	466557	2/9/88
1005	WATTS	466304	9/9/88

Figure 4.1 A database.

programmers. The **EMPLOYEES** file holds the basic information about each employee. A list of **DEPARTMENTS** and their staffing was later requested and a new file was established to hold the information and allow it to be printed. Some time later, there came a requirement to produce a duty-list showing the name and telephone number of each employee and the dates when they were on duty.

You will see that there is much duplication of data in such an arrangement, and not all of the data is consistent or correct. For example, the name – **SMITH** or is it **SMYTHE**? – is held on all three files. What happens if Miss Smith gets married and changes her name? We should have to change her name on every file. What happens if Mr Watts changes his telephone number and the Name and Address Update Program only changes it on the **EMPLOYEES** file? What about his name on the **DUTY-LIST**? Whenever there is a duplication of data in this way, there is a possibility that it will threaten the integrity of the system; one occurrence of the field might be changed whilst another occurrence might not be changed. In many computer systems, this duplication is quite uncontrolled, with each program creating and maintaining its own files quite oblivious to the other programs and files. This is why you may get several letters from an organization, one with your name spelled correctly and one with your name spelled incorrectly. To resolve this, each item of data should be held in one place only.

If we were to reorganize the files so as to avoid such duplication, then we might find that, whilst the **EMPLOYEES** file stays the same in this case, the other two files may look like those shown in Fig. 4.2.

Now, when the Duty-list has to be produced to show the name and telephone-number of the employee, the report program can read the records from the **DUTY-LIST** file to find the employee-number, and then use this to retrieve the employee's name and telephone-number from the **EMPLOYEES** file. If Miss Smith does

```
DUTY-LIST

 _____
|        |         |
| NUMBER | DATE    |
|_____|_____|
|        |         |
| 1001   | 2/9/88  |
| 1005   | 9/9/88  |
|_____|_____|
```

```
DEPARTMENTS

 _____
|        |         |
| DEPT   | EMP     |
|_____|_____|
|        |         |
| LAB    | 1001    |
| LAB    | 1006    |
| ADMIN  | 1003    |
| ADMIN  | 1005    |
|_____|_____|
```

Figure 4.2 Inverted lists.

Figure 4.3 Functional dependency.

change her name, or Mr Watts changes his telephone-number, the Name and Address Update Program will amend the fields on the **EMPLOYEES** file and the Duty-list program will subsequently pick up the correct information from there when it is needed. Such a collection of files accords with our definition of a database: all the data are accessible for the users, and there is only one copy of each piece of data.

A number of powerful techniques have been developed for analysing the data-requirements within the organization, for designing the files which hold those data, and for providing means by which they can be made accessible to programs and end-users alike. These offer a rigorous set of principles, the practice of which is known as information engineering.

In a moment, we shall look at the technique of normalization which is one of the procedures that you will carry out in order to arrive at a possible design for such a collection of files – a design for a database. Before we start, however, there are a couple of points which we must clarify.

4.2.1 Functional dependency

When we consider the data within the system, we often find that one piece of data is **dependent upon** another. If we think of a client record, then we can say that the Client-name is dependent upon the Client-number, because the Client-name can only be found **if** we know the Client-number. Such functional dependency can be shown diagrammatically as in Fig. 4.3. The individual attributes are represented by hexagons, and the dependency is shown by a line with an arrow-head pointing towards the dependent attribute.

The Client-address is also functionally dependent upon the Client-number. We can show this by the diagram in Fig. 4.4.

On a purchase order, we may find that the Order-quantity depends upon both the Order-number and the Product-number. This can be represented by the diagram shown in Fig. 4.5.

In turn, the Product-description is functionally dependent upon the Product-number. We can represent these last two facts by the diagram shown in Fig. 4.6. Other diagramming techniques would represent this last information in the manner showed in Fig. 4.7.

Functional dependency diagrams, such as these, can be a valuable tool when you are trying to clarify your thoughts about the interrelationship and the

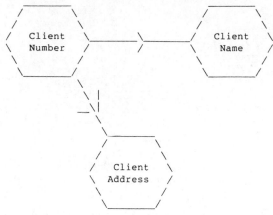

Figure 4.4 The Client-address and Client-name are functionally dependent upon the Client-number.

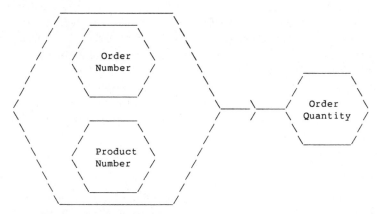

Figure 4.5 Order-quantity is functionally dependent upon the Order-number and Product-number.

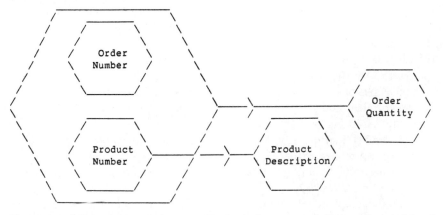

Figure 4.6 Order-quantity is functionally dependent upon Order-number and Product-number and Product description is functionally dependent upon Product-number.

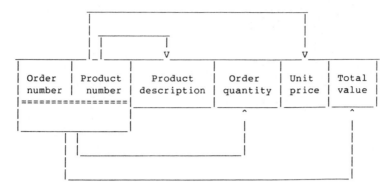

Figure 4.7 Alternative diagram representing the information in Fig. 4.6.

dependency of the various attributes in an entity. They show that, in these examples:

1. if we know the Client-number, then this uniquely identifies the Client-name
2. if we know the Client-number, then this uniquely identifies the Client-address
3. if we know the Order-number and the Product-number, then these uniquely identify the Quantity-ordered, and,
4. if we know the Product-number, then this uniquely identifies the Product-description.

We shall use this definition:

Functional dependency: an attribute, A, is functionally dependent upon another attribute, B, if attribute A can be uniquely identified when the value of attribute B is known.

We shall use the concept of functional dependency when we discuss data normalization.

4.2.2 Entity or file?

When we were discussing the data structure diagram, we referred to each box on the diagram as an entity. In physical terms, we may have been interpreting this as a file. Other words will come along. So perhaps we should think a moment about the meaning of these and other terms: **entity, item, attribute, file, record, field, data item, aggregate, occurrence.**

Unfortunately, there is a blurring in the meaning and the usage of these terms. Nevertheless, in broad terms, we can say that **entity, item** and **attribute** are used during the analysis and design phases of our work, when we are talking about conceptual or logical data models, whereas **file, record, field, data item, aggregate** and **occurrence** are used in connection with the physical realization of the logical models and during the programming activity.

In logical terms, an entity is made up of items, and these items are made up of

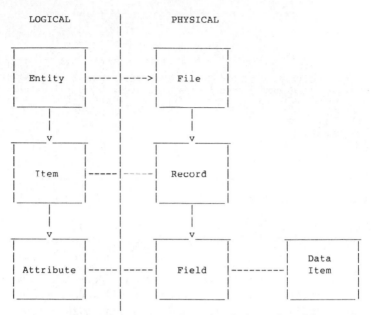

Figure 4.8 Distinction between logical and physical models.

attributes. In physical terms, a file is made up of records, and these records are made up of fields, or data items. Fig. 4.8 illustrates this. When the transition is made from logical to physical, one entity may be represented by several files as a result of the constraints of the particular operating system which we are using.

An occurrence is simply a real example of a record or a field. When we represent a format or an occurrence of a record, we shall separate the various fields by a colon. In practice, the fields may be fixed length and not physically separate, or they may be identifiable in other ways. Thus, if a record has the format

Client-number:Client-name:Credit-limit

then an occurrence of this record might be

1234:JONES, A.B.:1000.00.

Another occurrence of the Client-name field might be:

RICHARDSON-FITZPATRICK, E.W.

Client-name may be referred to as an attribute name or a field name.

An aggregate is a single data item, such as the occurrence 251288, which may be interpreted as representing several values, possibly day, month and year.

4.3   NORMALIZATION

When producing the conceptual data model – the data structure diagram – during the analysis stage, we looked at the entities in broad terms; we did not concern ourselves with the detailed data. By using the data relations and other information which we have gathered, we can now look more closely at the actual pieces of data which must be processed.

In many traditional systems – manual and computer systems – there is much duplication of data, as we saw when we discussed databases. This situation arises for a number of reasons:

- Each program was designed to read, process and create its own data files;
- It was considered preferable to hold several pieces of data on one record, rather than perform several operations to read the data from several different records;
- The usage of the data by one department of an organization – such as Sales – may have been considered to be distinct from the usage by another department – such as Personnel.

Each user has his or her own view of the data which the organization uses, and although the user is only concerned with the data within this local data model, each such view must now be considered as a part of the global data model.

When we are analysing the data for our system, in order to produce a consistent database, we have two objectives:

1. to ensure that each piece of data is accessible to any process which needs that data
2. to ensure that each piece of data is held in one place only

One of the steps in our data analysis – normalization – is designed to attain these objectives. The technique of normalization is a rule-based procedure. It will provide a cross-check for the data model which we built up earlier, and for the functional analysis which we shall perform later.

We can illustrate the process of normalization by considering the simple Sales Order form which is shown in Fig. 4.9.

4.3.1 Step 1 – the raw data

The first step in the normalization process is to list the raw data items. The Sales Order in Fig. 4.9 would yield the following attributes:

Order-number
Order-date
Delivery-date
Customer-number
Customer-name
Customer-address
Product-number
Product-description
Product-quantity
Unit-price
Order-line-total
Order-total

```
| ***** ACME FURNITURE COMPANY LIMITED *****              |
|                                                          |
|          ***** SALES ORDER *****                         |
|                                                          |
| ORDER NUMBER| 111111              ORDER-DATE| 02/02/87   |
|                                 DELIVERY DATE| 02/05/87   |
|                                                          |
|   CUSTOMER  | 33333                                      |
|             |                                            |
|             | JOHN SMITH AND CO LTD                      |
|             | 34 HIGH STREET, YORK                       |
|                                                          |
| | PRODUCT | DESCRIPTION |QTY | UNIT  | COST    |         |
| |         |             |    | PRICE |         |         |
| |  44444  | WOODEN CHAIRS|  5 | 66.00 | 330.00  |         |
| |  77777  | STEEL TABLES |  8 | 99.00 | 792.00  |         |
|                                                          |
|                            TOTAL      1122.00            |
|                                                          |
```

Figure 4.9 A sales order form.

```
SALES-ORDER (Order-number, Order-date, Delivery-date,
    Customer-number, Customer-name, Customer-address,
    (Product-number, Product-description, Product-quantity,
    Unit-price, Order-line-total), Order-total)
```

Figure 4.10 SALES-ORDER entity structure.

If we can recognize any attribute or attributes which uniquely identify the Sales Order – the key – then this will be underlined. The Order-number is the obvious choice here.

We shall use the notation in which the **SALES-ORDER** entity is illustrated in Fig. 4.10. This shows the name of the entity, the key attribute and the data attributes. Repeating groups are enclosed in parentheses.

4.3.2 Step 2 – first normal form

The next step in the normalization process is to remove the repeating groups. A repeating group is one or more attributes which may occur several times within the item.

In our Sales Order, there is such a repeating group – the order line – as shown in Fig. 4.11. Each occurrence of this group of data has the same importance as the others, and there may be one, two or any number of lines on one order.

44444	WOODEN CHAIRS	5	66.00	330.00
77777	STEEL TABLES	8	99.00	792.00

Figure 4.11 A repeating group of data.

This section of the order form is made up of (one or more) repetitions of the data group:

Product-number
Product-description
Product-quantity
Unit-price
Order-line-total

Therefore, we remove this repeating group and make this a separate entity. The key of the original entity becomes an attribute – normally a part of the key – of the new entity.

We now have two entities (Fig. 4.12) and since they do not contain any further repeating groups, these are said to be in the first normal form.

Each occurrence of the entity must have a unique key. The unique key for this new entity is a **compound key** made up of the Order-number from the original **SALES-ORDER** entity and the Product-number which identifies the particular

```
Order-number
Order-date
Delivery-date
Customer-number
Customer-name
Customer-address
Order-total

Order-number
Product-number
Product-description
Product-quantity
Unit-price
Order-line-total
```

SALES-ORDER (Order-number, Order-date, Delivery-date,
    Customer-number, Customer-name, Customer-address,
    Order-total)

ORDER-LINE (Order-number, Product-number, Product-
    description, Product-quantity, Unit-price, Order-line-
    total)

Figure 4.12 Two entities in the first normal form.

```
ORDER-LINE (Order-number, Line-number, Product-number,
   Product-description, Product-quantity, Unit-price,
   Order-line-total)
```

Figure 4.13 ORDER-LINE entity structure.

order-line in question. This is based on the assumption that any particular product is only ordered once on each order; if this is not so, then the key:

Order-number   Product-number

will not be unique. We should have to check this assumption with our users to ensure that it is valid. An alternative solution might be to allocate a unique LINE-NUMBER to each line on our Sales Order. This might yield the Order-line entity shown in Fig. 4.13.

4.3.3   Step 3 – second normal form

We discussed the idea of functional dependency in Section 4.2.1, and we shall use this concept at the next step in the normalization process:

For any data entities which have a compound key, remove any attributes which are not functionally dependent upon the entire key.

Looking at the **ORDER-LINE** entity of Fig. 4.12, we check the data attributes – not those of the key – to see which are functionally dependent upon the whole compound key (that is, those which are peculiar to this particular Order-line) and which are dependent upon only a part of the key.

Order-number
Product-number
Product-description – dependent upon Product-number only
Product-quantity – peculiar to this order line
Unit-price – dependent upon Product-number only
Order-line-total – peculiar to this order line.

We then remove those attributes which are not dependent upon the entire key – Product-description and Unit-price – and use them to establish one or more new entities. In this example, there will be only one new entity and this might have Product-number as its key.

We know that the Product-description is functionally dependent upon the Product-number because, given a value for the Product-number, 44444, for example, then we can obtain a unique value for the Product-description: WOODEN CHAIRS. However, the Product-quantity is dependent upon the entire key, because we must know both the Order-number, 111111, and the Product-number, 44444, in order to obtain the unique Product-quantity: 5. These two points are illustrated in the functional dependency diagram in Fig. 4.14.

When we have removed those attributes which are not functionally dependent

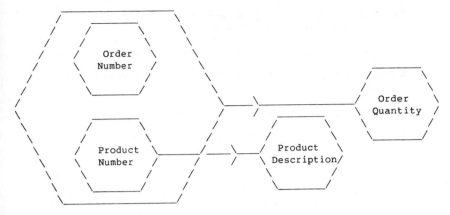

Figure 4.14 Functional dependency diagram.

```
SALES-ORDER (Order-number, Order-date, Delivery-date, Customer-
     number, Customer-name, Customer-address, Order-total)

ORDER-LINE (Order-number, Product-number, Product-quantity,
     Order-line-total)

PRODUCT (Product-number, Product-description, Unit-price)
```

Figure 4.15 Second normal form.

upon the entire compound key, our data are in the second normal form (Fig. 4.15).

4.3.4 Step 4 – third normal form

We use the idea of functional dependency again at the next step in the normalization process when we remove any data attributes which are functionally dependent upon other data attributes. Looking at the **SALES-ORDER** entity, we check the data attributes – not those of the key – to see which are functionally dependent upon other data attributes of that entity:

Order-number
Order-date
Delivery-date
Customer-number
Customer-name – dependent upon Customer-number
Customer-address – dependent upon Customer-number
Order-total

We then remove those which are dependent upon other attributes – Customer-

```
SALES-ORDER (Order-number, Order-date, Delivery-date,
   Customer-number, Order-total)

CUSTOMER (Customer-number, Customer-name, Customer-address)

ORDER-LINE (Order-number, Product-number, Product-quantity,
   Order-line-total)

PRODUCT (Product-number, Product-description, Unit-price)
```

Figure 4.16 Third normal form.

name and Customer-address – and use them to establish a new entity which has Customer-number as its key.

We know that the Customer-name is functionally dependent upon the Customer-number because, given a value for the Customer-number, 33333, for example, then we can obtain a unique value for the Customer-name: JOHN SMITH AND CO LTD. Similarly, given a value for the Customer-number, 33333, for example, then we can obtain a unique value for the Customer-address: 34 HIGH STREET, YORK.

We repeat this step for the **ORDER-LINE** entity, where Product-description and Unit-price are dependent upon Product-number. When we have considered all our entities and removed those attributes which are functionally dependent upon other attributes, our data is in the third normal form. These structures are shown in Fig. 4.16. The schema – map of the structure of this part of our database – and the relationships are represented diagrammatically in Fig. 4.17.

Some analysts use the term foreign key to indicate an attribute which is data in one entity and a key in another entity. A foreign key may be shown by prefixing the data attribute by an asterisk, as in the **SALES-ORDER** entity which is shown in Fig. 4.18, because the Customer-number is the key to the **CUSTOMER** entity.

4.3.5 Step 5 – consolidation

We have now derived the third normal form for our data. However, normalization is not concerned with just one entity in isolation. When we look at one input document as we have just done with the Sales Order, when we consider one report, or when we talk to the users in one functional area, we derive only a single local data model. A user in the Accounts functional area may be concerned only with the code-number, description and price of a stock-item, whilst another user in the Warehouse functional area may only be concerned with the dimensions of an item, its code-number and its location: two user-views of the data generating two individual – local – data models. We must now merge these separate local data models to produce the global data model for the organization – or at least that part of the organization which will be associated with our proposed system.

The normalization procedure is carried out for every document and every report – including those which are to be produced by the proposed system – for every functional area. By consolidating the individual local data models into a

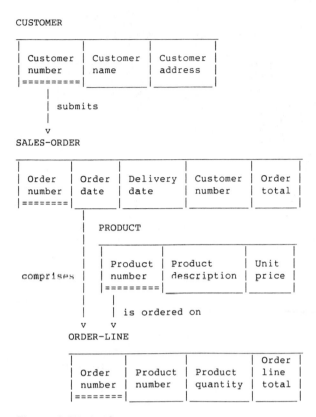

Figure 4.17 A schema.

SALES-ORDER (<u>Order-number</u>, Order-date, Delivery-date,
*Customer-number, Order-total)

Figure 4.18 Use of an asterisk to identify a foreign key in the data attributes.

single global data model, we can develop a flexible database whose properties include the accessibility of all necessary data and the elimination of situations in which the same piece of data is held in several places.

Let us suppose that, in addition to the sales orders shown above, the proposed system is to produce a **PRODUCT CATALOGUE**. The analyst's design for this report is shown in Fig. 4.19.

The normalization procedure will yield the entities shown in Fig. 4.20.

If we compare these structures with those shown in Fig. 4.16, we see that the **PRODUCT** entity derived from the Sales Order has the same key as this new **CATALOGUE** entity. We must now consider whether we should consolidate any entities which have the same key to give us a single **PRODUCT** entity.

PRODUCT (<u>Product number</u>, Product-description, Unit-price, Code)

PART	DESCRIPTION	LOCN	LAST USED	PRICE	QTY	CODE
0372	DESKS	MN/387	16/09/87	42.22	34	B70
		UK/101	01/02/87	42.22	56	
		UK2/9	31/03/87	42.22	20	
0567	STOOLS	MN/206	2/05/87	56.77	34	D4
		UK/20	29/07/86	56.77	32	
1000	CHAIRS	UK/614	7/10/87	58.75	55	L7
		MN/614	16/06/87	58.75	43	
1005	STOOLS	UK2/75	1/06/87	37.50	35	L8
1479	LADDERS	UK2/965	8/09/87	68.50	54	L8
		MN/100	11/02/87	68.50	30	

CATALOGUE (Part-Number, Description, (Location-code,
Last-used), Price, (Qty), Code)

Figure 4.19 Design for a Product Catalogue.

CATALOGUE (Part-Number, Description, Price, Code)

CATALOGUE-ENTRY (Part-Number, Location-code)

LOCATION (Location-code, Last-used, Qty)

Figure 4.20 Normalized CATALOGUE entity structures.

At this point, we must remember the important fact that various users and various situations may present us with the same data with different names. We can see that:

- Part-number and Product-number are synonyms
- Description and Product-description are synonyms
- Price and Unit-price are synonyms.

It is important for the analyst to be aware of such synonyms, otherwise the same piece of data may be held – redundantly – in several places, thus defeating one of the purposes of normalization of the data.

Another problem is the confusion brought about when the same name is used for two different items of data. For example, DATE may mean the date on which an order was placed on one entity, but it may mean the date on which we last withdrew items from stock on another entity. In this case, we might prefer to use longer, more explicit names such as SALES-ORDER-RECEIVED DATE and STOCK-LAST-USED-DATE. The analyst must always select attribute names

```
0372 MN/387
0372 UK/101
0372 UK2/9
0567 MN/206
0567 UK/20
1000 UK/614
1000 MN/614
1005 UK2/75
1479 UK2/965
1479 MN/100
```

Figure 4.21 Key-only entities.

carefully and with precision so as to avoid such homonyms within the database. The normalization of the **CATALOGUE** gave us a **CATALOGUE-ENTRY** entity:

CATALOGUE-ENTRY (Part-Number, Location-code)

This is a key-only entity, consisting of a key without any data attributes. Typical keys, based on the above data, would be as shown in Fig. 4.21.

When a key-only entity is encountered, you should consider whether or not the entity is useful. If a key-only entity serves no purpose, then we may discard it from our design. However, in this case the entity is indeed useful since it tells us which product is held in which location and which location holds which product. If we did not have this entity, then we should have to choose some other way of recording these two pieces of information. We could, for example, hold the Product-number in the **LOCATION** entity

LOCATION (Location-code, Product-number, Last-used, Qty)

and the link from Product-number to Location-code could be achieved by another entity

PRODUCT-LOCATION (Product-number, Sequence-number, Location-code)

of which typical occurrences might be as shown in Fig. 4.22.

A key which includes a non-real element like the Sequence-number in this example, is called a composite key by some analysts, whilst others do not distinguish between compound keys and composite keys.

```
0372 01 MN/387
0372 01 UK/101
0372 01 UK2/9
0567 01 MN/206
0567 01 UK/20
1000 01 UK/614
1000 01 MN/614
1005 01 UK2/75
1479 01 UK2/965
1479 01 MN/100
```

Figure 4.22 PRODUCT-LOCATION occurrences.

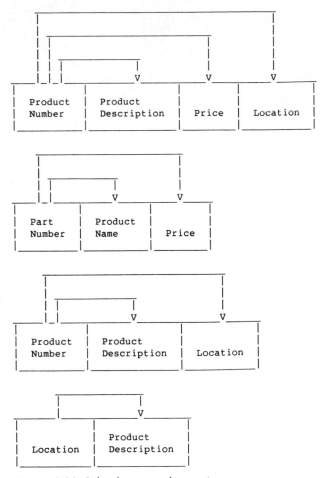

Figure 4.23 Sub-schemas and user-views.

Database management systems allow the various users – and this includes the programmers – to visualize and handle the data in their own way. Such views are independent of the physical way in which the data are actually held on the disk. For example, an entity which we may have produced as:

PRODUCT (<u>Product-number</u>, Product-description, Unit-price, Location)

may be regarded by the various users as any of the structures shown in Fig. 4.23, each group of users concerning themselves with their own larger or smaller subset of the contents of the entity.

Such a diagram represents the view that each user may have of the data. We are now including the programmers of the various sub-systems amongst the users of the database. One user may regard the Part-number as directing him directly to Part-description and Price, whilst another may think that the

Warehouse Location will direct her directly to the Product-description. At the programming level, each programmer's view is a sub-schema of the total data schema. In many cases, only the database administrator may see the complete schema – the overall map of the database.

4.3.6   Step 6 – dispersion

Whilst it may make sense to combine the attributes from several entities into a single entity, it may also make sense to fragment the attributes from one entity and disperse them into two or more separate entities. For example, the earlier steps of data normalization may suggest that an entity such as:

PRODUCT (<u>Product-number</u>, Product-description, Unit-price, Discount-code)

be established with the key and three data attributes as shown. But if we look at the nature of the attributes and the use which is made of them, we may, find that:

- The Unit-price is used more frequently than the Product-description;
- The Discount-code changes frequently whilst the rest of the information is relatively static;
- The applications which use the Product-description require fast response.

If we are able to identify such situations, then we must consider whether or not the entity should be fragmented. Some of the possible solutions – partial dispersion and complete dispersion – are shown in Fig. 4.24.

The latter solution – where each attribute is held on a separate entity – is arguably the most flexible. But in practice, it will be necessary to process two or more attributes at the same time, and dispersing the data in such a way may lead to many more disk input–output operations than will a set of entities which are organized differently.

The analyst must consider these points in the light of the physical environment which will be handling such files.

```
a) Partial dispersion

   PRODUCT-RATE (Product-number, Unit-price, Discount-
        code)

   PRODUCT-NAME (Product-number, Product-description)

b) Complete dispersion

   PRODUCT-PRICE (Product-number, Unit-price)

   PRODUCT-NAME (Product-number, Product-description)

   PRODUCT-CODE (Product-number, Discount-code)
```

Figure 4.24 Data dispersion.

4.3.7 Step 7 – arrangement

We have looked at the contents of the entities. It may also be worth paying attention to the sequence in which the attributes are arranged within the entity. For example, does it matter whether a **PRODUCT** entity is organized as:

PRODUCT (<u>Product-number</u>, Product-description, Unit-price)

or as

PRODUCT (<u>Product-number</u>, Unit-price, Product-description)

In almost every instance, where any importance is attached to the physical arrangement of the attributes, this is usually a consequence of the physical demands of the operating system. For example, it may be that the operating system accesses fields at the front of a record more quickly than those at the end. Thus, the Unit-price would be more easily accessible in the second of the above models.

Another point is relevant to those operating systems which allow variable-length fields and those which ignore trailing null fields of a record. In such environments, it may be advantageous to organize the fields so that those which are optionally empty – or null – are placed at the end of the record according to likelihood with which they will be empty. Thus, if we are holding an employee's name and address together with the marital status and the number of children, the structure shown in Fig. 4.25(b) is better than that shown in Fig. 4.25(a). If we can further arrange our coding such that a marital status of **SINGLE** is represented by null (because our investigation may have revealed that this is the

```
a) EMPLOYEE (Employee-number, Employee-name, Marital-status,
            Number-of-children, Employee-address)

   with occurrences such as:

   1007 : P.WALLACE : MARRIED : 3 : 44 WATER SIDE
   1234 : J.A.SMITH : MARRIED : 0 : 134 CORN LANE
   1346 : W.JENKINS : SINGLE : 0 : 76 HEY ST

b) EMPLOYEE (Employee-number, Employee-name, Employee-address,
            Marital-status, Number-of-children)

   with occurrences such as:

   1007 : P.WALLACE : 44 WATER SIDE : MARRIED : 3
   1234 : J.A.SMITH : 134 CORN LANE : MARRIED
   1346 : W.JENKINS : 76 HEY ST : SINGLE

c) Occurrences with SINGLE represented by null.

   1007 : P.WALLACE : 44 WATER SIDE : MARRIED : 3
   1234 : J.A.SMITH : 134 CORN LANE : MARRIED
   1346 : W.JENKINS : 76 HEY ST
```

Figure 4.25 Data arrangement.

most likely status in our specific application, as, for example, in a college registration system), then we can reduce our record size even more, as shown in Fig. 4.25(c), thereby saving space on our files.

It could be argued that, during the design stage, the analyst is only concerned with the logical structure of the records, and that the topics discussed here – consolidation, dispersion and arrangement – should be left to the later physical consideration. However, the points which we have raised indicate their importance and suggest that the analyst – or someone – must study the nature and the use of the data closely before the records are committed in this – or indeed any other – manner.

4.3.8 Step 8 – numerical dependency

Data normalization techniques were originally developed for use with relational databases which concern themselves with tables of data. Some of the results might conflict with our experience using non-relational databases. One example of this might be the totals which we have considered to be a part of the data which we must hold – the Order-total and the Order-line-total. If we hold our entities in the form derived above, then we can certainly reproduce the Sales Order form without any further processing.

In practice, however, it might be that we need not store the total value of the sales Order, Order-total: we could easily accumulate the individual Order-line-totals as we print each line of the order and then print this accumulated total at the end of the order. Going further, we might feel that even the Order-line-total is redundant since it can be calculated from the Product-quantity multiplied by the Unit-price.

It may be argued that the fact that we are holding what is essentially the same information in more than place conflicts with our original concept of a database. This raises the concept of numerical dependency. If formal data normalization has derived an attribute which is numerically or arithmetically dependent upon one of more of the other attributes, then you should consider whether or not it is necessary to hold this numerically dependent attribute. In our example, the Order-total and the Order-line-total are numerically dependent upon other fields.

If the reports and enquiries which make up our system need to know an individual total in order to satisfy an enquiry such as:

'Tell me the total value of Sales Order 111111'

then it may be more efficient to hold this total as a discrete attribute – as in our third normal form – in order to display it rather than calculate it for every enquiry. We may also need to hold the Order-line-total as a separate attribute if, for example, it is ever likely to have a special value, such as a special offer rate. In such a case it may not be the simple product of quantity and price.

However, if we shall only ever need to know the total in the context of a complete printed Sales Order, where we can calculate and accumulate the total as we produce the document, then there is probably no need to hold the total as a separate attribute within our database.

4.3.9   Performing the data normalization

The following points should be borne in mind when performing the data normalization:

1. The current documents and reports which are encountered within the system, together with the proposed documents and reports, are used to provide the necessary information;
2. List the raw data items as they appear on the document and reports;
3. Indicate a suitable key;
4. Indicate any repeating groups;
5. Remove the repeating groups and establish a new entity; indicate a suitable key for the new entity;
6. For any entities which have a compound key, remove any attributes which are not functionally dependent upon the entire key and establish a new entity; indicate a suitable key for the new entity;
7. Remove any attributes which are functionally dependent upon other attributes and establish a new entity; indicate a suitable key for the new entity;
8. Consider where any numerically dependent fields need to be held explicitly, and ask yourself whether it is necessary to hold any computed fields, such as totals, which can be calculated from other parts of the database;
9. Consider the consolidation and fragmentation of the resulting entities; you might combine any entities with identical keys, and disperse complex entities into a static part and a volatile part;
10. Consider the implications which a particular database management system may have on your entity (file) structure;
11. When you have finished, go back and check the new entities which you have created at steps (5), (6), (7) and (8) to confirm that they are consistent with steps (4) onwards;

The resulting normalized data relationships will subsequently be used to derive the data model for the system.

4.3.10   Example 1

We are required to perform a normalization of the data in the order form shown in Fig. 4.26.

1. The documents and reports within the system are used to provide the necessary information. In this example, we are using a sample order form.

2. List the raw data items as they appear on the document and reports:
   Name
   Refno.
   Address
   Item-number
   Description

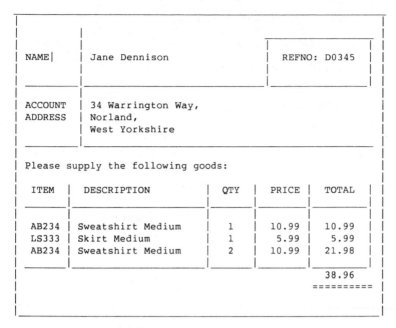

Figure 4.26 An order form.

Qty
Price
Total
Order-total
3. Indicate a suitable key:
   Refno.
4. Indicate any repeating groups:
   Name
   Refno.
   Address
   Item-number – repeating
   Description – repeating
   Qty – repeating
   Price – repeating
   Total-repeating
   Order-total
5. Remove the repeating groups and establish a new entity. Indicate a suitable
   key for the new entity:

Name	Refno.
Refno.	Item-number
Address	Description
Order-total	Qty
	Price
	Total

```
| D0345 | AB234 | Sweatshirt Medium | 1 | 10.99 | 10.99 |
| D0345 | LS333 | Skirt Medium      | 1 |  5.99 |  5.99 |
| D0345 | AB234 | Sweatshirt Medium | 2 | 10.99 | 21.98 |
```

Figure 4.27 A repeating data group.

However, the key made up of Refno, and Item-number would not be unique in this situation. It would give us the occurrences shown in Fig. 4.27 in which the first and the third entries have the same key.

The simplest way in which we can resolve this is to use an artificial element in the key. If we imagine that the lines of the order are numbered sequentially, then we could use this line-number as a part of the key.

Name	Refno
Refno	Line-number
Address	Item-number
Order-total	Description
	Qty
	Price
	Total

6. All the data attributes in the new entity are dependent upon the entire key.
7. Remove any attributes which are functionally dependent upon other data attributes. There would seem to be some connection between the Name and the Address. We could resolve this by either

   (a) inventing an artificial client number and using this as a key for a new client entity, or
   (b) using the Name as the key for the new client entity.

After discussing this with the users, we find that most orders are one-off and we do not need to hold the client's details outside the Order entity.

The Order-line entity has some functionally dependent data attributes: Description and Price are dependent upon the item-number. We remove these to create a new product entity.

Finally, we are left with the entities and the structures shown in Fig. 4.28. Note that we have moved the key attributes of the **ORDER** entity to the conventional place at the front of the entity.

8. Consider the consolidation and fragmentation of the resulting entities – we might consider combining any entities with identical keys, breaking complex entities into a static part and a volatile part. However, in this case there would seem to be no real justification for changing these final structures.

ORDER (Refno, Name, Address, Order-total)

ORDER-LINE (Refno, Line Number, Item Number, Qty, Total)

PRODUCT (Item Number, Description, Price)

Figure 4.28 ORDER, ORDER-LINE and PRODUCT entity structures.

Since we are only dealing with a single document here, the normalization has probably gone as far as we need go.

4.3.11 Example 2

We are required to perform a normalization of the data in the video library catalogue shown in Fig. 4.29.

1. The documents and reports within the system are used to provide the necessary information. In this example, we are using a part of the catalogue.
2. List the raw data items as they appear on the document and reports:
   Video-number
   Title
   Recent-title-indicator
   Weekly-rate
   Daily-rate
   Weekend-rate
   Duration
3. Indicate a suitable key
   Video-number
4. There are no repeating groups.
5. There are no compound keys.
6. Remove any attributes which are functionally dependent upon other attributes. If this requires you to establish a new entity, then indicate a suitable key for the new entity.
   If we look closely at the data, we can see that there seems to be some connection between the Recent-title-indicator and the hire rates. A recent title, indicated by an asterisk, has weekly, daily and week-end hire rates of £4.00, £1.50, and £1.75 respectively, whilst a less-recent title has the hire rates of £3.00, £1.00, and £1.50.

VIDEO NUMBER	TITLE	RECENT TITLE	HIRE RATE WEEK	HIRE RATE DAY	HIRE RATE WK-END	MINS
700	SUNDAY II	*	4.00	1.50	1.75	120
056	WHISPERERS		3.00	1.00	1.50	60
078	SALAD IN ROME		3.00	1.00	1.50	145
340	THE THING		3.00	1.00	1.50	120
600	WATER MARGIN	*	4.00	1.50	1.75	60
734	RAMBO XCIX	*	4.00	1.50	1.75	220
098	CARRY OUT		3.00	1.00	1.50	140
534	YES, SIR	*	4.00	1.50	1.75	140

Figure 4.29 A video library catalogue

```
CATALOGUE (Video Number, Title, Recent Title Indicator,
          Duration)

RATE (Recent Title Indicator, Weekly-rate, Daily-rate,
      Weekend-rate)
```

Figure 4.30 CATALOGUE and RATE entity structures.

```
WEEKRATE (Recent Title Indicator, Weekly-rate)

DAYRATE (Recent Title Indicator, Daily-rate)

WEEKENDRATE (Recent Title Indicator, Weekend-rate)
```

Figure 4.31 WEEKRATE, DAYRATE and WEEKENDRATE entity structures.

After checking with our users that this is always the case, we can derive the entities shown in Fig. 4.30.

When we come to implement these entities as a physical model, we may find that we have to review the nature of the Recent-title-indicator. The choice of an asterisk to indicate a recent title and blank to indicate a less-recent title might be unacceptable on some computer systems. We may have to use other values, such as R (recent) and X (less-recent).

7. Consolidate the resulting entities – you might consider combining any entities with identical keys, breaking complex entities into a static part and a volatile part.

Since it may be that, in our new system, we shall never require all the hire rates at the same time, we could argue the case for having this information held on three separate entities, as shown in Fig. 4.31.

Since we are only dealing with a single document here, the normalization has probably gone as far as we need to go.

4.3.12   Choosing the schema

When we are pursuing the course of normalization towards file design, many of the decisions which we must make will reduce to a choice between saving space on disk and saving time in processing.

We can illustrate this by looking at data which are used by an accounting system to record the postal addresses and the delivery addresses of clients. In some instances, both accounts and deliveries will be sent to the same address. In others, there will be two different addresses, accounts being sent to one place and goods being delivered at another. There are several possible models. We shall consider three:

1. hold both addresses
2. hold one or two addresses

3. hold one address and a flag to indicate the presence of a second address on a second file.

Fig. 4.32 illustrates these. Typical occurrences – with one and with two addresses – are shown.

We can now look at the relative advantages and disadvantages of these three possibilities.

(a)   *Space requirements*

Version (1) wastes considerable space in cases where both addresses are the same. Furthermore, duplication of data means that the integrity of the data is at risk.

Version (2) is good because there is no duplication.

Version (3) is not so good, because we need extra space for the **FLAG** and for the Client-number which is used on the **SECOND-ADDRESS** file.

(b)   *Processing requirements*

Version (1) is good because one read operation will retrieve all we need to know about any particular client.

Version (2) is not bad, and a process would do a simple check – if there is no Delivery-address then use the Postal-address.

Version (3) is not good. A process would have to read a record, check the setting of the **FLAG** and then do a second read if required.

Another aspect of processing which might direct us to select one possibility rather than another is the nature of the processing. If the files are going to be processed serially, or if a query language is to be used, we may find it better to adopt, say, version (1) rather than version (2).

A further point which we must consider is the relative proportion of clients with one address to those with two addresses. We should review the earlier comments – on space requirements and processing requirements – for the three situations where a large number of clients have a single address, where a large number of clients have two addresses, and where there are roughly equal proportions of each. Can you think of any other data models which might be used in this application?

4.4   PROPOSED DATA STRUCTURE DIAGRAM

During the process of normalization, we were forced to make certain assumptions about the nature of the data:

- only one product appears on each sales order
- no more than ten products can be ordered at one time
- one storage location holds only one product
- the same price applies to the product at each location
- everyone has a name shorter than 25 characters in length.

1) Hold both addresses

ADDRESS

Client-number	Postal-address	Delivery-address
1234	34 HIGH ST	34 HIGH ST
1235	10 GROVE RD	106 LITTLE ST

2) Hold one or two addresses

ADDRESS

Client-number	Postal-address	Delivery-address
1234	34 HIGH ST	
1235	10 GROVE RD	106 LITTLE ST

3) Hold one address and a flag to indicate the presence of a second address on a second file

ADDRESS

Client-number	Postal-address	Flag
1234	34 HIGH ST	NO
1235	10 GROVE RD	YES

SECOND-ADDRESS

Client-number	Delivery-address
1235	106 LITTLE ST

Figure 4.32 Possible data models.

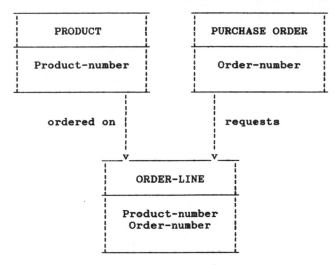

Figure 4.33 Proposed data structure diagram.

We must, of course, confirm our assumptions with the users, and be prepared to modify the design in the light of their replies.

Finally, we shall use the entity structures to produce a new data structure diagram – the proposed DSD. This is a logical view of the data and will later be modified in the light of any physical requirements imposed by the operating system which we shall be using. A typical DSD is illustrated in Fig. 4.33. As before, the boxes on the DSD represent the entities and the entity name is written inside the box. You may also indicate the record key inside the box.

We now have a picture of the data and the relationships between the data which we shall use in our proposed system.

4.4.1 Sizing information

As Fig. 4.34 shows, sizing information may be included on the data structure diagram.

This information includes:

- the average record length (r) for each entity
- the average number of records in the file (n) for each entity
- the total file size (f) for each entity, where f is the product of r and n
- and, for detail entities, the average number of occurrences of detail items for each occurrence of a master entity (o).

An example is shown in Fig. 4.35.

Use of the data structure diagram in this way can throw valuable light on the size of the files. In the above illustration, the figure of 2000 records on the INVOICE-DETAIL file is derived from 200 (the number of records on the INVOICE-

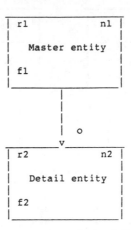

Figure 4.34 Sizing information.

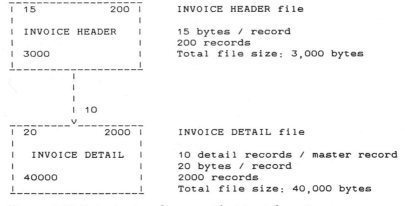

```
  _____
| 15              200 |          INVOICE HEADER file
|                     |
| INVOICE HEADER      |          15 bytes / record
|                     |          200 records
| 3000                |          Total file size: 3,000 bytes
|_____|
          |
          |
          |
          | 10
  _____v_____
| 20             2000 |          INVOICE DETAIL file
|                     |
|  INVOICE DETAIL     |          10 detail records / master record
|                     |          20 bytes / record
| 40000               |          2000 records
|_____|          Total file size: 40,000 bytes
```

Figure 4.35 Data structure diagram with sizing information.

HEADER file) multiplied by 10 (the number of occurrences of the detail for each master). For each master entity, therefore, we need to know the the average record length and the average number of records in the file, and for each detail entity, we need to know the average record length and the average number of occurrences for one occurrence of the master entity. From these figures, it is possible to fill in the rest of the information. Conversely, if we know the average record length for the master entity and all the information about the detail entity – the average record length, the average number of records in the file and the average number of occurrences – then it is again possible to fill in the rest of the information.

4.4.2 Producing the proposed data structure diagram

The following points should be borne in mind when producing the data structure diagram for the proposed system:

1. The results of data normalization are used to provide the necessary information about the identity and the contents of the entities;
2. There is a box for each entity recognized;
3. Each box contains the name of the entity and the names of the key attribute(s) for that entity;
4. Entities which have a compound key are the details of master entities which have the elements of the compound key as their key; if these masters do not exist, then they must be established and added to the diagram;
5. Add any operational entities which are necessary to create entry points for access paths within the diagram;
6. Add the master-detail and other relational links to the diagram;
7. If you are using a database management system, such as **CODASYL**, which uses relationships to achieve the master-detail linkage, then you should name the relationships on your diagram. Otherwise, you may not feel that these are necessary;
8. You may need to show sizing information on the diagram. This will include:
   (a) the average record length for each entity
   (b) the average number of records in the file for each entity
   (c) the total file size for each entity
   (d) for detail entities, the average number of occurrences of detail items for each occurrence of a master entity.

The resulting data structure diagram is used to verify other stages in the analysis of the system, and will serve as a means of cross-checking and corroborating your data flow diagram. The data structure diagram and the data flow diagram are the most valuable documents which our methodology produces. They will form the basis for the new system.

4.5 PHYSICAL FILE MANAGEMENT

We have now derived our data structure diagram, following the principles of normalization. Unfortunately, we have to live in the real world – as it is, and not as we would like it to be. When we implement our logical model, we must contend with the various database management systems and file handlers, and we must live according to the rules and constraints which they impose. So the next step is to produce the physical data structure diagram. This is constructed from the normalized data relationships by taking into account the nature of the particular file handler which is to be used and any other non-functional consider-ations – such as operational entities and security facilities – which may affect the picture.

Some Database Management Systems, such as **CODASYL**, can handle entities and relationships with ease, as we shall see in Chapter 7. On other systems, records are retrieved simply by building a key and then reading the record by means of that key. Let us see how our relationships stand up to this organization.

4.5.1   One-to-one relationships

The existence of a one-to-one relationship implies that either of the items in the relationship can be identified directly from the other. This is achieved by holding the key of the one somewhere within the data of the other.

For one-to-one relationships – not optional relationships – cross-referencing is usually achieved by keying both entities on the same key, as shown in Fig. 4.36. Corresponding records are then matched since they have the same key.

For other one-to-one relationships – including optional – the key of one entity

```
PERSONNEL (Staff-number, Name, Address, Date-of-birth,
          Number-of-children)

PAYROLL (Staff-number, Rate-of-pay, Tax-code, Hols-due
         Hols-taken)

SALARY (Staff-number, Gross-to-date, Net-to-date, Tax-
        to-date)
```

Typical occurrences:

```
PERSONNEL
2003 : STEELE, A : 14 BATTINSON STREET, LINCOLN : 29/07/87

PAYROLL
2003 : 12000 : 128L : 25 : 10

SALARY
2003 : 10560 : 6000 : 4560
```

Figure 4.36 One-to-one relationship.

```
PROJECT (Project-number, Project-name, Manager-number)

MANAGER (Staff-number, Name, Address, Project-number)
```

Typical occurrences:

```
PROJECT
PGA101 : P.G.ANSTEE STOCK FORECASTING : 2003

MANAGER
2003 : STEELE, A : 14 BATTINSON STREET, LINCOLN : PGA101
```

Figure 4.37 Example of a one-to-one relationship – 1.

is held in the other entity as an attribute and vice versa. An example of this situation was illustrated in Fig. 3.20 with an optional relationship between a **PROJECT** and a **MANAGER**. The entities may have the structure and occurrences shown in Fig. 4.37.

If a manager has not yet been assigned to the project, then the occurrences would be as shown in Fig. 4.38.

4.5.2 One-to-many relationships

A one-to-many relationship implies that the item in the master entity can be identified from an item in the detail entity. This is achieved by storing the key of the master somewhere in the detail. Let us look at the normalized forms and occurrences shown in Fig. 4.39.

Note the arbitrary choice of the character '/' to separate the elements of the physical key. If the elements of the key are of fixed length, then there may not be any need for such a separator.

Thus, for any Order-detail, such as 1200/400, we could find the Order, 1200, and also the Product, 400, to which it relates.

```
PROJECT
PGA101 : P.G.ANSTEE LTD STOCK FORECASTING

MANAGER
2003 : STEELE, A : 14 BATTINSON STREET, LINCOLN
```

Figure 4.38 Example of a one-to-one relationship – 2.

```
ORDER (Order-number, Customer-number, Date, Order-
       total)

PRODUCT (Product-number, Description, Unit-price)

ORDER-DETAIL (Order-number, Product-number, Quantity,
              Total)
```

Typical occurrences:

```
ORDER
1200 : 355 : 290189 : 87.00

PRODUCT
400 : RED PLASTIC TABLE : 27.00

ORDER-DETAIL
1200/400 : 2 : 54.00
1200/300 : 1 : 33.00
```

Figure 4.39 One-to-many relationship.

However, a one-to-many relationship also implies that all detail items which relate to a particular master can be retrieved directly, and without reading all the records in the detail serially. In the above example, we cannot find the Order-details from the data in the Order item:

1200:355:290189:87.00

Therefore, a downwards master-to-detail linkage mechanism must be used in order to achieve this. The following methods of linking are possible:

1. Building the keys of the detail file from the key of the master together with a sequence number, in order to keep the keys unique, as shown in Fig. 4.40. Great care must be taken with this implementation when the detail file is a link-entity and is a member of more than one relationship, and when that relationship needs to be exploited. Do we need to know all the products which are currently on orders? If the answer is 'Yes', then this problem can be resolved by the next solution.

2. By using another file to link downwards. The records here would have a primary key which is the same as the master and carry the key of the detail as an attribute. The entities would now be as shown in Fig. 4.41.

   In practice, we would probably not duplicate the data which is also held in the key. Thus, the entities and the occurrences would probably be like those shown in Fig. 4.42.

3. By storing the keys of the detail records in the master item as a multi-valued attribute. This conflicts with the fundamental principle of the first normal form, but since it can be handled effectively on some operating systems, there is no reason to ignore it. The entities and occurrences, therefore, might look like those shown in Fig. 4.43.

   This illustration uses a bracket] to separate the various multi-values. The dots... indicate that there are other orders for this product. Multi-valued downward pointers have the particular advantage that some file handlers and

```
ORDER (Order-number, Customer-number, Date, Order-
     total)

PRODUCT (Product-number, Description, Unit-price)

ORDER-LINE (Order-number, Sequence-number, Quantity,
     Total)
```

Typical occurrences:

```
ORDER
1200 : 355 : 290189 : 87.00

ORDER-LINE
1200/001 : 400 : 2 : 54.00
1200/002 : 300 : 1 : 33.00
```

Figure 4.40 Example of a one-to-many relationship – 1.

ORDER (Order-number, Customer-number, Date, Order-
    total)

PRODUCT (Product-number, Description, Unit-price)

ORDER-DETAIL (Order-number, Product-number, Quantity,
    Total)

ORDER-LINE (Order-number, Sequence-number, Order-
    number, Product-number)

PRODUCT-LINE (Product-number, Sequence-number, Order-
    number, Product-number)

Typical occurrences:

ORDER
1200 : 355 : 290189 : 87.00

PRODUCT
300 : GREEN CHAIRS : 33.00
400 : RED PLASTIC TABLE : 27.00

ORDER-DETAIL
1200/400 : 2 : 54.00
1200/300 : 1 : 33.00

ORDER-LINE
1200/001 : 1200/400
1200/002 : 1200/300

PRODUCT-LINE
400/304 : 1200/400
300/765 : 1200/300

Figure 4.41 Example of a one-to-many relationship – 2

ORDER-LINE (Order-number, Sequence-number, Product-
    number)

PRODUCT-LINE (Product-number, Sequence-number, Order-
    number)

Typical occurrences:

ORDER-LINE
1200/001 : 400
1200/002 : 300

PRODUCT-LINE
400/304 : 1200
300/765 : 1200

Figure 4.42 Example of a one to many relationship – 3

```
ORDER (Order-number, Customer-number, Date, Order-
    total, (Product-number))

PRODUCT (Product-number, Description, Unit-price,
    (Order-number))

ORDER-DETAIL (Order-number, Product-number, Quantity,
    Total)
```

```
Typical occurrences:

ORDER
1200 : 355 : 290189 : 87.00 : 400 ] 300

PRODUCT
300 : GREEN CHAIRS : 33.00 : ... ] 1200 ] ...
400 : RED PLASTIC TABLE : 27.00 : ... ] 1200 ] ...

ORDER-DETAIL
1200/400 : 2 : 54.00
1200/300 : 1 : 33.00
```

Figure 4.43 Example of a one-to-many relationship – 4.

query languages can accommodate them easily, using them to link downwards without doing a serial pass through the detail.

4.5.3 Security

The security of the sytem is not implemented at any one stage, but must be held at the back of your mind throughout the data analysis and the functional analysis activities. If we look at the general aspects of controlling the security of the data and of the programs, we see that the patterns of access and possible controls on that access can become very complicated indeed. The protagonists in the discussion are:

1. the data files which are to be made accessible
2. which of these data files are to be made available for reading
3. which of these data files are to be made available for updating
4. the programs and processing which are to be provided
5. how the programs are to access the data
6. the users to whom these are to be made available
7. the physical location of the terminals from which access can be gained.

In many instances the analyst cannot do this in isolation, but must liaise closely with the user to determine how the security characteristics are to be allocated – **how who** is to be allowed to do **what** with **which** data and **where** and **when**. A formal means of going about this is to produce lists of:

- all the data items which are to be held on file; this can be produced after the earlier parts of the data design have been completed
- all the functions which are to be provided; this can be produced when the function catalogue and the function maps are being derived during the functional analysis
- how the functions are to access the data
- all the users who are to have access to the system
- how the functions are to be distributed to the users

The resultant security matrix will provide information when deciding the security needs of the proposed system.

4.6 ENTITY DESCRIPTIONS

The information derived during the data normalization process is now used to produce your entity descriptions. These show the keys and the likely data contents of the attributes – fields – which make up the entities. They may also show the expected volumes of data. You may find that the entity descriptions will change as the analysis of the system proceeds:

1. new attributes may be added
2. attributes may be moved from one file to another
3. the nature of the attributes may be changed
4. the format of the attributes may be changed
5. redundant or obsolete attributes may be removed from files.

A typical entity description for the **CLIENT** entity is shown in Fig. 4.44. The information shown on the form is:

1. the entity reference – a unique identifier which will be used on the data flow diagrams
2. key – a K is written alongside the attribute, or attributes, which make up the record-key
3. the attribute sequence-number – shown for the data (non-key) attributes
4. attributes – the names of the attributes, or fields, which comprise the entity
5. format – an indicator of the maximum length and the nature of the attribute: whether it is alphabetic (A), numeric (N) or alphanumeric (X)
6. comments – any special notes or comments about the attribute.

It will also be valuable to give an example of the type of data which might be encountered in each attribute, as illustrated in Fig. 4.45. This will avoid possible misunderstandings.

If an attribute comprises a repeating group, then the analyst will also specify:

7. the average length of the multi-values
8. the average number of multi-values
9. the maximum number of multi-values in the attribute.

```
                        ENTITY DESCRIPTION
----------------------------------------------------------------

ENTITY REFERENCE: D8

ENTITY DESCRIPTION:   CLIENT

COMMENTS:
-------------------------------------------------------------
       I               I         I
ATTR   I   ATTRIBUTE   I FORMAT  I  COMMENTS
-------I---------------I---------I---------------------------
       I               I         I
  K    I CLIENT-NUMBER I   4N    I leading zeroes
       I               I         I
  1    I CLIENT-NAME   I   30A   I
       I               I         I
  2    I CLIENT-ADDRESS I  100X  I
       I               I         I
  3    I CLIENT-PHONE  I   20X   I
       I               I         I
  4    I CREDIT-LIMIT  I   10N   I Pence
-------I---------------I---------I---------------------------
```

Figure 4.44 Entity description.


```
                        SAMPLE DATA
----------------------------------------------------------------

ENTITY REFERENCE: D8

ENTITY NAME: CLIENT
----------------------------------------------------------------

K CLIENT-NUMBER:   0077

1 CLIENT-NAME:     SMITH, JOHN WILLIAM

2 CLIENT-ADDRESS:  56, ALLBY CLOSE, WATLINGFORD, HAMPSHIRE, AN6 6N/

3 CLIENT-PHONE:    ANDOVER 999666

4 CREDIT-LIMIT:    20000
----------------------------------------------------------------
```

Figure 4.45 Sample data.

When designing files for a specific operating system or environment, it may also be relevant to include:

10. any formatting codes – such as left filled with zeroes or right filled with blanks
11. any help messages or user messages
12. any format checking which is to be performed by the system.

As with the other documents and tools which we use in our structured methodology, the entity description is subject to continuous review. Its importance and value suggest that it is best if this information is transferred to the computer documentation files – or a data dictionary – as soon as possible, and held on-line so that the current version is immediately available to all concerned. held on-line so that the current version is immediately available to all concerned.

4.6.1 Producing the entity descriptions

The following points should be borne in mind when producing the entity descriptions:

1. The descriptions are based on the entity structures produced by the data normalization activity;
2. The name of the entity is shown at the head of the form;
3. An entity reference is given so that this entity can be clearly identified on the data flow diagrams;
4. There is one entry in the form for each attribute (data item) in the entity;
5. At this stage the entries contain your first thoughts about:
   (a) an indication of whether the attribute is the key, or a part of the key
   (b) a name for the attribute; this may be required by the programmers or by any data dictionary which you will use
   (c) the length and format of the attribute
   (d) any comments concerning the nature of the data;
6. As you maintain your entity descriptions, it is a good plan to maintain a similar list showing typical occurrences of the attributes in the entity.

The resulting entity descriptions are used as a basis for the design of the files for the system, and are used to cross-check the decisions which you make as you develop the data flow diagrams and the processing descriptions for the system.

4.7 SUMMARY

Our primary data analysis tool is the principle of data normalization. This enables us to derive a preliminary data model for the proposed system.

Thus far, we have been thinking in terms of ideas and conceptual models of our data, but now we are now making the transition from this idealized picture across to the physical files. The data model may have to be modified in order to fit in with any constraints which the physical computer system and its database management system may impose upon us.

As we produce our data model, we also derive the entity descriptions, showing the contents of the records on our files. However, even this data model is not final. We may have to change it further as a result of the processing demands which we shall identify during the next phase of functional analysis.

4.8   QUESTIONS

4.1.   What are the aims of data normalization?

4.2.   Describe one advantage and one disadvantage which data normalization presents for:
   (a) the user
   (b) the systems analyst
   (c) the applications programmer.

4.3.   Write down the steps which are followed when producing the third normal form of a set of data.

```
- - - - - - - - - - - - - - - - - - - - - - - - - - - - - - - - - - - - - - - - - - -

Rte   From...... To........ Reg ..... Cont  Chrge Date....
                                            Rate

- - - - - - - - - - - - - - - - - - - - - - - - - - - - - - - - - - - - - - - - - -

102   Lincoln    Leeds      ABC 123 A ALO9  D     13/09/88
                                      PHO1  A
                                      ALO7  E
                                      ALO5  B
003   Manchester Lincoln    PQR 123 A PHO5  D     13/09/88
                                      PHO8  C
                                      AM10  C
103   Lincoln    York       PQR 123 A PHO3  C     14/09/88
                                      PHO7  A
                                      AM10  C
302   York       Norwich    DEF 123 A PHO9  E     14/09/88
                                      PH10  F
003   Manchester Lincoln    PQR 123 A ALO7  E     15/09/88
                                      PHO3  C
                                      ALO5  B
                                      PHO5  D
                                      ALO9  D

- - - - - - - - - - - - - - - - - - - - - - - - - - - - - - - - - - - - - - - - -
```

Figure 4.46 Traffic manager's log book.

4.4.   A road haulage company has a number of vehicles and a number of containers which it uses to transport goods around the country. Based upon the data in the section of the traffic manager's log book which is shown in Fig. 4.46, derive a set of entities in third normal form. The column headings are Route number, Starting point, Destination, Vehicle registration number, Container number, Container charge rate, and the date of the journey.

4.5.   Using the data given in the order form shown in Fig. 4.9, create examples of some occurrences of the entities shown in Fig. 4.47.

```
ORDER (Name, Refno, Address, Order Total)

ORDER-LINE (Refno, Item Number, Sequence Number, Qty,
    Total)

PRODUCT (Item Number, Description, Price)
```

Figure 4.47 ORDER, ORDER-LINE and PRODUCT entities.

4.6. Using the data given in the video library catalogue shown in Fig. 4.29, create examples of some occurrences of the entities, and the possible alternative entities, shown in Fig. 4.48.

```
CATALOGUE (Video Number, Title, Recent Title Indicator,
    Duration)

RATE (Recent Title Indicator, Weekly Rate, Daily Rate,
    Weekend Rate)

The possible alternative entities are:

WEEKRATE (Recent Title Indicator, Weekly-rate)

DAYRATE (Recent Title Indicator, Daily-rate)

WEEKENDRATE (Recent Title Indicator, Weekend-rate)
```

Figure 4.48 CATALOGUE and RATE entities.

```
a) RATE entity

    RATE (Vehicle-number, 20-mile-rate, 50-mile-rate,
        100-mile-rate)

b) Alternative structures

    RATE20 (Vehicle-number, 20-mile-rate)

    RATE50 (Vehicle-number, 50-mile-rate)

    RATE100 (Vehicle-number, 100-mile-rate)
```

Figure 4.49 Alternative RATE entity structures.

4.7. Each vehicle owned by a car hire company has a set of charge rates according to the distance travelled by the client. It has been decided to represent this by the **RATE** entity shown in Fig. 4.49(a). What would be the advantages and disadvantages, if we had used the entities shown in Fig. 4.49(b) instead?

How would the two designs cope, if we later required to hold rates for 200-mile journeys? How could we modify the two designs, if we later required to hold the total mileage done by that vehicle each week? What other data models could be used?ezl

4.8. A supply system has to hold three addresses for its clients: the account is sent to one address; the goods are sent to a second address; the statement is sent to a third address. For some clients, two or all three of the addresses may be the same.

(a) Suggest at least two possible data structures which could represent this information.

(b) What are the advantages of each – in terms of record size and processing speed?

4.9. Draw a single functional dependency diagram for the entities shown in Fig. 4.50.

ORDER (<u>Order-number</u>, Client-number, Order-total)

CLIENT (<u>Client-number</u>, Client-address, Credit-limit)

ORDER-LINE (<u>Line-number</u>, <u>Order-number</u>, <u>Part-number</u>, <u>Sequence-number</u>, Quantity, Line-total)

PART (<u>Part-number</u>, Description, Price)

STOCK (<u>Part-number</u>, Stock-quantity, Location)

Figure 4.50 ORDER, CLIENT, ORDER-LINE, PART and STOCK entities.

4.10. A seat reservation system for a certain bus company holds information about the clients, the vehicles, the seat reservations, and the vehicle types. The average record sizes are client (60 bytes), vehicle (120 bytes), reservation (40 bytes), vehicle type (20 bytes). In the company's fleet, there are 76 buses with 50 seats; 42 buses with 65 seats; 22 buses with 20 seats; 10 buses with 16 seats; 5 buses with 10 seats.

Draw a data structure diagram for these entities, and add the sizing information based upon these figures.

4.11. The country of Acmay is to install a computer system to process its telephone directory. The entries are to appear as shown in Fig. 4.51.

There are about 7 million subscribers in Acmay. Design suitable entities to hold the data.

4.12. The telephone directory system introduced in Question 4.11 is to be extended so that a classified directory can also be produced. This will allow an entry such as that shown in Fig. 4.52 to appear in the section on **BUTCHERS** and also in the section on **MEAT IMPORTERS**. Modify your solution to Question 4.10 to allow this.

```
Bancroft, A.L, P.O.Box 1332 ............ Tokay 4001
Bank of Acmay Limited
    Head Office, 34 Jones Boulevard ... Acmay 10229
    Bambay Township Branch, 26 Caraway Rd,
        Bambay ...................... Acmay 46755
    Martin Square ................... Acmay 18223
    Tokay Branch, 1002 Tokay Highway ... Tokay 1822
    Urumbay Branch .................... Urumbay 10
Banks, Mrs Clara, 123A Fortescue Mansions,
    Tokay Highway ..................... Tokay 9811
Banxi, Abraham, Butcher, 49 Jones Boulevard,
    Fontan District ................... Acmay 8665
Banxi, Dr Abraham, P.O.Box 1999 ........ Acmay 9122
Banxi, Mirham, 49 Jones Boulevard ...... Acmay 8665
```

Figure 4.51 Telephone directory.

```
Banxi, Abraham, 49 Jones Boulevard, Fontan
    District ......................... Acmay 8665
```

Figure 4.52 Classified telephone directory entry.

```
Abbay to Acmay .................. Mon 15:30
Acmay
    Abbay ....................... Mon  8:30
    Bambay ...................... Wed  6:30
    Comay ....................... Tue 11:00
    Domay ....................... Wed 13:00
    Saimbay ..................... Fri  9:00
    Tokay and Urumbay ........... Thu 12:00
    Urumbay via Tokay ........... Thu 12:00
Bambay
    Acmay ....................... Wed 10:30
    Urumbay ..................... Sat  7:00
Comay to Acmay .................. Tue 17:23
Domay to Acmay .................. Wed 15:30
Saimbay to Acmay ................ Fri 21:35
Tokay to Acmay .................. Fri  9:30
Urumbay
    Acmay via Tokay ............. Thu 19:45
    Bambay ...................... Sat 14:12
    Tokay ....................... Thu 19:45
```

Figure 4.53 Railway timetable.

4.13. In Acmay, the street names frequently change in order to commemorate popular people. For example 'Jones Boulevard' is about to be renamed 'Urumguay Passage'.

How would your data design for the telephone directory situation handle such changes? Can you amend it to make the process of changing street names easier?

4.14. The railway authority in Acmay has problems in producing a reliable timetable. They would like to use a computer system to help them and they would like the timetable to look something like that shown in Fig. 4.53. Design a set of entities which could be used to record this information.

4.15. A doctor already holds his patients' records on a computer system. Fig. 4.54(a) shows the current file structure. This reflects the contents of the patient's record card which might look like that shown in Fig. 4.54(b). Produce a normalized design for the entity or entities which you would use.

```
PATIENT (National-insurance-number, Surname, (First Names),
         Title, Address, Telephone-number, Date-of-last-visit,
         (Contact, Next-of-kin-telephone-number, Relationship)
         (Date-of-visit, Symptoms, Comments, Medication)
         (Date-of-hospitalisation, Hospital-name, Reason,
(a)      Date-left, (Name-of-doctor))
```

```
National Insurance Number:  ZZ 11 22 33 A

Name: Jones, Mary Elizabeth, Miss

Address: 12 Main Street, Bexhill, Sussex

Telephone: 01-999 4500

Last Visit: 7 July 1987

Contact: Mrs Alice Smith, 01-999 4500, Mother
         Miss Mary Johnson, 01-999 3456, Friend

Visits:
----------------------------------------------------------------
         |                |             |                      |
01/01/85 | Cold           |             | Paracetamol          |
03/03/85 | Headache       | Migraine?   | Paracetamol          |
07/07/86 | Sunburn        |             | Calamine lotion      |
12/07/86 | Headache       |             | Migraway             |
07/07/87 | Vaccinations   | Travelling  | Smallpox vaccine     |
         |                |             |                      |
----------------------------------------------------------------

Hospital Visits:
--------------------------------------------------------------------------------
         |              |             |          |          |            |
01/10/84 | Whittington  | Minor Burn  |          | 02/10/84 | Dr Jobson  |
         |              |             |          |          | Dr Oddson  |
         |              |             |          |          |            |
--------------------------------------------------------------------------------
01/11/84 | Whittington  | Remove sutures  | 01/11/84 | Dr Bodson  |
(b)      |              |                 |          |            |
--------------------------------------------------------------------------------
```

Figure 4.54 PATIENT entity.

4.16. Get a copy of any official form, such as an invoice, a membership form, a bank statement, a catalogue or a timetable, and produce possible entity structures in third normal form.

5

Structured systems design – functional analysis

After the initial investigation and the subsequent systems analysis, your task now is to ensure that the design addresses the users' requirements – both in terms of data and the functions.

In Chapter 4, we produced our data model during the data analysis activity. In the present chapter, we shall look at the processing which our system is to perform – the functional analysis. We shall use the following definition:

Functional analysis: the analysis of data and the ways in which they are associated, and of the processing requirements of the functional areas, disregarding any physical constraints or limitations.

5.1 PROCESS, FUNCTION OR PROGRAM?

When we expanded the data flow diagram (DFD) into a number of lower-level diagrams, we referred to the boxes as process boxes. Shortly, we shall start to talk about functions and modules, and later, during the programming stage, we shall encounter the terms program and subroutine. So what do we mean by these words, and how do they all relate to each other? The diagram in Fig. 5.1 shows a rough correspondence between these terms, and this will be sufficient for our present purposes.

In general terms, we can say that:

- Each process box on the low-level DFD is equivalent to one of the processes which we shall consider during the design stage;
- Each such process is equivalent to one option on the sub-system menu;
- Each process may comprise one or more functions;
- Each function is equivalent to a program, or some other user facility such as a report or a query language enquiry;
- Each function may comprise one or more modules;
- Each program may comprise one or more subroutines;
- Each module is approximately equivalent to a subroutine.

We are now ready to consider the way in which the processes and the functions of our system are designed.

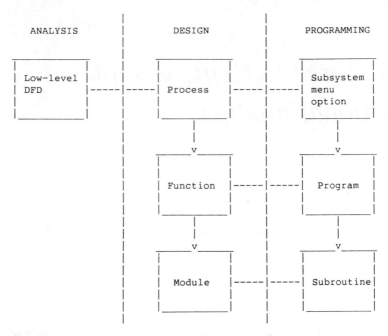

Figure 5.1 Functions or programs?

5.2 PROPOSED DATA FLOW DIAGRAM

We must now look at the DFD for the current system and amend this to produce the proposed DFD. This will include:

1. The boundaries of the required system.
   It may be that the user does not want us to implement all parts of the current system. She may, for example, want the stock control but not the stock ordering elements to be implemented, or she may want to calculate the wages and cash due, but she may prefer her clerks to decide how the coins and banknotes are to be made up in the wages packets.

   Those parts of the system which are not to be included will be shown as external entities outside the system boundary of the DFD.
2. Existing processes which have been changed as a result of our thoughts during the intermediate stages discussed in Interlude 1.
3. New processes which are added as a result of the problems and requirements list which we have been maintaining.
4. New processes which must be added in order to preserve the integrity of the database. These will be identified from the entity/function matrix as we proceed.

This step produces the proposed DFD which shows the functional requirements of the system and will make the largest contribution to the design of the proposed system.

The components of the proposed DFD are the same as before: external entities, process boxes, data flows and data stores. The general rules for drawing the proposed DFDs are as we saw in Chapter 3, except for one or two slight differences:

1. It may not be sensible to include the name of the functional area – Accounts or Wages Department – in a process box if that process is accessible to several users in different functional areas. In such cases, just show the identity-number and the process title.
2. Any physical resources should be represented by the information on the documents which accompany them.
3. Most, if not all, of the data stores will be D-types (see section 3.3.2), representing on-line computer files.

5.2.1 Producing the proposed data flow diagram

The following points should be borne in mind when producing the DFDs for the proposed system:

1. It will normally be possible to use the DFD for the current system as a foundation for the proposed DFD.
2. The nature of the elements on this new DFD will be the same as before: external entities, processes, data flows and data stores.
3. Come to a written agreement with your users as to which parts of the current system are to be within the boundary of your proposed system.
4. Come to a written agreement with your users that the remaining parts of the current system are not to be within the boundary of the proposed system. This removes any misunderstandings which may arise.
5. Review your problems and requirements list to see if it is possible to modify any of the existing processes to solve some of the problems or meet some of the requirements indicated there. You will then reflect these modifications on your DFD.
6. Review any remaining problems and requirements on your list and add new processes to solve those problems or meet those requirements. You will then show these additions on your DFD.
7. Add any new processes which are necessary to maintain the integrity of the database. You will have identified these from the event/function matrix, as described in the next section.
8. Use the data stores which have come about as a result of the data normalization.
9. Ensure that all data coming into the system triggers a process – one event triggers one process.
10. Using the rule of no more than ten processes per DFD, decompose your design into top level, intermediate-level, and low-level DFDs.
11. Review these DFDs with your users.

The DFD and the data structure diagram are the most valuable documents which our methodology produces. They will form the basis for the new system.

5.3   ENTITY/FUNCTION MATRIX

It is important to remember that the data model and the process model are two aspects of the same system. They both work together. The entity/function matrix ties up these two aspects and is a valuable part of the system documentation. Since the matrix may enable you to identify any gaps in your system, it will also contribute to the overall design. On this matrix, each process box – or function – in the low-level DFD is cross-referenced to each entity, showing whether the entity is created, amended, or deleted by that function. Fig. 5.2 illustrates this.

The functions are written one on each row of the matrix, and the name of the entities are written above the columns. The DFD reference number may also be shown. At the intersection, a letter is written to show whether that function:

I inserts/adds/creates records on that entity
M modifies/changes that entity
L looks at that entity
D deletes records from that entity

If a certain function can perform more than one action on an entity – it may allow the user to insert then modify an entity, for example – then a combination of these letters will be written:

I/M

If a single function affects several entities, then the appropriate code(s) are written in all the relevant entity columns.

This document has a number of benefits:

1. If an entity is changed, it is a simple matter to identify those processes which may be affected by the changes.

FUNCTION		CLIENT	ORDER	O/LINE	STOCK	D F D r e f
SOP01	Process a new order	I/M	I	I	M	1.1
SOP02	Cancel an existing order	L	M	M	M	1.3
SOP07	Amend an existing order		M	M	M	1.4
SOP09	Print all orders	L	L/M	D	L	1.2

Figure 5.2 Entity/function matrix.

This is particularly important when using those operating systems which do not provide automatic program/file cross-reference utilities.
2. It is possible to ensure the entity integrity, that is, the complete processing of each entity.

There must be a function which creates each (occurrence of the) entity. In the above example, we see that we need a further function – ADD NEW STOCK – which will Insert records on the STOCK entity, because there is no I in the STOCK column.

There must be a function which eventually deletes each (occurrence of the) entity. Precautions can be taken to ensure that the records on each entity are deleted at some point, otherwise the files will get bigger and bigger until they overflow. In the above example, we see that there are no provisions for deleting records from the ORDER, STOCK or CLIENT entities – there is no D in any of these columns. We must then check our investigation, possibly referring back to the users to see what they wish to do about this. It may be that CLIENT and STOCK records are never deleted, but an annual archiving process may be needed to clear down the ORDER entity.
3. We can see the impact of changing a record layout, since we can quickly see which processes are affected. This will give us an indication of the costs (the number of programs) involved if, for example, a file layout is to be reorganized.

We must now add any new processes to our DFD and ensure that it is consistent with the entity/function matrix.

5.3.1 Producing the entity/function matrix

The following points should be borne in mind when producing and using the entity/function matrix:

1. The matrix is initially derived from the data structure diagram, the entity descriptions and the data flow diagrams.
2. The matrix shows which entities are processed by which functions.
3. The entity names are used as the column headings.
4. Each row heading will show the function reference number (this will be inserted later when the function catalogue has been produced), the function title and the DFD reference number.
5. The cells at the intersections of the rows and columns contain one or more of the following codes:

   I if the function inserts/adds/creates records on that entity
   M if the function modifies/changes that entity
   D if the function deletes records from that entity
   L if the function simply looks at that entity without any other processing

6. You should then check the entries in each column to see that each entity experiences the processes of I at least one M or L, and D. If there are any

omissions in this entity life cycle, then you should investigate and amend your data flow diagrams to accommodate these.

The matrix serves two purposes: firstly, it allows you to check the integrity of the processing when designing the system by ensuring that each entity is created, used and ultimately deleted; secondly, it allows you to see the scope of the impact which any changes in the entity structure may have on the processing routines, and vice versa.

5.4   FUNCTION CATALOGUE

The function catalogue is derived from the proposed DFDs. It provides a brief description of each of the functions which accomplish the processes described there. There will be an entry in the function catalogue for each process box on the low-level DFD, specifying:

1. a unique identity number for the function; this is usually an alphanumeric identifer and may eventually become the name of the program which performs the function
2. a brief descriptive title for the function
3. a process reference number to cross-reference the function to the low-level DFD
4. an indication of whether it is to be either
   (a) an on-line function (O), in which the user makes a transaction and it is processed immediately – the computer asking for, accepting, and responding to the user's input data, or
   (b) a batch function (B), in which, after initiation by the user, the computer will perform one or more operations repetitively on many similar sets of data – possibly calculating the salaries of all employees or producing a set of bank statements – without further intervention from the user
5. a short verbal description of the function; the detailed description of the

FUNCTION CATALOGUE

FUNCTION REF	FUNCTION TITLE	DFD REF	TYPE	DESCRIPTION
SO103	RETURN GOODS	2.4.1	O	Accept details of returned goods
SO104	ACKNOWLEDGE RETURNED GOODS	2.4.2	B	Print letters acknowledging returned goods

Figure 5.3 Function catalogue.

function's action will be given later in the function description and the module description.

Some typical entries in the function catalogue are shown in Fig. 5.3.

When we are considering this task of functional decomposition, two obvious questions are 'How do you know whether a process is made up of several functions or not?' and 'How do you know what these functions are?' We can answer these by reminding ourselves that, in many cases, one low-level DFD process will represent one function. In other cases, a single process such as:

ADD A NEW ORDER

may require us to execute a function which will add the details of the new order to the **ORDER** file, as we cited above. It may then require a further function to print an acknowledgement of that order. We may very well have decomposed the **ADD A NEW ORDER** process on our low-level DFD. However, if we had not done this, here and in other areas of our work, the structured methodology will provide checks for the analyst. Any functions which we fail to recognize here will reveal themselves later when we produce our module catalogue.

There is another point which we must mention at this stage: every system should have a set of routines to allow users – not to mention analysts and programmers – to display and interrogate the contents of records on the various files. Unless such routines are an integral part of the functional requirements, in order to simplify the picture, it is not customary to indicate these on the DFDs. One reason for this is that they may be one-off needs and not triggered by any specific event. The same may be true of other functions, such as routine reports and the emergency amendment of records. All such functions should have an entry in the function catalogue if they are to be a permanent feature of the system. If they are not documented, they may get lost or forgotten (and possibly even duplicated and re-written each time a need arises). Consequently, they will not be considered if the main system is amended at any time and may thereby jeopardize the data and the processing.

5.4.1 Producing the function catalogue

The following points should be borne in mind when producing the function catalogue:

1. It may be helpful – although not strictly correct – if you interpret the word function as program or user-facility in this context;
2. You will use the proposed DFDs to provide the information;
3. Make a list of all the process boxes on the DFDs;
4. In most cases, each process box gives rise to one entry in the function catalogue;
5. Look at each process box on the low-level DFDs and decide whether it can be achieved by a single function or whether it should be decomposed into several functions,

6. Include these functions in the catalogue;
7. Include any file enquiry or file maintenance functions which will be required;
8. For each entry, include:
   (a) a unique identity number
   (b) a title for the function
   (c) the reference number of the process box to which the function relates
   (d) an indication of whether it is an on-line function or a batch function
   (e) a brief description of what the function does.

The resulting function catalogue is used to derive the function descriptions. It will also serve as an index to the function descriptions.

5.5   FUNCTION DESCRIPTIONS

The function descriptions are derived from the entries in the function catalogue. They specify the details of the system's functional requirements, one function description for each function.

The function description is divided into a number of sections each relating to a part of the diagram shown in Fig. 5.4.

1. a verbal definition of the function
2. the specifications of the input messages for the function
3. the specifications of the output messages for the function
4. details of the data and the files which are used by the function

Let us look at these in detail.

5.5.1   Function definition

The definition of the requirements of the function will include:

1. a verbal description of the function, in user terms

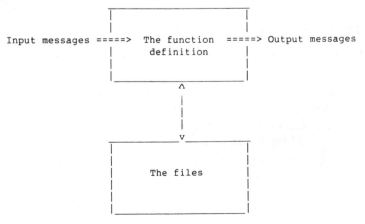

Figure 5.4 The function description.

2. an indication of whether this is to be an on-line function or a batch function
3. a technical description – a minispec – of the function, including details of the calculations and other operations which are performed; this may be presented in the form of a plain text, as we discussed when we were looking at the process narrative in Chapter 2, although there are many advantages in using a structured style, such as structured English, which we shall look at in section 5.5.7
4. the frequency with which the function is used; for example, this might be as required, or when goods inward notes are received, or at the end of the day's business
5. any associated operations – such as loading special stationery – which must be performed before this function is invoked
6. any associated operations – such as unloading a specific magnetic tape – which must be performed after this function has terminated
7. any associated functions which must be performed before this function is invoked; for example, it may be necessary to invoke a Sales Summary function before an End-of-day Report is initiated
8. any functions which must be performed after this function has terminated.

Remember that a function need not be performed by a program: a Sales Report might be produced by a Report Generator; an Explanatory Message might be generated by a word-processing utility; a Customer Enquiry might be handled by a Query Language sentence. If any of these are to be used, this should be indicated in the function description.

5.5.2 Input message specifications

As Fig. 5.4 shows, each piece of data which the user presents to the function is conventionally called an input message. Each item of input data can be regarded as the subject of a transaction, a transaction being defined as the sequence of operations in which:

1. the computer prompts the user
2. the user enters one or more items of input data
3. the computer accepts that data
4. the computer responds to that data.

The design for your function may be based upon the sequence of the transactions – the transaction dialogue – that handle the data of the function.

Because of the possible ambiguity, we shall use the terms with their traditional meanings: the noun **input** will refer to the data which the user submits to the computer, and the noun **message** will refer to the information which the computer displays to the user.

The specification of the input will include:

1. the source of the input data – this might be the name of a form or a document, such as the goods inward note
2. screen layouts – if the function is to be developed by prototyping, then detailed

SYSTEM: STOCK CONTROL   SUB-SYSTEM: PRODUCTS

PROCESS: PS/1.1 ADD A NEW PRODUCT

FIELD NAME	VALIDATION	MESSAGE	ACTION
PART.NUM		P.PS.004	
	If not numeric	X.PS.005	Re-input
	If not 0001-9999	X.PS.005	Re-input
	Less than 4 digits	W.PS.008	Pad out with leading zeroes and re-display
	Greater than 4 digits	X.PS.005	Re-input
	Exists on PROD099 file	X.PS.007	Re-input

Figure 5.5 Input data specification.

MESSAGES

SYSTEM: STOCK CONTROL   SUB-SYSTEM: PRODUCTS

REFERENCE	TEXT
P.PS.004	ENTER PART NUMBER (0001-9999)
X.PS.005	PART NUMBER MUST BE FOUR DIGITS
X.PS.006	PART NUMBER NOT ON PRODUCT FILE
X.PS.007	PART NUMBER ALREADY EXISTS ON PRODUCT FILE
W.PS.008	PART NUMBER PADDED TO FOUR DIGITS

Figure 5.6 Messages.

screen layouts may not be necessary at this stage, as we shall discuss in detail later

3. the prompt messages to be displayed – an example is shown in Fig. 5.5
4. the names of the data fields which are to be entered by the user
5. any validation which is performed on the data
6. the error messages and warning messages which are to be displayed in the event of invalid data – an example is shown in Fig. 5.6
7. a description of the action which is to be taken in the event of invalid data
8. some indication of the volume of the transactions – for example, thirty new orders per day.

When you are constructing the messages for your system – be they headings, prompt messages, warning messages, or error messages – it is worth considering that they be held on a file outside the coding of the program. A major advantage of this practice is that the text of the messages can be changed more easily. Thus, a sequence such as

READ MESSAGEX.PS.005 FROM MESSAGE-FILE
PRINT MESSAGEX.PS.005

or possibly a call to a message-display module

CALL PSMSG(005)

would replace

PRINT 'PART NUMBER MUST BE FOUR DIGITS'

and if the text of the message were ever to be changed – possibly for cosmetic reasons or to respond to the user's own jargon – then you need only change the message held on the text file, and this would be reflected throughout the system.

5.5.3 Input considerations

There are some general considerations which, whilst they do not relate directly to the function description, are important at the systems design stage. For those readers who are new to systems design, we shall look at; input data design, forms design, screen layouts, and some general operator considerations. Experienced analysts may wish to omit this section.

(a) *Input data design*

A most important requirement of information entered into the computer is that it should be accurate – or as accurate as possible. One of the means by which we might get closer to this ideal is by removing the number of ways by which the data can be inaccurate. Data may be entered incorrectly for many reasons, but essentially these reduce to the data being mis-read from the input documents, or the data being mis-typed into the computer. The scope for mis-reading and mis-interpreting the input data can be minimized by careful design of the input documents. The scope for mis-typing the input data can be minimized by keeping the actual text which the user has to enter to a bare minimum, and by checking and confirming the data. The data can be checked by using check-digit techniques, and by extensive vetting routines within the program. The program checking can obviously extend to the verification of the format and nature of the data. It is a simple matter for the program to detect that JOHN SMITH and 33/12/1989 are invalid values for a date, but how can we be sure, for example, that 12/1/1989 is the correct date? Should it be the 12th January or the 1st December? If this is the data on which a sales order was received, then our program might be able to check this against today's date and reject it if there is more than, say, 30 days' difference.

We could ask the user to approve all the data before they are accepted for further processing, and confirm that he does, in fact, wish to proceed. Or we could offer the opportunity to amend any parts of the information. But since the user probably thinks that he has typed it correctly anyway, such a step may only be appropriate for glaring mis-typing errors. We can perhaps stimulate the user by re-displaying the input data in a way which makes it easier to recognize errors.

We could adopt a similar approach in the case of a customer number, for example. After accepting the customer number and checking that it is in the correct format – this might be four numeric digits – our program would retrieve the record from the file and then display the customer name and address so that the user may compare these with information shown elsewhere on the input document.

Fig. 5.7 shows a structured English sequence for the sort of processing which could be carried out when accepting keyboard input data.

```
loop
    display prompt
    accept the user's data
    if there is an error-message displayed
    then
        clear the current error-message
        clear the flag which indicates the presence of
            an error-message on the screen
    endif
    validate the user's data
    if the user's data is valid
    then
        redisplay the user's data in correct format
    else
        clear input data field
        display error-message showing the incorrect data
            and the reason for rejection
        set the flag which indicates the presence of
            an error-message on the screen
    end
repeat until the user's data is valid
```

Figure 5.7 A data input and validation design.

(b)   *Screen layouts*

The effort which you must put into designing your screen layouts depends upon the answers to two questions.

1. Will you be using a screen painter?
   A screen painter package is a valuable tool enabling you to design your screen layouts on-line. It will allow you to draw a picture of the screen and move text strings around the screen and place them where you wish. When your final screen has been designed, the utility will produce a hard-copy of the screen layout and this can be included in the documentation. An example of such a layout is shown in Fig. 5.8. Many fourth generation language tools and application generators incorporate such facilities.
   Systems are also available to generate program code from the screen layout, and this code can then be incorporated into the application program as required.

2. Will you be developing the screen in a prototyping manner?
   If you are going to develop the fine detail of your screen layouts whilst the user is sitting with you at the terminal, then only the briefest details of the screen contents will be necessary at this stage. The positioning of the text and messages and of the input and output fields can be determined later, in

```
             1         2         3         4         5         6         7
    12345678901234567890123456789012345678901234567890123456789012345678901234 5
    ++++++++++++++++++++++++++++++++++++++++++++++++++++++++++++++++++++++++++++++
 1:                       ** SALES ORDER PROCESSING ROUTINE **
 2:
 3:CLIENT NUMBER: xxxx        CLIENT NAME: xxxxxxxxxxxxxxxxxxxxxxxxxxxxxxxxxx
 4:
 5:ORDER DATE: dd/mm/yy                              DELIVERY DATE: dd/
 6:
 7:PRODUCT CODE    DESCRIPTION                       QTY      PRICE
 8:
 9:xxxx           xxxxxxxxxxxxxxxxxxxxxxxxxxxxxxxxxxxx  xxxx   xxxxx.xx   xxx
 0:xxxx           xxxxxxxxxxxxxxxxxxxxxxxxxxxxxxxxxxxx  xxxx   xxxxx.xx   xxx
 1:xxxx           xxxxxxxxxxxxxxxxxxxxxxxxxxxxxxxxxxxx  xxxx   xxxxx.xx   xxx
 2:xxxx           xxxxxxxxxxxxxxxxxxxxxxxxxxxxxxxxxxxx  xxxx   xxxxx.xx   xxx
 3:xxxx           xxxxxxxxxxxxxxxxxxxxxxxxxxxxxxxxxxxx  xxxx   xxxxx.xx   xxx
 4:xxxx           xxxxxxxxxxxxxxxxxxxxxxxxxxxxxxxxxxxx  xxxx   xxxxx.xx   xxx
 5:xxxx           xxxxxxxxxxxxxxxxxxxxxxxxxxxxxxxxxxxx  xxxx   xxxxx.xx   xxx
 6:xxxx           xxxxxxxxxxxxxxxxxxxxxxxxxxxxxxxxxxxx  xxxx   xxxxx.xx   xxx
 7:xxxx           xxxxxxxxxxxxxxxxxxxxxxxxxxxxxxxxxxxx  xxxx   xxxxx.xx   xxx
 8:xxxx           xxxxxxxxxxxxxxxxxxxxxxxxxxxxxxxxxxxx  xxxx   xxxxx.xx   xxx
 9:xxxx           xxxxxxxxxxxxxxxxxxxxxxxxxxxxxxxxxxxx  xxxx   xxxxx.xx   xxx
 0:
 1:                                         TOTAL ORDER VALUE: xxxxx
 2:
 3:xxxx messages go here xxxxxxxxxxxxxxxxxxxxxxxxxxxxxxxxxxxxxxxxxxxxxxxxxxxxx
 4:
    ++++++++++++++++++++++++++++++++++++++++++++++++++++++++++++++++++++++++++++++
    12345678901234567890123456789012345678901234567890123456789012345678901234 5
             1         2         3         4         5         6         7
```

Figure 5.8 A screen format.

consultation with the users. We look at the subject of prototyping in Section 7.10.

If the answers to both these questions are NO, then you must design your screen layouts in the traditional manner, using a pencil and squared paper or screen formatting sheets.

(c) *Operator considerations*

Most modern computer systems serve users who are sitting at a VDU terminal; batch processing represents a very small proportion of some systems. If communication between the user and the computer is to be enjoyable, or at least endurable, the analyst must give a lot of thought to how that communication is to be achieved. The term user-friendly is now so overworked and abused that it has lost any value it had, but the analyst should strive to ensure that the users truly consider the system to be less user-hostile than it might be. If user reaction – during testing or after implementation – indicates any areas which could be improved, then this should be considered.

When we discuss the function map later in this chapter, we shall consider the various ways which the facilities are offered to the user. This may be via a menu structure, it may be within a completely closed system, or it may be at a lower level where the user invokes programs and queries language enquiries directly. We shall also discuss the provision of help facilities which users may invoke if they are in doubt at any point. When you are designing help facilities, try to be as brief – though as useful – as possible. You can do this by offering your user the opportunity to get a long or a short response. Thus, if the user enters '?' to seek help on what is expected of him or her the program may respond:

Enter unit price of product. Press M for more help

A further input of M, in this case, will provide an explanation at greater length.

As with error messages, it is a good plan to hold the text of the help messages outside the program. A word-processing facility – either the standard software or a module which you have produced – can be useful in handling the formatting and justification of the text of your messages.

Another area in which the psychological aspects of the user–machine interface must be considered is in connection with the response time. When a user invokes an operation via the keyboard, the amount of time which he or she is prepared to wait before becoming impatient is proportional to the complexity of the task as that user sees it. If I am using a travel agent's terminal to find the details of any holidays that are available for next week, for example, then I will expect a fairly quick response. But if I want details of any seven-day holidays in Crete costing less than £300, I am prepared to wait a little longer.

If there is really nothing that can be done to speed up a process, then you could display a message acknowledging the request and asking the user to wait. You might even echo the request, by displaying a message such as that shown in

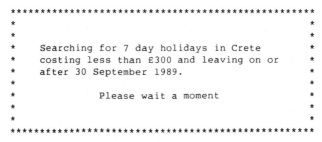

Figure 5.9 A courtesy message.

Fig. 5.9. This would give me something to think about whilst I'm waiting to find out about my holiday.

5.5.4 Output message specifications

In most cases, the output from a function will take the form of a displayed or a printed report – a sales analysis, a set of departmental statistics, a batch of salary cheques or a set of invoices.

As the example in Fig. 5.10 shows, that part of the function description which relates to the specification of the output should include:

1. the title of the report
2. the names of the files that are used in the report

```
                     OUTPUT SPECIFICATIONS


SYSTEM: STOCK CONTROL          SUB-SYSTEM: PRODUCTS


PROCESS: PS/2.7 PRODUCT CATALOGUE


REFERENCE: PS02007             | FILE: PROD009

TITLE: CURRENT PRODUCT STATUS
```

SEQ	FIELD NAMES	HEADING	WIDTH	TOTAL	C-B	SORT
1	PROD.NUM	CODE	10			3
2	PROD.DESC	DESCRIPTION	50			
3	PROD.DEPOT	DEPOT CODE	10		PAGE	1
4	PROD.QTY	QUANTITY	10			
5	PROD.VAL	VALUE	10	Y		
6	PROD.TYPE	PRODUCT TYPE	20		LINE	2

Figure 5.10 Output specifications

3. the identity of the data fields that are to appear on the report
4. an indication of the conditions under which any control breaks are to be made
5. an indication of the data fields that are to be totalled
6. an indication of the sequence into which the entries on the report are to be sorted, or the order in which the salary cheques are to be printed
7. report layouts – if the function is to be developed by prototyping, or if a query language is being used, then detailed report layouts and control break information may not be necessary at this stage.

It may also include:

8. the number of copies of the output
9. the destination of the output – for example, one copy of the sales statistics may be distributed to the Sales Manager and one copy to the Librarian
10. some indication of the volume of the output – possibly in terms of the number of printed pages – and of the turnaround time which is anticipated for the processing.

5.5.5   Data and file specifications

The description of the files which are used by the function should include:

1. the names of the files
2. the structure and contents of the records
3. the size and number of the records on the files
4. the action which is performed upon the files: additions, changes or deletions
5. if data are written to a work-file, then the layout of that file should be given
6. any demands which the database management system may make, such as maintenance of entry points and pointers.

In most cases, this information is provided on the entity/function matrix, the entity descriptions and the data structure diagram, and need not be repeated in a separate document.

5.5.6   Processing considerations

Minor details of the processing will inevitably be gathered as the investigation proceeds – even though the analyst may not be ready for such detail at the time. If this happens, it should be recorded as a narrative description, or in one of the other forms described below. For the same reasons, any thoughts on processing and reporting requirements could be recorded on what will become the function catalogue, as described in Section 5.4.

Traditional flowcharting techniques do still have their place in process design. However, the modularization of the system means that each module becomes smaller and simpler, and flowcharts now have their greatest benefit when they are used to help the programmer clarify any complex piece of processing or a sequence of complex decisions which have to be performed.

5.5.7 Structured English

The processing to be performed by a program or a module can be specified on the function descriptions by means of structured English sentences. This takes advantage of structured programming facilities: sequence, selection and iteration.

- sequential processing statements – sequence
- if structures – selection
- case structures – selection
- for structures – iteration
- loop structures – iteration

One intention of structured English is that it shall be intelligible to the untrained user so as to allow the analyst to confirm the tasks to be performed. For this reason, there is a minimum of jargon and formality in the language. The statements are written in free-form – albeit stylized – English, with keywords to highlight the constructions being used. There may be slight differences between the various versions of structured English which you encounter, but these will never affect its intelligibility. Another intention is that structured English shall be precise enough to convey the requirements to the programmer who will subsequently write the program. For this reason, the structures which are used are very close to those of formal programming languages. Fig. 5.11 shows some examples.

In this illustration, we have highlighted the keywords, although this is not necessary in practice.

By means of a sequence of top-down refinements, structured English allows the design for a function to be transformed into a form which is very near to the final coding produced by the programmer. To illustrate this, let us consider a system which will enable a tennis club to process the receipt of membership renewal subscriptions and produce a report on the payments received. We start off with a top-level design for the system which might be:

1 read in the payments
2 update the membership records
3 print a report of the payments received

This structured English design is sufficient to enable the users to see what is happening, and it may, in fact, be a simple paraphrasing of what already happens in the current clerical system. Each step in our design comprises a step number, followed by a brief text description of the action carried out.

The original top-level design will go through several refinements before it can be transformed into a computer language. At each refinement, one or more of the steps will be expanded.

1. **if** constructions can be represented by a sequence such as:

   ```
   if tax-code is less than zero
   then
       display 'invalid tax code found' message
   else
       calculate the tax due
   endif
   ```

2. **case** constructions can be represented by a sequence such as:

   ```
   case depending upon option
       option = A : add value to total
       option = S : subtract value from total
   else
       display 'invalid option' message
   endcase
   ```

3. **for** constructions can be represented by a sequence such as:

   ```
   for all records
       add price to total
   endfor
   ```

4. **loop** constructions can be represented by one of the sequences:

   ```
   loop until price less than 0
       add price to total
       ask user for price
   endloop
   ```

   ```
   loop while price not less than 0
       add price to total
       ask user for price
   endloop
   ```

   ```
   repeat until price less than 0
       add price to total
       ask user for price
   endrepeat
   ```

   ```
   repeat while price not less than 0
       add price to total
       ask user for price
   endrepeat
   ```

Figure 5.11 Structured English constructs.

As you derive your design, you will make a number of assumptions. In the top-level design, for example, we have assumed that:

- all the payments are valid
- none of the cheques will bounce
- all the payments are for existing members
- one payment is for one membership renewal
- the input data collected with each payment include membership information which will enable us to associate each payment with the proper membership record.

You may find that some of your assumptions are wrong, and you will then have to modify your design to accommodate these.

Let us look at our top-level design and start to refine it, beginning with step 2:

update the membership record.

This might involve several steps:

2.1 for all payments

2.2   update the membership record

We must add another step to control the 'for all payments' statement in step 2.1. This is the keyword **endfor**. You can see that the step numbers 2.1, 2.2 and 2.3 indicate how the new steps derive from the original step number 2. The text of step 2.2 has been indented to indicate its subordinate relationship to steps 2.1 and 2.3. Our new version is shown in Fig. 5.12.

```
1        read in the payments
2.1      for all payments
2.2          update the membership record
2.3      endfor
3        print a report of the payments received
```

Figure 5.12 Design for membership payments system – 1.

Refining step 2.2, we get the design shown in Fig. 5.13.

```
1        read in the payments
2.1      for all payments
2.2.1        read in the details
2.2.2        change the subscription status on the
             member's record
2.2.3        accumulate the amount paid
2.3      endfor
3        print a report of the payments received
```

Figure 5.13 Design for membership payments system – 2.

If we test the logic of this design, we will see that we need to rationalize the places at which we read in the details. When we have done this, we get the design shown in Fig. 5.14.

```
1          read in the first payment
2.1        for all payments
2.2.1.1        read in the membership number
2.2.1.2        find the member's record
2.2.2          change the subscription status on the
               member's record
2.2.3          accumulate the amount paid
2.3.1          read in the next payment
2.3        endfor
3          print a report of the payments received
```

Figure 5.14 Design for membership payments system – 3.

```
* Set counters to zero and open files
0.1        Initialize counters
0.2        Open files
1          Read in the first payment
2.1        For all payments
* Process all the payments
2.2.1.1        Read in the membership number
2.2.1.2        Find the member's record on file
2.2.2          Change the subscription status on
               the member's record
2.2.2.1            Write the member's record back to the file
2.2.3          Accumulate the amount paid
2.3.1          Read in the next payment
2.3        Endfor
* Print final report when all payments have been processed
3          Print a report of the total payments received
3.1        Close files
* End of job
```

Figure 5.15 Design for membership payments system – 4.

```
*
* Function to process the tennis club membership payments
*
0.0        Routine: Membership Payments
0.1        Initialize counters
0.2        Open files
0.2.1      If files cannot be opened successfully
0.2.2      Then
*
* Abandon the function
*
0.2.3          Display catastrophe message
0.2.4          Stop
0.2.5      Endif
1          Read in the first payment
2.1        Repeat while there are payments to process
2.2.1.1        Read in the membership number
2.2.1.2        Find the member's record on file
*
* Is member's record there?
*
2.2.1.2.1      If member's record cannot be found
2.2.1.2.2      Then
2.2.1.2.3          Display warning message
*
* Ignore payment if record not found
*
2.2.1.2.4      Else
*
* Process details if record found
*
2.2.2              Change the subscription status on
                   the member's record
2.2.2.1            Write the member's record back to the file
2.2.3              Accumulate the amount paid
2.2.1.2.5      Endif
2.3.1          Read in the next payment
2.3        Endrepeat
3          Print a report of the total payments received
3.1        Close files
4          Exit: Membership Payments
```

Figure 5.16 Design for membership payments system – 5.

Although the very nature of a structured English design implies that it should be easy to read, comments may be used, if required. Our final refined version might look like that shown in Fig. 5.15.

Some analysts use other keywords such as: routine, repeat while, repeat until, endrepeat, exit and stop. Using these, we might derive the design shown in Fig. 5.16.

In order to make the structured English closer to the final program, you may use actual function names, data names and file names, as shown in Fig. 5.17.

```
*
*  Function to process the tennis club membership payments
*
1     Routine: MEMBERSHIP.PAYMENTS
2     Initialize counters: TOTAL.PAID
3     Open files: MEMBER, PAYMENT
4     If files cannot be opened successfully
5     Then
*
*  Abandon the function
*
6            Display catastrophe message: TCM001
7            Stop
8     Endif
9     Read in the first PAYMENT
10    Repeat while there are payments to process
11           Read in the membership number: MEMBER-NUMBER
12           Find the MEMBER record on file
*
*  Is member's record there?
*
13           If MEMBER record cannot be found
14           Then
15                  Display warning message: TCM002
*
*  Ignore payment if record not found
*
16           Else
*
*  Process details if record found
*
17                  Change the subscription status on the MEMBER
                    record
18                  Write the MEMBER record back to the file
19                  Accumulate the amount paid
20           Endif
21           Read in the next PAYMENT
22    Endrepeat
23    Print a report of the total payments received
24    Close files: MEMBER, PAYMENT
25    Exit: MEMBERSHIP.PAYMENTS
```

Figure 5.17 Design for membership payments system – 6.

If we were using an on-line system, then we could derive an alternative solution based upon the original design. This might look like that shown in Fig. 5.18.

The most important features of structured English are

1. it can be read and understood by users who have no special programming expertise

2. the indentation reveals the structure of the design
3. the step numbers reveal the way in which the design evolved
4. it can be used as a basis for the design of the final program.

```
0.1     Initialize counters
0.2     Open files
1.1     Ask the user for the membership-number
1.2     Loop until membership-number is END
1.5         Read in the details of the amount pad
2.1         Change the subscription status on the
            member's record
2.2         Accumulate the amount paid
1.7         Ask the user for the membership-number
1.8     Endloop
3       Print a report of the payments received
```

Figure 5.18 Design for membership payments system – 7.

5.5.8   Example 1

Let us develop another structured English design.

We are required to produce a function that will add details of a telephone booking to the room reservation file for a hotel. Let us start with the initial design:

```
1       get the guest's details
2       find an available room
3       update the reservations file with the guest's
        details
4       ask the guest to send in a written confirmation
5       update the reservations file showing that this
        is a provisional booking and that we are
        awaiting written confirmation
6       send a written acknowledgement of the
        provisional booking to the guest
```

Figure 5.19 Design for a hotel reservation system – 1.

```
1       Get the guest's details
2.1     Find an available room
2.2     If there is an available room
2.3     Then
3           Update the reservations file with
            the guest's details
4           Ask the guest to send in a written
            confirmation
5           Update the reservations file showing
            that this is a provisional booking and
            that we are awaiting written confirmation
6           Send a written acknowledgement of the
            provisional booking to the guest
2.4     Else
2.5         Apologize to the guest
2.6     Endif
```

Figure 5.20 Design for a hotel reservation system – 2.

1 get the guest's details
2 find an available room
3 update the reservations file with the guest's details

After further consultation with our user, we may learn that some additional
actions are to be taken, producing the design shown in Fig. 5.19.

```
1        Get the guest's details
2.1      Find an available room
2.2      If there is an available room
2.3      Then
3            Update the reservations file with the
             guest's details
4.1          If payment accompanies the reservation
4.2          Then
4.3              Update the reservations file showing
                 that payment has been received
4.4              Produce a printed confirmation
4.5          Else
4.6              Ask the guest to send in a written
                 confirmation
5                Update the reservations file showing that
                 this is a provisional booking and that we
                 are awaiting written confirmation
6                Send a written acknowledgement of the
                 provisional booking to the guest
4.9          Endif
2.4      Else
2.5          Apologize to the guest
2.6      Endif
```

Figure 5.21 Design for a hotel reservation system – 3.

```
1        Get the guest's details
2.1.1    Get and validate check-in date
2.1.2    Get and validate room requirements
         (single, double, twin)
2.1.3    Loop for all rooms of type required
2.1.4        Check if room available on required date
2.1.5    Endloop
2.2      If there is an available room
2.3      Then
3            Update the reservations file with the guest's
             details
4.1          If payment accompanies the reservation
4.2          Then
4.3              Update the reservations file showing that
                 payment has been received
4.4              Produce a printed confirmation
4.5          Else
4.6              Ask the guest to send in a written confirmation
5                Update the reservations file showing that
                 this is a provisional booking and that we are
                 awaiting written confirmation
6                Send a written acknowledgement of the
                 provisional booking to the guest
4.9          Endif
2.4      Else
2.5          Apologize to the guest
2.6      Endif
```

Figure 5.22 Design for a hotel reservation system – 4.

Successive possible refinements – and possible modifications to the users' requirements – are shown in Figs 5.20–22.

1. We refine step 2 to cater for no suitable room being available (Fig. 5.20);
2. We refine step 4 to cater for the situation where the guest pays for the accommodation when making the reservation (Fig. 5.21);
3. We refine the process of searching for an available room (Fig. 5.22).

This may be sufficient level of detail to enable the programmer to produce the program code directly, or we may need to go into more detail about the files which we shall use. For example, we may have to elaborate upon the methods for searching for the room at step 2.1.4 or upon the action to be taken at step 2.5 if there are no rooms available.

5.5.9 Example 2 – designing a module

In this example, we are required to produce a module which will accept an alphanumeric string, such as

ALEXANDER GRAHAM BELL

or

LOUISA M. ALCOTT

or

LEWIS CARROLL

and extract the **surname**.

A top-level design may be as shown in Fig. 5.23.

Note that we have made two assumptions about the data: there will always be a

```
1        get the whole string
2        loop until there are no more characters
3            scan for spaces
4            store following word
5        repeat
6        display the latest word
```

Figure 5.23 Top-level design to extract a surname.

```
1        get the whole string
2.1      get first character of the string
2.2      if there is no character
2.3      then
2.4          exit
2.5      else
2.6          loop until there are no more characters
3                scan for spaces
4                store following word
5.1              get next character
5.2          repeat
6            display the latest word
2.7      endif
```

Figure 5.24 Refined design to extract a surname.

non-null string to process; there will always be at least one space. Further refinements – to overcome these assumptions – might be:

1. Remove the first assumption, continuing the process only when there is a character present, and then tidy up the loop control mechanism by using this character (Fig. 5.24);
2. Remove the second assumption, and then initialize, build and display the surname (Fig. 5.25).

The design is for a module, and not an independent function, so we amend our design to accommodate this. We specify that there is one input parameter, we have called this **STRING**, and there is one output parameter, we have called this **SURNAME**.

Note that solution (2) in Fig. 5.25 assumes that the character string does not end in spaces. How could we modify the design to handle this problem?

Once the module has been defined, then it may be utilized in other structured English designs. Other designs will make use of this module by means of a statement such as:

GET.SURNAME (fullname, surname)

We shall look at the identification and the description of such modules when we consider the module catalogue and the module description later.

```
Module: GET.SURNAME

Input parameter: STRING

Output parameter: SURNAME
```
```
1.1     set SURNAME to null
2.1     get first character of the STRING
2.2     if there is no character
2.3     then
2.4         do nothing
2.5     else
2.6         loop until there are no more characters in
            STRING
3.1             if the current character is a space
3.2             then
3.3                 set SURNAME to null
3.4             else
4.1                 append current character to end of
                    SURNAME
3.5             endif
5.1             get next character
5.2         repeat
2.7     endif
9       return
```

Figure 5.25 Design for GET.SURNAME module.

```
                 SALES FIGURES 1989
                 ==================
                    JAN 15051
                    FEB 15049
                    MAR 15523
                    APR 16645
                    MAY 17670
                    JUN 25478
                    JUL 22025
                    AUG 18976
                    SEP 14864
                    OCT 9863
                    NOV 8336
                    DEC 5862


                 SALES FIGURES 1989
                 ==================
             JAN *************
             FEB *************
             MAR *************
             APR **************
             MAY ***************
             JUN ************************
             JUL *********************
             AUG *****************
             SEP *************
             OCT ********
             NOV *******
             DEC ****

                 SALES FIGURES 1989
                 ==================
    25K                      ***
    24K                      ***
    23K                      ***
    22K                      *** ***
    21K                      *** ***
    20K                      *** ***
    19K                      *** ***
    18K                      *** *** ***
    17K                  *** *** *** ***
    16K              *** *** *** *** ***
    15K *** *** *** *** *** *** *** ***
    14K *** *** *** *** *** *** *** *** ***
    13K *** *** *** *** *** *** *** *** ***
    12K *** *** *** *** *** *** *** *** ***
    11K *** *** *** *** *** *** *** *** ***
    10K *** *** *** *** *** *** *** *** ***
     9K *** *** *** *** *** *** *** *** *** ***
     8K *** *** *** *** *** *** *** *** *** *** ***
     7K *** *** *** *** *** *** *** *** *** *** ***
     6K *** *** *** *** *** *** *** *** *** *** ***
     5K *** *** *** *** *** *** *** *** *** *** *** ***
     4K *** *** *** *** *** *** *** *** *** *** *** ***
     3K *** *** *** *** *** *** *** *** *** *** *** ***
     2K *** *** *** *** *** *** *** *** *** *** *** ***
     1K *** *** *** *** *** *** *** *** *** *** *** ***

        JAN FEB MAR APR MAY JUN JUL AUG SEP OCT NOV DEC
```

Figure 5.26 Graphical output possibilities.

5.5.10   Output considerations

Let us consider those aspects of the process description which relate to the output data and the results.

In practice, the output from most commercial applications is the printed document. Several million pages of printed reports are produced every day. Are all of these pages actually read? Are they read by everyone who receives a copy? There is a strong case for restricting the printed output from a system. Apart from the economics of printing the pages and throwing them away unread or partly read, there is the fact that too much printed matter devalues the information that it contains. It is much better to provide a manager with just the information he needs, for example

TOTAL PROFIT YEAR TO DATE: £1,023,225

rather than embedding this figure in hundreds of pages of analysis and cost breakdowns. Wherever possible, offer your users a choice as to the quantity of information which they receive and the depth to which the breakdown is needed.

Is it necessary to print the output at all? Would the users not be just as happy with displayed figures? They will certainly be happy when they know that this displayed figure shows the sales as they were 5 min ago, whereas the printed report may only show last week's figures.

Even printed and displayed output can be made more accessible and clearer by using graphic devices. A plotter is ideal, but even screens and printers can produce simple bar-charts and pie-charts to present information. Fig. 5.26 is an example showing the same information in three forms. Any of these be displayed or printed.

Another form of output, the KWIC – KeyWord In Context – report, is particularly valuable when the user is seeking a reference of which only a part is known. Fig. 5.27 shows how such a report might be used to find the title of one of Charles Dickens's novels.

5.5.11   Report layouts

The specification for printed reports will include:

1. the title of the report
2. the position and contents of the actual text items which are to appear on the report, including headings, prompts and messages: are the date, the time and the page-number to be shown?
3. the position and length of all data fields which are to be shown
4. details of the control breaks: is the report to skip to a new page for each customer?
5. details of the totals which are to be maintained and printed: are sub-totals and grand-totals to be shown?
6. details of the sorting sequence: are the employee details to be sorted by department, and within each department are they to be sorted by descending salary rates?

```
REF   TITLE _____ |_____
                            |
2007                        BARNABY RUDGE
2011                        BLEAK HOUSE
2002             SKETCHES BY BOZ
2002             SKETCHES BY BOZ
2009            A CHRISTMAS CAROL
2009                      A CHRISTMAS CAROL
2008               MARTIN CHUZZLEWIT
2014      A TALE OF TWO CITIES
2001              DAVID COPPERFIELD
2006          THE OLD CURIOSITY SHOP
2001                        DAVID COPPERFIELD
2010                        DOMBEY AND SON
2013               LITTLE DORRIT
2017 THE MYSTERY OF EDWIN DROOD
2017       THE MYSTERY OF EDWIN DROOD
2015              GREAT EXPECTATIONS
2016         OUR MUTUAL FRIEND
2015                        GREAT EXPECTATIONS
2012                        HARD TIMES
2011                BLEAK HOUSE
2013                        LITTLE DORRIT
2008                        MARTIN CHUZZLEWIT
2016                  OUR MUTUAL FRIEND
2017                  THE MYSTERY OF EDWIN DROOD
2005                        NICHOLAS NICKLEBY
2005             NICHOLAS NICKLEBY
2006                THE OLD CURIOSITY SHOP
2004                        OLIVER TWIST
2016                        OUR MUTUAL FRIEND
2003         THE PICKWICK PAPERS
2003              THE PICKWICK PAPERS
2007              BARNABY RUDGE
2006   THE OLD CURIOSITY SHOP
2002                        SKETCHES BY BOZ
2010            DOMBEY AND SON
2014                      A TALE OF TWO CITIES
2012                HARD TIMES
2004            OLIVER TWIST
2014         A TALE OF TWO CITIES
```

Figure 5.27 KWIC – keyword-in-context report.

As with screen layouts, the effort which you must put in to designing your report layouts depends upon the facilities which are available to you and the environment in which you and your users will be working. Many fourth generation language tools and application generators include report design facilities and will enable you to produce a hard-copy dummy report for use in your documentation. As before, if you are intending to design your reports by prototyping in collaboration with the users, then only the briefest details of the report contents will be necessary at this stage. The actual positioning of the fields can be determined later.

By far the greatest simplification in the production of reports, and of report programs, is the advent of query languages. Query languages are usually supported by a database management system and, as we shall see when discuss the subject in more detail in Chapter 7, they enable you to generate reports, and your users to make *ad hoc* enquiries by means of simple statements such as

LIST OVERDUE INVOICES SHOWING NAME DATE-DUE AND TOTAL AMOUNT

which might produce the report shown in LISTING of Fig. 5.28.

If you do not have automatic report formatting facilities at your disposal, then you must specify the report layouts in the traditional manner, using pencil and squared paper or printer formatting sheets, as shown in Fig. 5.29.

5.5.12 Producing the function descriptions

The following points should be borne in mind when producing the function descriptions:

1. Every entry in the function catalogue is used to produce one function description.
2. The narrative descriptions, flowcharts, decision tables and other information, which you gathered during your investigation and analysis, are used to provide the details of the processing that is to be performed by the function.

```
INVOICES NAME...................................... DATE-DUE... AMOUNT

  1750     HIGGINS, A                     12 FEB 1989    2.52
  1799     HIGGINS, A                     01 SEP 1989    9.96
  1736     JOHNSON AND WATLING            05 MAR 1989    6.50
  1738     JOHNSON AND WATLING            30 APR 1988    8.02
  1790     JOHNSON AND WATLING            09 JUL 1987    2.56
  1797     JOHNSON AND WATLING            17 FEB 1989    9.28
  1744     KEYES PARTNERS                 08 NOV 1989    1.21
  1746     KEYES PARTNERS                 18 FEB 1989    8.26
  1751     KEYES PARTNERS                 03 AUG 1989    9.81
  1753     KEYES PARTNERS                 19 DEC 1987    9.41
  1775     KEYES PARTNERS                 04 FEB 1988    5.69
  1777     KEYES PARTNERS                 06 SEP 1989    1.65
  1791     KEYES PARTNERS                 30 APR 1987    8.96
  1795     KEYES PARTNERS                 26 DEC 1988    8.01
  1748     MOTTLINGHAM                    19 OCT 1987    6.24
  1754     MOTTLINGHAM                    04 SEP 1989    5.52
  1793     SMITH AND CO                   05 FEB 1989    1.71
  1739     WILSON-BATLEY LTD              21 FEB 1988    2.12
  1742     WILSON-BATLEY LTD              10 NOV 1988    3.41
  1752     WILSON-BATLEY LTD              22 JUL 1988    4.72
                                                        ======
                          TOTAL AMOUNT OUTSTANDING      115.56
```

Figure 5.28 Query language report

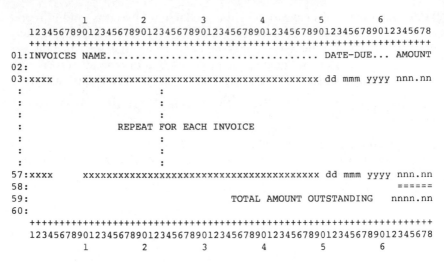

Figure 5.29 Report layout.

Each function description will contain:

3. a verbal description of the function
4. an indication of whether this is to be an on-line function or a batch function
5. a technical description of the function. The full processing details should be given in a form such as structured English
6. any operations which must be performed before or after this function
7. any other functions which must be performed before or after this function
8. input specifications for batch and on-line functions:
   (a) the names of the data fields that are to be entered by the user
   (b) the prompt messages to be displayed
   (c) any validation which is performed on the data
   (d) the error messages and warning messages which are to be displayed
   (e) a description of the action which is to be taken when errors are detected
   (f) screen layouts
   (g) the names of the files
   (h) the action which is performed upon the files
   (i) if data are written to a work-file, then the layout of that file should also be declared
9. output specifications for batch and report functions, including:
   (a) the title of the report
   (b) the position and contents of the actual text that is to appear on the report, including headings, prompts and messages
   (c) the position and length of all data fields which are to be shown
   (d) details of the control breaks
   (e) details of the totals which are to be maintained and printed
   (f) details of the sorting sequence

The resulting function descriptions are used to derive the function maps, and they will also be the basis for the programmers' work.

5.6   FUNCTION MAPS

A function map – sometimes known as a Visual Table of Contents – is used to document the physical layout and interfacing of the various routines which make up the system. It is based upon the contents of the function catalogue and will represent the menu structure to be used in the construction of the system, showing the paths which your users will take in order to obtain a specific process or function. In most instances, one element on a function map will represent one process on a DFD. If this is so, the function map is simply a tree-structure version of the DFD. However, you may remember that we said our DFDs probably would not contain details of:

- simple file enquiry processes
- routine reports
- *ad hoc* reports

These may be absent from the DFDs since they are not processes that are triggered by any specific event. If the proposed system contains any such facilities, then they will indeed appear on the function map. Some of your functions may appear more than once on the function map; this will be because you may want to offer them at more then one place. For example, a function to

AMEND A CUSTOMER RECORD

may be available as a direct operation when a customer's address or telephone number changes. But it may also be available from within the function to

ADD A NEW CUSTOMER RECORD

in case the operator has made a mistake in entering the source data for the new record.

In some operating systems, it is possible for a user to invoke programs directly, by typing in a command such as

RUN PAYROLL45

or your users may be able to make enquiries via a query language simply by typing in commands such as

LIST THE NAME, AGE, ADDRESS OF STAFF

or they may be able to produce a copy of a printed document by means of a word processing package invoked by a command such as

WORDPLAY SECTION 7.3

If these facilities are available in your environment, then you must now decide whether they are to be offered to your end-users directly – in the manner shown here – or whether they will be invoked indirectly via the menu structure of your function map. It is strongly recommended that, wherever possible, you keep the end-users within the framework of your function map and that you demand that the user goes through the menu structure to arrive at functions which merely invoke each of the commands shown. If you were to allow the user to invoke the commands directly, then mistakes may occur. What would happen if the user were to type

RUN PAYROLL54
LIST THE NAME, AGE, ADDRESS OF STOCK
WORDPLAY SECTION 3.7

and would the user know how to recover from what has been done? Could any of these commands be dangerous or jeopardize the security or integrity of the system?

By holding your users within the framework of your function map, you can control all the activities which are attempted, and you can also restrict and vet their activities to ensure that these are acceptable and consistent. If you want your users to enjoy the flexibility which a query language affords, then you could consider providing a function which will assist the user to generate a valid enquiry.

Having made the decision to contain all or a part of your users' activities within your control, you must now decide where you are going to place the individual facilities within the overall framework. Are you going to have a **REPORTS** branch on your menu tree-structure which allows the users to choose from

STOCK-REPORT
ORDER-REPORT
OUTSTANDING-ORDER-REPORT
CLIENT-REPORT

or is the **STOCK-REPORT** to be made available through the **STOCK-PROCESSING-MENU**, the **ORDER-REPORT** and **OUTSTANDING-ORDER-REPORT** through the **ORDER-PROCESSING-MENU**, and so on? This question can only be answered by knowing how your users work. Is a **STOCK-REPORT** likely to be done at about the same time as an **ORDER-REPORT**? If so, then you might group these together on an **REPORT-MENU**. Is a **STOCK-REPORT** likely to be done at about the same time as a **STOCK-FILE-AMENDMENT**? If so, then you might group these together on the **STOCK-PROCESSING-MENU**. These is, of course, no reason why you should not offer **both** facilities, and have the **same** function accessible from two different points on your function map.

The top-level DFD will be used to derive the system function map, as shown in Fig. 5.30. This is another example of the Jackson Diagram which we met in Chapter 1.

The intermediate and low-level DFDs will be used to produce successively more detailed function maps. Fig. 5.31 shows a function map based upon the intermediate DFD for the Sales Orders section of this main menu.

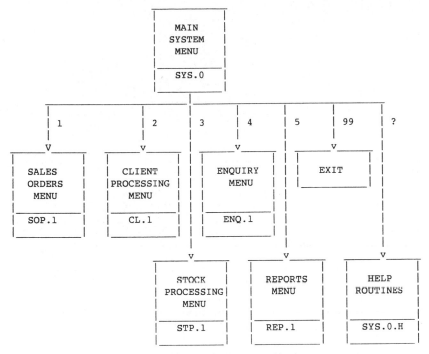

Figure 5.30 Function map – Jackson diagram.

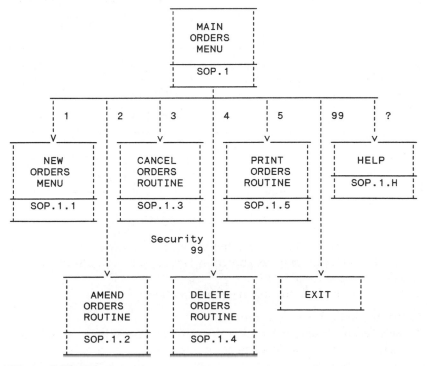

Figure 5.31 Function map.

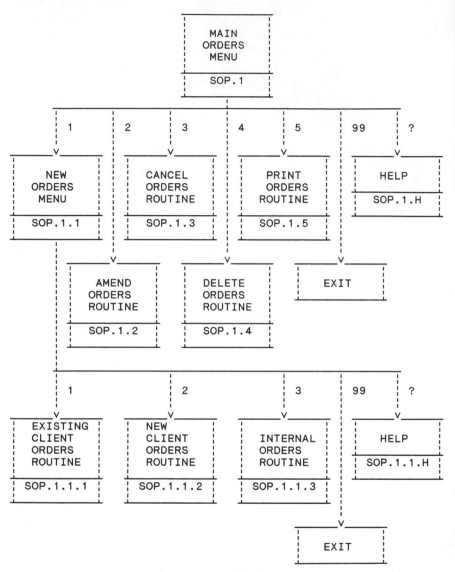

Figure 5.32 Function map showing several levels.

If your system is not too large, then it may be possible to show two – or even three – levels on one map, as shown in Fig. 5.32. More than this can become difficult to produce and to read.

These maps provide the following information:

1. the title of each menu or process
2. the reference number for each menu or process – this is used as a cross-reference to the other documentation relating to the process.

3. a help routine for each menu – this is a simple routine which the user can invoke if he is not sure what the choices on the menu mean. Such help routines will generate simple explanatory messages.
4. an exit routine for each menu – this is simply a way of passing control back up to the previous (higher-level) menu or, in the case of the top-most menu, a way of leaving the system entirely.

Help routines and the Exit routines should be provided for every menu.

5. option codes – it is possible to show the option codes – or control codes – which the user must enter in order to reach each routine from the appropriate menu. This is a good place at which to standardize the user facilities that you will offer.

```
Main system menu (SYS.0)
|
|_1__Main sales orders menu (SOP.1)
|    |
|    |_1__New orders menu (SOP.1.1)
|    |   |
|    |   |_1__Existing client orders routine (SOP.1.1.1
|    |   |
|    |   |_2__New client orders routine (SOP.1.1.2)
|    |   |
|    |   |_3__Internal orders routine (SOP.1.1.3)
|    |   |
|    |   |_99_Return to main menu (SOP.1.1)
|    |   |
|    |   |_?__Help routine (SOP.1.1.H)
|    |
|    |_2__Amend order routine (SOP.1.2)
|    |
|    |_3__Cancel orders routine (SOP.1.3)
|    |
|    |_4__Delete orders routine (SOP.1.4) [Security 99]
|    |
|    |_5__Print orders routine (SOP.1.5)
|    |
|    |_99_Return to main system menu (SOP.1)
|    |
|    |_?__Help routine (SOP.1.H)
|
|_2__Client processing menu (CL.1)
|
|_3__Stock processing menu (STP.1)
|
|_4__Enquiry menu (REP.1)
|
|_5__Reports menu (REP.1)
|
|_99_logoff the system
|
|_?__Help routine for system menu (SYS.0.H)
```

Figure 5.33 Function map – structured list.

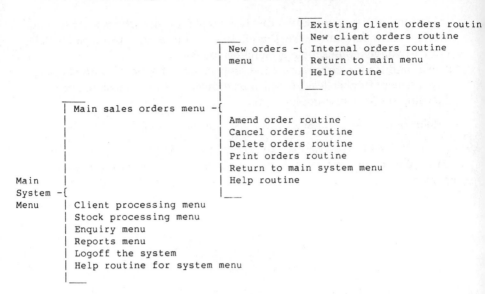

Figure 5.34 Function map – Warnier-Orr diagram.

In the function maps shown here, we have used option 99 as a means of returning to the previous menu, and the question mark as a means of soliciting help.

6. security codes – if certain options are to be restricted to authorized users, then this could be shown as in Fig. 5.31, where the **DELETE ORDERS** routine is only accessible to users with a security code of 99. The security code could be controlled by the program according to the user-identity or terminal location or by some other parameter.

If any special system software is used, or a mixture of languages, then this too will be indicated on the function maps.

Because the maps can become rather large and difficult to draw, you may prefer to produce the function map in one of the alternative formats illustrated in Fig. 5.33 and Fig. 5.34.

5.6.1 Producing the function maps

The following points should be borne in mind when producing the function maps:

1. The function catalogue and the function descriptions are used to provide the necessary information.
2. The function map represents the menu structure which the user will navigate in order to reach a particular function.
3. The functions should be grouped together logically: those for the Accounts Department separated from those for the Stock Control Clerks, the report functions on a separate menu from the processing functions.

4. You may feel that a particular facility – or even an entire menu – should be made available at more than one point in the menu structure. This will avoid your users having to go up and down branches of the menu structure to reach a particular facility. If so, indicate this on the map.
5. When a DFD process box is decomposed into smaller processes on a lower-level DFD, then that process generally corresponds to a menu on the function map.
6. The function map shows the names and reference numbers of the functions.
7. A help routine is provided for each menu.
8. An exit option is provided for each menu in order to return to the higher-level menu.
9. Indicate the option codes on the function map. This will enable the map to serve as a user training document.
10. Indicate any security codes on the function map. This will indicate the security level which is necessary to access any privileged processing.

The resulting function maps are used by the programmers to provide the linkage mechanism by which the users access the functions. They will also be of value to the end-users, showing how the processing is reached.

5.7 MODULE CATALOGUE

The function maps are used to document the physical layout and interfacing of the various routines which make up the system. We now need a more detailed representation of the physical system – the module catalogue. This will enable us to identify the various components – subroutines and functions – that will be required by the system. We develop the module catalogue by identifying any processing that is common to the various functions, and we ensure that the modules which perform such common processing are shared wherever possible. In many cases this part of the design activity will be carried out by the programmers.

The **LISTING** in Fig. 5.35 shows the structured English description of a function to **ADD STOCK RECORDS**.

We now look at this list and mark:

1. the file processing modules
2. the data input modules
3. the data validation modules
4. the calculation and processing modules
5. the display and output modules.

We have used asterisks to indicate such routines in Fig. 5.35. We then make a list of all these modules:

1. accept and verify part-number
2. display input form on screen
3. display data on screen

```
accept and verify part-number                                    ***
repeat until part-number is END
    if part-number is on the stock file
    then
            display input form on screen                         ***
            display data on screen                               ***
    else
            display input form on screen                         ***
            accept and verify description                        ***
            accept and verify unit-price                         ***
            accept and verify quantity-in-stock                  ***
            ask user if he wants to amend the stock record  ***
            if he wants to amend
                then
                    amend the stock record                       ***
            endif
            ask user if he wants to add the stock record   ***
                or abandon
            if he wants to add
            then
                    write stock record on the stock file    ***
            else
                    print message to indicate abandonment   ***
            endif
    endif
endrepeat
```

Figure 5.35 Design for stock addition function.

4. display input form on screen
5. accept and verify description
6. accept and verify unit-price
7. accept and verify quantity-in-stock
8. ask user if he wants to amend the stock record
9. amend the stock record
10. ask user if he wants to add the stock record
11. write stock record on the stock file
12. print message to indicate abandonment.

This list is used to produce a **module catalogue** and when supported by the **module maps** this will form a valuable means of communication between the analyst and the programmers.

In addition to the **ADD STOCK RECORD** function, there would also be a function to **AMEND STOCK RECORDS**, as shown in the **LISTING** in Fig. 5.36. We produce a list of the modules for that function in the same manner.

From this, we produce the module list:

1. accept and verify Part-number
2. display input form on screen
3. display data on screen
4. ask user if he wants to amend this Stock-record
5. accept and verify Description

```
accept and verify part-number                            ***
repeat until part-number is END
    if part-number is on the stock file
    then
            display input form on screen                 ***
            display data on screen                       ***
            ask user if he wants to amend this stock record ***
            loop until user doesn't want to amend
                    accept and verify description        ***
                    accept and verify unit-price         ***
                    accept and verify quantity-in-stock  ***
                    amend the stock record               ***
                    write the stock record on the stock file ***
                    ask user if he wants to amend further ***
            endloop
    else
            display error message                        ***
    endif
endrepeat
```

Figure 5.36 Design for stock amendment function.

6. accept and verify Unit-price
7. accept and verify Quantity-in-stock
8. amend the Stock-record
9. write the Stock-record on the Stock-file
10. ask user if he wants to amend further
11. display error message
12. endrepeat

Comparing the two lists, we find that there are several modules which are common to both these functions.

- accept and verify Description
- accept and verify Part-number
- accept and verify Quantity-in-stock
- accept and verify Unit-price
- amend the Stock-record
- ask user if he wants to amend further
- ask user if he wants to amend this Stock-record
- display input form on screen
- display data on screen
- display error message
- print message to indicate abandonment
- repeat until part-number is **END**
- write the stock record on the Stock-file

We continue to do this for the other functions in the function catalogue. We must of course ensure that the functions are the same. A vague **Amend record** may mean **Amend the stock level record** in one part of the system, and **Amend the order-line record** in another part. When we are certain that the various usages of the module are identical and unambiguous, then there are a number of choices available:

1. We may include the statement – or statements – which perform the modules *in situ* within every function that requires them.
2. We may include the statements as an internal subroutine within every function that requires them.
3. We may include the statements as a single external routine which is accessible to every function that requires them.

Which of these – statement, internal routine or external routine – you or the programmers choose is largely a matter of experience. There are no hard and fast rules. One solution will mean more duplicated coding than another. The questions that influence whether a module should be independent are:

1. Is the module used on a large number of occasions by any of the functions?
2. Is the module used by a large number of functions?
3. Will the module contain a large number of program statements?
4. Is the module complex?
5. Is the module likely to be changed in the future?
6. Is the action of the module hardware dependent?
7. Is it likely to change if the system is implemented on another operating system or with different hardware?
8. Is the module likely to modified if the system is made available to other users? This is particularly appropriate when designing software which is to be supplied to many different users.

If the answer to these is **YES**, then the module should be a candidate for becoming a free-standing module. In programming terms, we are now looking at the individual **SUBROUTINES, FUNCTIONS** and **PROCEDURES** to which you will pass control by means of **GOSUB, CALL** and other program control statements.

Typical of the routines which you might consider for extraction and establishment as independent modules are:

- display a specific screen input form
- display a particular error message
- display a heading with the time and date
- prompt, accept input, and re-display the input
- verify the format of a specific data item
- read a specific record and possibly change the format of any data items
- ready a particular output device
- change a specific field on a specific type of record
- change the format of any data items and write a specific record
- amend a specific type of record
- any routines which are dependent upon the hardware and/or the software which you use – or which you may use in the future.

The module catalogue can be developed from the list of modules into a form

MODULE CATALOGUE

```
 --------- ----------------------------------------- -----------
         |                                         |
 MODULE  | MODULE DESCRIPTION                      | Used in
 REF     |                                         |
 --------|-----------------------------------------|-----------
         |                                         |
 SOPS001 | Accept and verify description           | SOP.1.1.1
         |                                         | SOP.1.1.2
         |                                         | SOP.1.2
 SOPS002 | Accept and verify part-number           | SOP.1.1.1
         |                                         | SOP.1.1.2
         |                                         | SOP.1.2
 SOPS005 | Amend the stock record                  | SOP.1.1.1
         |                                         | SOP.1.1.2
         |                                         | SOP.1.1.3
 --------|-----------------------------------------|-----------
```

Figure 5.37 Module catalogue.

similar to that of the function catalogue, as shown in Fig. 5.37. The module catalogue is used to produce the module descriptions.

5.7.1 Producing the module catalogue

The following points should be borne in mind when producing the module catalogue:

1. The module catalogue identifies common routines which can be extracted and established as modules to be called upon as and when required;
2. The function descriptions are used to provide the necessary information to produce the module catalogue;
3. You must now consider each function description in turn and:
   (a) identify any file processing routines, specifying the file and the action— read, write or update – which is carried out
   (b) identify any data input routines
   (c) identify any data validation routines
   (d) identify any calculation and processing routines
   (e) identify any routines which are likely to be complex or difficult to write
   (f) identify any routines which perform an action which is likely to be required – in the same form or in a slightly modified form – in more than one function
   (g) identify any display, output and reporting routines in each function
   (h) identify any routines which are hardware or software dependent;
4. These lists are then co-ordinated for all the functions, and common modules are extracted and considered for isolation as independent modules;
5. The module catalogue is derived from these lists. It shows a unique identifier and the description of each module, and the identities of the functions which use that module.

The resulting module catalogue is used to derive the module descriptions and the final program specifications.

5.8   MODULE DESCRIPTION

For each module shown on the module catalogue, there will be a detailed module description of the processing which it performs. Much, if not all, of this will be drawn from the appropriate function description(s):

1. a description of what the module does and the operation of the module
2. a detailed description of the processing involved; this may be a structured English passage, or it may include flowcharts, decision tables and formulae in cases where there is complex or complicated processing to be performed
3. a cross-reference to the low-level DFD
4. the nature and sequence of parameters used by the module
5. input parameters, that is, data values which are passed to the module
6. output parameters, that is, data values which are passed from the module
7. exit and error links, stating the conditions under which each is taken
8. any screen layouts appropriate to the module
9. any report layouts appropriate to the module
10. any validation which takes place in the module
11. error messages and error codes returned by the module
12. reference to the files – and entity descriptions – which are concerned with the module.

In many cases, the programmers may have the responsibility for the production of the module catalogue and the derivation of the module descriptions.

5.8.1   Producing the module descriptions

The following points should be borne in mind when producing the module descriptions:

1. The module catalogue and the function descriptions are used to provide the necessary information.
2. There is a module description for each module.
3. The details of the module description are based upon the relevant parts of the function descriptions and will be extended to show the detailed action of the module.
4. The module description will include specifications of the input parameters which are to be passed to the module and the results which are passed out of the module.
5. The parameter specifications will describe the significance, the sequence and the format of the parameters.
6. The description should include details of the functions which will use that

module. This will be of use in assessing the scope of the impact if the module is later modified.

These module descriptions together with the function descriptions will constitute the program specifications.

5.9 MODULE MAPS

The function maps are used to document the physical layout and interfacing of the various routines which make up the system, and can be used in user-training to show the interaction of the various functions. The **module map** takes this to a lower level showing the modules which are called – and possibly shared – by the functions, but it is primarily a document for communication between the analyst and the programmer, and between the programmer and the maintenance programmer.

Because this step towards modularization is, in some part, dependent upon the programming environment, some systems development teams require that the programmers rather than the analyst produce the module catalogue and the module maps.

The module map is developed by adding the information held in the module catalogue, showing which functions call which modules, to the function map. The result is a chart of a similar format to the function map, except that option codes are not usually shown.

We can illustrate this by looking at the Main Sales Order function which appeared in the function maps. Let us imagine that our module catalogue identified the following functions:

Accept and vet option (SOPS102)
Amend orders record (SOPS105)
Display a menu (SOPS101)
Display orders screen (SOPS104)
Open orders file (SOPS103)
Produce heading (SOPS106)

The resultant module map might be represented as a Jackson Diagram, or a structured list like that shown in Fig. 5.38.

There is no significance in the arrangement of the modules on the module map. All the modules which may be used by a function are included and no special convention is necessary to indicate that a certain module is optional or conditional.

For clarity, we have used a double vertical line to link the function and its modules to distinguish these from the linkage between the menus and the functions. You can indicate those modules which are used in more than one function by an asterisk, as we have done here, or by a number indicating how many functions share that module.

The possible number of modules which the system uses can produce a complex

```
Main sales orders menu (SOP.1)
|    ||
|    ||___ Display a menu (SOPS101) *
|    ||___ Accept and vet option (SOPS102) *
|
|___ New orders menu (SOP.1.1)
|    |   ||
|    |   ||___ Open orders file (SOPS103)
|    |   ||___ Display a menu (SOPS101) *
|    |   ||___ Accept and vet option (SOPS102) *
|    |
|    |___ Existing client orders routine (SOP.1.1.1)
|    |    ||
|    |    ||___ Display orders screen (SOPS104) *
|    |    ||___ Amend orders record (SOPS105) *
|    |
|    |___ New client orders routine (SOP.1.1.2)
|    |    ||
|    |    ||___ Display orders screen (SOPS104) *
|    |    ||___ Amend orders record (SOPS105) *
|    |
|    |___ Internal orders routine (SOP.1.1.3)
|    |    ||
|    |    ||___ Display orders screen (SOPS104) *
|    |    ||___ Amend orders record (SOPS105) *
|    |
|    |___ Return to main menu (SOP.1.1)
|    |
|    |___ Help routine (SOP.1.1.H)
|
|___ Amend order routine (SOP.1.2)
|    ||
|    ||___ Display orders screen (SOPS104) *
|    ||___ Amend orders record (SOPS105) *
|
|___ Cancel orders routine (SOP.1.3)
|    ||
|    ||___ Display orders screen (SOPS104) *
|    ||___ Amend orders record (SOPS105) *
|
|___ Delete orders routine (SOP.1.4)
|    ||
|    ||___ Display orders screen (SOPS104) *
|    ||___ Amend orders record (SOPS105) *
|
|___ Print orders routine (SOP.1.5)
|    ||
|    ||___ Produce heading (SOPS106)
|
|___ Return to main system menu (SOP.1)
|
|___ Help routine (SOP.1.H)
```

Figure 5.38 Module map.

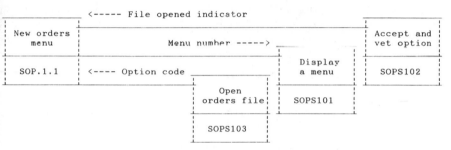

```
Main sales orders menu (SOP.1)
 ¦    ¦¦
 ¦    ¦¦   Menu-number ----->
 ¦    ¦¦___ Display a menu (SOPS101) *
 ¦    ¦¦
 ¦    ¦¦___ Accept and vet option (SOPS102) *
 ¦         <----- Option-code
 ¦
 ¦___ New orders menu (SOP.1.1)
 ¦     ¦   ¦¦
 ¦     ¦   ¦¦___ Open orders file (SOPS103)
 ¦     ¦   ¦¦   <----- File-opened-indicator
 ¦     ¦   ¦¦
 ¦     ¦   ¦¦   Menu-number ----->
 ¦     ¦   ¦¦___ Display a menu (SOPS101) *
 ¦     ¦   ¦¦
 ¦     ¦   ¦¦___ Accept and vet option (SOPS102) *
 ¦     ¦        <----- Option-code
 ¦     ¦
```

```
                 <----- File opened indicator
 _____
¦                ¦                                  ¦             ¦
¦ New orders     ¦                                  ¦ Accept and  ¦
¦   menu         ¦       Menu number ----->  _____  ¦ vet option  ¦
¦_____¦_____¦     ¦_¦_____¦
¦                ¦                          ¦Display¦¦            ¦
¦   SOP.1.1      ¦ <---- Option code  _____ ¦a menu ¦¦   SOPS102   ¦
¦_____¦_____¦    ¦_¦_____¦¦_____¦
                                     ¦Open   ¦¦
                                     ¦orders file¦¦  SOPS101
                                     ¦_____¦_¦_____
                                     ¦
                                     ¦ SOPS103
                                     ¦_____
```

Figure 5.39 Module maps showing parameters.

module map. For this reason, it is best to show only a few functions – and their modules – on any one map.

It is also practicable to show the data values which are passed to and from the various modules. This is illustrated in the section shown in Fig. 5.39.

5.9.1   Producing the module maps

The following points should be borne in mind when producing the module maps:

1. the function maps and the module catalogue are used to provide the necessary information;
2. the map shows which modules are called by which functions;
3. all modules which can be called by the main function are included on the map;
4. the general organization of the map is similar to that of the function maps;
5. the data parameters passed between the main function and the module – and back – are indicated along the connecting lines;
6. the sequence in which the modules are connected to the main function is not significant;
7. an asterisk or a numeric counter may be used to indicate that a module is used by more than one function

5.10 SUMMARY

The functional analysis is performed firstly by disregarding any physical constraints or limitations, and later by considering the way in which the conceptual processes become physical programs and subroutines. The DFD is our primary source and from it we identify the processes and the associated functions within the proposed system, all the time cross-checking this with the data model derived during the data analysis.

The entity/function matrix is a valuable tool for identifying – and adding to the DFD – any functions which may be necessary to ensure the integrity of the database.

From the DFD, we develop the function catalogue, the function descriptions and the function maps.

The development and production of the module catalogue, the module maps, and the module descriptions, may be the work of the systems designer. In some circumstances, however, this task may be left to the programming team.

We have now reached the end of the systems design phase of our activities.

5.11 QUESTIONS

5.1. Write a structured English description corresponding to the following narrative:

>   The sales clerk totals the prices of the items on the order and enters this on the customer's account as a debit. She then checks the customer's name and address card to see where the goods are to be delivered. If the client lives more than fifty miles from the depot then a delivery charge of 2% is added to the order. The delivery charge is then debited to the customer's account. But if the customer's business over the last three months is more than five times the value of the current order, then no delivery charge is made. If a delivery charge is made, then it is credited to the general carriers account.

5.2. You are designing a system which will investigate the use that customers make of a new AcmeSuper supermarket. The management of AcmeSuper are interested in the following aspects:
(a) How large is the customer's family?
(b) How far does the customer travel to reach the supermarket?
(c) How often does the customer visit the supermarket?
(d) How much do they spend per visit?
(e) Which other local stores does the customer visit?
(f) Is there any special product which the customer buys from this supermarket?
(g) Are the shopping hours convenient?

(h) Are there any improvements which the customer would like to see at the supermarket?

(i) What newspapers does the customer read?

Design a form which an interviewer might use to collect this information. We shall refer to this system in subsequent questions.

5.3. Design a screen which could be used to input the information collected on the forms which you designed in the solution to the last question.

5.4. The systems analyst has provided the following written description:

The number of days' holiday to which an employee is entitled depends upon how long he has worked with the company at the start of the holiday year. The holiday year runs from 1st January to 31st December. If he has worked less than 1 year, then he gets one and two-thirds days for every complete month. If he started after 30th October in the previous year, then he gets no holidays this year. If he has worked more than one year, then he gets twenty days' holiday. If he has worked more than five years, then he gets an extra two days, and if he has worked more than ten years, he gets a further three days.

Indicate how this could be represented in:
(a) a flowchart
(b) a decision table
(c) a sequence of structured English.

5.5. A road haulage company has a number of vehicles. A vehicle is used to carry containers. There are two types of containers: a large container which carries two container-units, and a small container which carries one container-unit. Obeying the regulations given below, write a structured English sequence to print a list of the maximum and minimum number of container-units that a vehicle may carry, for unladen weights in the range 4–24 tons. Assume that the unladen weight is an integer number of tons.

If the unladen weight of the vehicle is less than or equal to 5 tons, then it can only carry two containers. If the unladen weight is greater than 5 tons, then it can carry three containers, plus two extra containers for every full 5 tons unladen weight over the initial 5 tons. If a large container is present, then only one more large container can be carried. No vehicle may carry all large or all small containers.

5.6. Design a structured English sequence which will scan an address of the form:

43 HIGH STREET, LINCOLN, LN2 3NN

to obtain the post code. In this example it would return the value:

LN2 3NN

5.7.   Write a structured English sequence to describe the validation which is to be performed on the data input to the AcmeSuper analysis system.
Establish a set of prompt messages, error messages and other messages which are to be displayed to the operator as the data are being entered.

5.8.   Suggest some ways in which you might present the information collected by the AcmeSuper analysis system. Describe one advantage and one disadvantage for each of the methods which you propose.

5.9.   You are preparing the function description for a routine which will accept data about new students for a correspondence college and add these to a file. The data are to be held in records of the format – and occurrences – shown in Fig. 5.40. Design the input screen(s) and write a structured English description of the validation and other processing which are to be performed. You should also define any messages which are to be displayed to prompt, to warn and to correct the users' actions.

```
STUDENT (Student-number, Surname, Initials, Sex,
        Address-line-1, Address-line-2, Address-line-
        3, Date-of-birth)

COURSE (Course-code, Course-description)

ENROLLMENT (Student-number, Course-code, Date-
        enrolled)
```

STUDENT

| | 13477 | WARWICK | AB | M | 13 HAMP ST | DENTON | M55 5ET | 260968 | |

COURSE

| | AM12 | EUROPEAN ART 1310-1400 | |

ENROLLMENT

| | 13477 | AM12 | 071087 | |

Figure 5.40 STUDENT, COURSE and ENROLLMENT entities.

5.10. A **CLIENT** entity contains the name and addresses of clients, each client being identified by a Client-number. A **PRODUCT** entity contains the description of products and a repeating group representing the Client-numbers of those clients who have placed orders for the product during the last year. Inverted entities, **CLIENT-PRODUCT** and **GROUP-PRODUCT**, are maintained. The entity structures are shown in Fig. 5.41.

Write structured English sequences to handle the following demands:
(a) Produce a list of the names and addresses of all clients who have placed orders for product number 1234.

```
CLIENT (Client-number, Name, Address, Credit-
    limit)


PRODUCT (Product-number, Description, Product-
    group, Reorder-stock-level, (Client-number))

CLIENT-PRODUCT (Client-number, (Product-number))

GROUP-PRODUCT (Product-group, (Product-number))
```

Figure 5.41 CLIENT, PRODUCT, CLIENT-PRODUCT and GROUP-PRODUCT entities.

```
*  function to add a new record to the personnel file
1       open personnel file
2       if file can't be opened
3       then
4           display error message
5           abandon processing
6       endif
7       display personnel screen
8       prompt for and accept the personnel number
9       loop until personnel = END
10          if number is valid
11          then
12              prompt for, accept and validate name
13              prompt for, accept and validate address
14              prompt for, accept and validate date of
                birth
15              prompt for, accept and validate
                starting date
16              ask if amendments are ok
17              if amendments are ok
18              then
19                  convert date of birth and starting
                    date to internal format
20                  write personnel record to disk
21                  display 'action complete' message
22              else
23                  display 'action abandoned message'
24              endif
25          else
26              display 'invalid personnel number'
27          endif
28          prompt for and accept the personnel number
29      endloop
```

Figure 5.42 Design for a function to add a new record to the personnel file.

(b) Produce a list of the descriptions of all products in Product-group A12 which have been ordered by client number 9881.

5.11. Draw a function map which might represent the processing related to the Acme Credit Company which is described in the questions to Chapter 3.

```
* function to change a record on the personnel file
1        open personnel file
2        if file cannot be opened
3        then
4            display 'file cannot be opened' message
5            abandon processing
6        endif
7        display personnel screen
8        prompt for and accept the personnel number
9        loop until personnel = END
10           if number is valid
11           then
12               read personnel record from disk
13               convert birthdate and start date to
                 external format
14               display the personnel details
15               ask user if record is to be amended
16               if record is not to be amended
17               then
18                   display 'no action taken' message
19               else
20                   ask user which field is to be changed
21                   loop until no more fields to be changed
22                       case depending upon which field
23                           case name is to be changed:
24                               prompt for, accept and validate name
25                           case address is to be changed
26                               prompt for, accept and validate address
27                           case birthdate is to be changed
28                               prompt for, accept and validate birthdate
29                           otherwise
30                               display 'invalid field' message
31                       endcase
32                       ask user which field is to be changed
33                   endloop
34                   ask if amendments are ok
35                   if amendments are ok
36                   then
37                       convert birthdate and start date to
                         internal format
38                       write personnel record to disk
39                       display 'action complete' message
40                   else
41                       display 'action abandoned message'
42                   endif
43               else
44                   display error message
45               endif
46           endif
47           prompt for and accept the personnel number
48       endloop
```

Figure 5.43 Design for a function to change a record on the personnel file.

5.12. Functions are to be produced to add records to a file using data entered by the user, to display the contents of a record, amend the contents of a record, and delete a record from the file.

List the modules which you think would be used in each function, and indicate which modules could be common to two or more of the functions.

5.13. The designs shown in Fig. 5.42 and Fig. 5.43 have been produced for two separate functions. Produce a module catalogue identifying those pieces of processing which you feel could be taken out and developed as separate modules.

5.14. Produce a module map for the two functions based upon your answer to the previous question.

5.15. The structured English design in Fig. 5.44 relates to a module which is to be used to update the records about patients at a clinic. The information held about the patients includes: the surname, the full given names, the address, the telephone number, the date of the last visit, the name of the patient's doctor and the name of the next of kin. Refine the design as far as you can. At each stage, write down any assumptions which you are making.

```
*
* module to amend a patient's record
*
1      display blank patient record form
2      prompt for and accept patient's reference number
3.1    loop until no more patients
4           read patient's record
* process this patient's record
5.1         loop for all changes
* accept changes
5.2         endloop
6           ask if user wants to file changed record
7.1         if response is NO
7.2         then
7.3              do nothing
7.4         else
7.5              write patient's record away
7.6         endif
3.2    endloop
```

Figure 5.44 Design for a module to amend a patient's record.

6

Structured programming

The function and module descriptions which the programmer receives from the systems analyst describe the input, the output, the data and the processing involved in the system. The data may be presented as a set of entity descriptions or file layouts.

It should be remembered that modern systems do not consist solely of coded programs. Some of the functions may be accomplished by software packages: utility programs, word processing, query languages, report generators, and many others. We shall look at some of these in Chapter 7.

This chapter is presented for those programmers, and would-be programmers, who need to extend their experience (if any) into the current commercial programming environment. Experienced programmers may ignore this chapter.

The analyst may express the required processing in a number of ways:

- structured English
- flowcharts
- decision tables

The programmer should obviously be familiar with whichever tool is to be used in his or her own environment, and should also be able to transform the analyst's descriptions into working program code.

One of the most well-known techniques for developing computer programs is that of structured programming. A structured program is a one which is composed of a set of discrete units. The processing path flows from one unit to the next, each unit having a single entry point and a single exit point. This is shown in Fig. 6.1.

Compare this with the **spaghetti coding** of the **non-structured** program shown in Fig. 6.2. It is obvious that the flow of control in such an inextricable program is difficult to follow. If a problem occurs within such a program – say at statement 1001 – then it will be a very tedious process to unravel the maze in order to discover how and why the processing reached that particular point. Neither will it be an easy task trying to correct the problem. In the structured program, on the other hand, we know that statement 1001 can only have been reached by the gradual flow of processing down from the top of the program, and any error can be much more easily located and corrected.

In this context, we could define:

Unit: a sequence of one or more constructions in which there is only one entry point to the unit and one exit point from the unit.

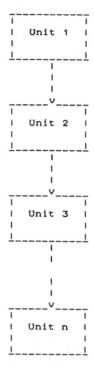

Figure 6.1 A structured program.

Such a unit could comprise elements which fall into one or more of the categories:

- sequence
- selection
- iteration.

Although the surface structures – the coding – by which these are represented depend upon the language used, the following structures are frequently encountered in current third generation programming languages.

1. A **sequence** is a single unit which performs its work, and then passes control to the next physical unit in the program.
   (a) A simple statement, such as input/output statements and assignment statements, as shown in Fig. 6.3.
   (b) A call to an internal subroutine, such as **GOSUB**, as shown in Fig. 6.4.
   (c) A call to an external routine, procedure or function, by means of statements such as CALL, PROC or PROCEDURE. Since such a call implies that the processing returns to the unit, it does not conflict with our definition

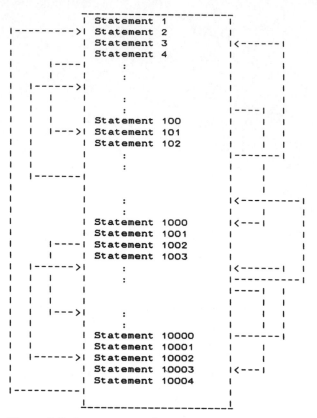

Figure 6.2 An unstructured program.

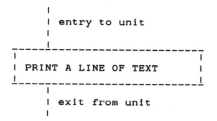

Figure 6.3 A sequence construct – 1.

2. A **selection** is a unit which tests for one or more conditions and according to the result(s) of the test takes one or more courses of action, and then passes out of the unit.

   (a) An **IF**-type construction with one of two possible outcomes returning to a common flow on leaving the unit, as shown in Fig. 6.5.

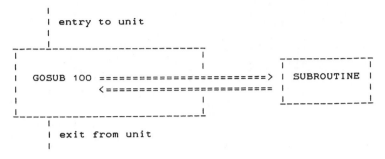

Figure 6.4 A sequence construct – 2.

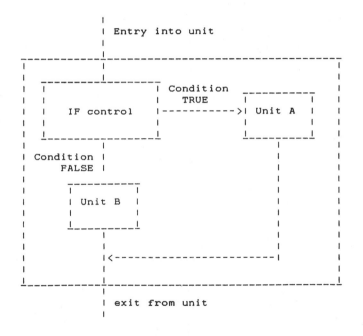

Figure 6.5 A select construct – IF.

(b) A **CASE**-type construction with two more possible outcomes returning to a common flow on leaving the unit. The construction shown in Fig. 6.6 consists of three case-tests but, in practice, any number of tests may take place. The **IF**-type construction is really a special instance of the **CASE** with one or two outcomes.
3. An **iteration** is a unit which performs a certain process repeatedly until a specified condition is reached. When this condition is reached, control passes out of the unit.

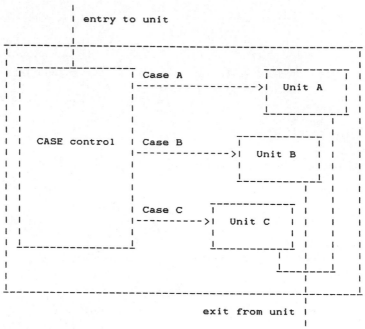

Figure 6.6 A select construct – CASE.

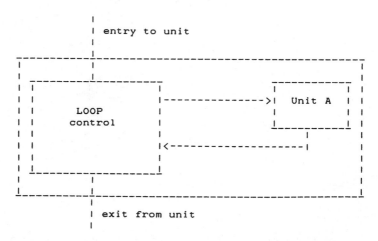

Figure 6.7 An iteration construct – LOOP.

(a) A **FOR**-construction. Fig. 6.7 shows a **FOR** construction in which Unit A is repeated whilst a control variable takes all values in a specified range. When the control variable attains the value at the end of the range, the iteration stops and control passes out of the unit.

(b) A **LOOP-UNTIL** construction. Fig. 6.8 shows a **LOOP-UNTIL** construction, in which Unit A is repeatedly executed until a specified condition is true. When the condition is satisfied, control passes out of the unit.

(c) A **LOOP-WHILE** construction. Fig. 6.9 shows a **LOOP-WHILE** construction, in which Unit A is repeatedly executed while a specified condition is true. When the condition is no longer satisfied, control is passed out of the unit.

Logically, the **LOOP-UNTIL** and **LOOP-WHILE** are very similar, except that one tests for the reverse of the condition tested by the other.

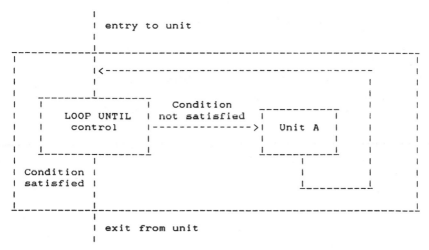

Figure 6.8 An iteration construct – LOOP UNTIL.

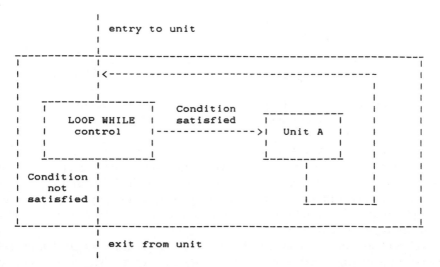

Figure 6.9 An iteration construct – LOOP WHILE.

6.1   STRUCTURES IN PRACTICE

In the following sections, we see how these constructions may be implemented in PASCAL, COBOL and in structured English.

6.1.1   Structures in PASCAL

Fig. 6.10 shows some examples of these constructions in PASCAL, a programming language which was specially designed to allow structured principles to be put into practice.

6.1.2   Structures in COBOL

Fig. 6.11 shows some examples of how these constructions might be represented in standard COBOL 1974.

Until recently, **COBOL** made very few concessions to some of the structures which we have been looking at. However, the Draft Proposed Revised X3.23 American National Standard Programming Language **COBOL**, puts forward a number of changes which, amongst other things, provide for a new **EVALUATE** statement to represent the **CASE** construction. This is illustrated in Fig. 6.12. The new proposals also include a large number of **END** statements which terminate the various structures more clearly than does the full-stop. Some of these are also shown in Fig. 6.12.

6.1.3   Structures in structured English

If the analyst has developed the processing decriptions in structured English, the transition from the design to the final coding will be much easier than if they were expressed in, say, a piece of written narrative.

Fig. 6.13 shows some examples of how these constructions might be represented in structured English.

6.1.4   Exception conditions

There is one occasion on which the rule of one-entry – one-exit to each unit may be broken. That is when we detect an exception – or error – condition which may prevent further processing.

If we adhere strictly to structured programming principles, on detection of an error we should have to set an error-switch and only complete the processing of subsequent units according to the setting of this switch. As a result, the coding could become very messy and the execution time unnecessarily protracted. Such exceptions may be handled more neatly by leaving the main processing flow completely, as shown in Fig. 6.14.

This will normally be achieved by the use of a **GOTO** statement, the *bête noire* of structured programming, but a boon in such instances. The destination on leaving the unit depends upon the logic of the program. Processing may pass to

An IF construction:

```
| IF ClientBalance < ClientLimit          |
| THEN                                     |
|     WRITE (ClientAccountNumber,' is overdrawn')  |
| ELSE                                     |
|     WRITE (ClientAccountNumber,' is in the black')  |
|                                          |
```

A CASE construction:

```
| CASE Number OF                           |
|     1:2:3: WRITE (Number,' is 1 or 2 or 3');  |
|     4:5:6: WRITE (Number,' is 4 or 5 or 6');  |
|     7:8: WRITE (Number,' is 7 or 8')     |
| END                                      |
|                                          |
```

A FOR construction:

```
| FOR Counter := 1 TO 100 DO               |
|     Total := Total + Value[Counter]      |
|                                          |
```

A LOOP-UNTIL construction:

```
| REPEAT                                   |
|     BEGIN                                |
|         Total:=Total+Value[Counter];     |
|         Counter:=Counter+1               |
|     END                                  |
| UNTIL Value[Counter] = 0 or Counter > 99 |
|                                          |
```

A LOOP-WHILE construction:

```
| WHILE Value[Counter] <> 0 AND Counter < 100 DO  |
|     BEGIN                                |
|         Total:=Total+Value[Counter];     |
|         Counter:=Counter+1               |
|     END                                  |
|                                          |
```

Figure 6.10 Surface structures in Pascal.

An IF construction:

```
    IF AGE > 16 AND AGE < 65
        MOVE VALID-AGE TO AGE-INDICATOR
    ELSE
        MOVE INVALID-AGE TO AGE-INDICATOR .
```

A CASE construction:

```
    IF OPTION = "A"
        MOVE "ADD" TO CHOICE
        ELSE
            IF OPTION = "D"
                MOVE "DELETE" TO CHOICE
                ELSE
                    IF OPTION = "C"
                        MOVE "CHANGE" TO CHOICE .
```

A FOR and LOOP UNTIL construction:

```
    PERFORM VARYING COUNT FROM 1 BY 1 UNTIL COUNT=10
        ADD SALES-FIGURES(COUNT) TO TOTAL
```

Figure 6.11 Surface structures in Cobol – 1.

The EVALUATE construction:

```
    EVALUATE OPTION
        WHEN "A"
            MOVE "ADD" TO CHOICE
        WHEN "D"
            MOVE "DELETE" TO CHOICE
        WHEN "C"
            MOVE "CHANGE" TO CHOICE
        WHEN-OTHER
            GO TO ENTER-OPTION .
```

Proposed Cobol statements having a closing END-

```
    ADD       ...     END-ADD
    COMPUTE     ...     END-COMPUTE
    DIVIDE    ...     END-DIVIDE
    EVALUATE    ...     END-EVALUATE
    IF    ...     END-IF
    IF    ...  .  ELSE ... END-IF
    MULTIPLY  '  ...     END-MULTIPLY
    PERFORM     ...     END-PERFORM
    SEARCH    ...     END-SEARCH
    SUBTRACT    ...     END-SUBTRACT
    UNSTRING    ...     END-UNSTRING
```

Figure 6.12 Surface structures in Cobol – 2.

An IF construction:

```
 _____|_____
|                                                               |
|   IF AGE > 16 AND AGE < 65                                    |
|   THEN                                                         |
|      MOVE VALID-AGE TO AGE-INDICATOR                           |
|   ELSE                                                         |
|      MOVE INVALID-AGE TO AGE-INDICATOR                         |
|   ENDIF                                                        |
|                                                               |
|_____|
                              |
```

A CASE construction:

```
 _____|_____
|                                                               |
|   CASE DEPENDING UPON OPTION                                  |
|      OPTION = "A" | MOVE "ADD" TO CHOICE                      |
|      OPTION = "D" | MOVE "DELETE" TO CHOICE                   |
|      OPTION = "C" | MOVE "CHANGE" TO CHOICE                   |
|   ELSE                                                         |
|      DISPLAY 'INVALID OPTION' MESSAGE                          |
|      SET ERROR SWITCH                                          |
|   ENDCASE                                                      |
|                                                               |
|_____|
                              |
```

A FOR construction:

```
 _____|_____
|                                                               |
|   FOR ALL RECORDS                                             |
|      ADD SALES-FIGURES TO TOTAL                               |
|   ENDFOR                                                       |
|_____|
                              |
```

A LOOP construction:

```
 _____|_____
|                                                               |
|   INPUT VALUE                                                 |
|   LOOP UNTIL VALUE = 0                                        |
|      ADD VALUE TO TOTAL                                        |
|      INPUT VALUE                                               |
|   ENDLOOP                                                      |
|_____|
                              |
```

Figure 6.13 Surface structures in structured English.

some standard error-handling unit within the program, as shown in Fig. 6.15(a). Alternatively, the processing may return to the start of the program, as shown in Fig. 6.15(b).

6.1.5 Which language?

The choice of language – or languages – in which a given system is to be written is largely dependent upon the environment in which the application is to be used,

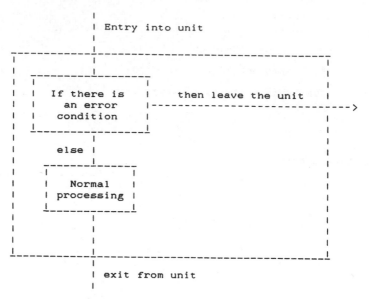

Figure 6.14 Exception conditions – 1.

the operating system which is to be used and the assemblers, interpreters or compilers which are available to handle the language.

We must remember that the point of using a programming language is to make the program development more efficient and more cost-effective by:

1. reducing the time taken to code the program
2. allowing symbolic coding with meaningful data names and routine names
3. encouraging recognized techniques, such as structured programming
4. making the program easier to read and verify
5. reducing the number of opportunities for programming errors to occur
6. providing a good compiler to highlight any naïve errors
7. simplifying the location and correction of errors
8. improving the maintainability of the program
9. improving the portability of the system to other computers.

To satisfy these criteria, and with freedom from any other constraints, it is obviously appropriate to select as high-level a language as possible. In almost every case, Assembler can be discarded as a serious contender.

There are, of course, other media for producing a processing function, as we shall see.

6.1.6 Structured design and fourth generation languages (4GL)

The examples which we have just seen and the structured English designs produced in Chapter 5 assumed that the systems were going to be written in third

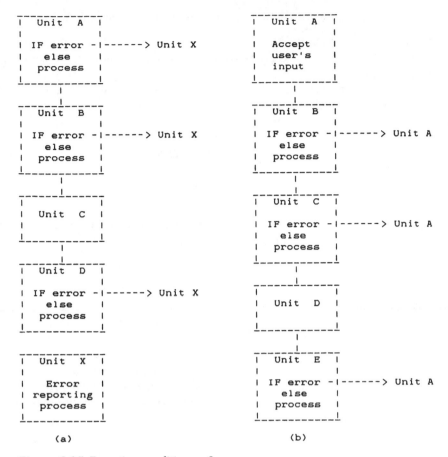

Figure 6.15 Exception conditions – 2.

generation languages. Each design represented a sequence of operations which could be converted directly into program code – BASIC COBOL or PASCAL, for example. The advent of the automated techniques which we shall look at in Chapter 7 now makes it possible for a system to include large elements of non-coded processing: word-processing may be used to display program messages; a standard spreadsheet package may be incorporated within an accounting system; more and more commercial systems are looking towards fourth generation languages.

How do these impact on the designs which we have produced earlier? The analyst's function maps and module maps indicate which elements of the system are to be handled by which software. The programmers' responsibility is to ensure that they are familiar with this software and with the ways in which they are linked together.

When required to transfer a structured English design into an operational function, the programmer will start by indicating those parts of the design which the 4GL, or other software, will handle automatically. These may include:

1. file processing – opening files, reading records, reporting on missing or duplicate records, writing records away after processing, linking records into relationships
2. routines for performing calculations and manipulating data
3. validation of input data
4. formatting of data read from – and written to – files
5. routines for handling screen and printed output
6. routines for producing reports and responding to user queries
7. menu structure and program linkage
8. processing control and exception conditions – terminating and abandoning an operation

Having highlighted these on the design, the remaining parts are those which require the special attention of the programmer.

6.2 MODULAR PROGRAMMING

Modular programming is the technique of writing a program as a series of independent units or modules, passing control from one to another to perform the overall task of the program. This is not quite the same as structured programming, although it is possible to write each structure (or unit in our earlier discussion) – or group of contiguous structures – as a separate program module. These separate modules can then be invoked in turn from a main controlling program, as illustrated in Fig. 6.16. Here we see how the control program passes control to Module 1. When the processing within Module 1 is complete, control is returned back to the main program. From here, control is passed to Module 2, then back to the main program, and so on.

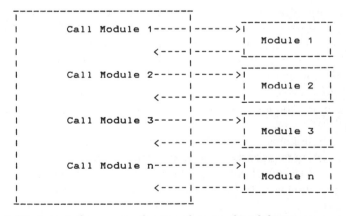

Figure 6.16 A control program, showing the use of modular programming.

In this case, the main control program would consist simply of a set of call statements:

Call module 1
Call module 2
Call module 3
⋮
Call module *n*

The separate modules may in turn pass control to other (lower-level) modules. Constructing the main program as a series of modules has several important advantages:

1. The structure of the main processing can be seen more clearly, and is therefore more understandable, than with a large inextricable program;
2. The task of writing the separate modules can be allocated to a number of programmers;
3. Complex routines, or those whose efficiency is important to the total processing, can be written by experienced programmers, leaving the simpler routines to trainee and junior staff;
4. The programmers need only concern themselves with one module at a time, and can concentrate their attentions on the input data to that module, the processing done by that module, and the output results produced by that module;
5. Each module can be designed, written, compiled (or generated) and tested separately;
6. During testing of the module, a simple harness can be constructed which will provide test input values to the module, call the module, and then verify the output results produced;
7. During testing of the system, a dummy module can be constructed – returning valid results – until such time as the real module is ready for use;
8. Maintenance of the overall program is more easily carried out; modification or enhancement of a single module does not affect the rest of the system, any amended module can be amended and tested in isolation;
9. The control and monitoring of the development of the system is simplified, since the time and resources required to produce the individual modules can be more easily estimated and scheduled;
10. Economic benefits can accrue if a module can be used in more than one part of the system.

We described the analyst's tasks of identifying modules in Chapter 5, when we were looking at the module catalogue, the module maps and the module descriptions. Programmers should always be aware of opportunities to move a particular process to a separate module, and for this reason, they are advised to read the relevant parts of Chapter 5.

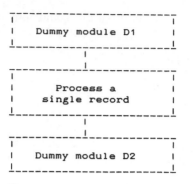

Figure 6.17 Program inversion – 1.

6.2.1   Program inversion

The concept of **program inversion** utilizes the features of modularization to develop a program, and is particularly suitable for programs which process a large number of records on a file. The first version of the program is written so that it processes a single record. A typical layout is shown in Fig. 6.17. A dummy module, D1, is placed at the beginning of the program, and may be used to allow the programmer to enter test data for processing by the main module. Then follows the main module to process the record. Finally comes another dummy module, D2, which may simply display the results of the processing.

When this version has been tested and is found to work correctly, the dummy module D1 is replaced by one or more modules which perform the necessary file initialization – such as opening the files – and which also read in a record from the file. This new version is then tested and corrected as necessary. The dummy module D2 is then replaced by one or more modules which control the processing of all the records and carry out the final housekeeping – such as closing the files, reporting control totals and other end-of-job processing. Finally we arrive at a structure like that shown in Fig. 6.18.

6.3   SUMMARY

Now, that the systems analyst has designed the proposed system, we proceed to programming. Current data processing has provided a large number of tools and techniques for the programmer.

Of these, modular programming and structured programming are probably the best established. A modularized design make it much easier to develop, test and maintain a complete system. Structured programming produces individual modules which are easier to develop and maintain.

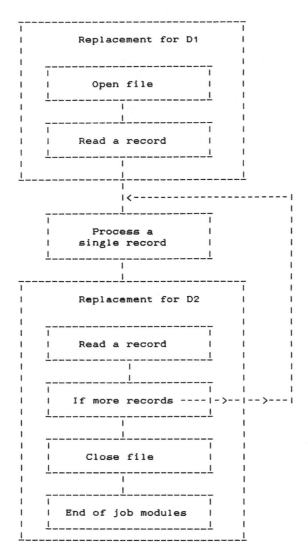

Figure 6.18 Program inversion – 2.

6.4 QUESTIONS

6.1. You have been asked to rewrite the BASIC program shown in Fig. 6.19. Produce an equivalent structured English design.

6.2. Take the design which you produced as your solution to Question (1) and code it in a language of your choice.

6.3. It is now required to amend the records used in the previous questions so

```
10 PRINT "WHAT IS THE NAME OF THE FILE"
20 INPUT F$
30 IF F$="END" THEN STOP
40 OPEN F$ ON-ERROR GO TO 500
50 PRINT "WHAT IS THE RECORD KEY"
60 INPUT K$
70 IF K$="END" THEN GO TO 10
80 READ F$, K$, R$ ON-ERROR GO TO 520
90 N$=R$[1,20]
100 A$=R$[21,50]
110 D$=R$[51,62]
120 PRINT N$
130 PRINT A$
140 PRINT D$
150 C=0
160 PRINT "CHANGE WHICH FIELD? NAME / ADDRESS / DATE / END"
170 INPUT X$
180 IF X$="NAME" THEN GO TO 260
190 IF X$="ADDRESS" THEN GO TO 330
200 IF X$="DATE" THEN GO TO 400
210 IF X$="END" THEN GO TO 230
220 GO TO 320
230 IF C=1 THEN GO 470
240 PRINT "RECORD UNCHANGED"
250 GO TO 50
260 PRINT "ENTER NEW NAME"
270 INPUT M$
280 IF M$="" THEN GO TO 310
290 N$=M$
300 C=1
310 PRINT N$
320 GO TO 390
330 PRINT "ENTER NEW AGE"
340 INPUT B$
350 IF B$="" THEN GO TO 380
360 A$=B$
370 C=1
380 PRINT A$
390 GO TO 460
400 PRINT "ENTER NEW DATE"
410 INPUT Y$
420 IF Y$="" THEN GO TO 450
430 D$=Y$
440 C=1
450 PRINT D$
460 GO TO 160
470 WRITE K$, N$, A$, D$ ON F$
480 PRINT "RECORD CHANGED"
490 GO TO 10
500 PRINT "CANNOT OPEN FILE"
510 GO TO 10
520 PRINT "CANNOT FIND RECORD"
530 GO TO 50
540 END
```

Figure 6.19 A BASIC program.

that they hold additional fields: a telephone number of up to twenty characters in length; a number representing the salary, of up to six characters in length. Amend your solution to allow these fields to be added or changed.

6.4. Pascal's triangle, illustrated here, is important in mathematics. In each successive row of the triangle, each term except the first and last is the sum of the two terms to the left and right above it. A program is to be written to generate and display Pascal's triangle. A possible design is shown in Fig. 6.20. Refine the design as necessary.

Produce a coded version of the design in a language of your choice.

```
*
* To print Pascal's triangle
*
*                           1   1
*                         1   2   1
*                       1   3   3   1
*                     1   4   6   4   1
*                   1   5   10   10   5   1
*                 1   6   15   20   15   6   1
*
* uses two lists list1 and list2
*

1     set first two elements in list1 to 1
2     set first element in list2 to 1
3     set list.counter to 2
4     loop 20 times
5         for all values of p from 2 to list.counter
6             set element p in list2 equal to the sum of
              element p-1 and element p of list 1
7         endfor
8         append 1 to end of list2
9         print list2
10        add 1 to list.counter
11        interchange list1 and list2
12    endloop
```

Figure 6.20 Pascal's triangle.

6.5. Produce a structured English design for a module called **REMOVE** which will accept two variables called **STRING** (of any length) and **CHARACTER** (a single character), and then remove all occurrences of the **CHARACTER** from **STRING**. Thus, the statement:

REMOVE ('THE CAT SAT ON THE MAT', 'E')

would return the string:

TH CAT SAT ON TH MAT

6.6. Modify your **REMOVE** module so that the variable **CHARACTER** can be more than one character in length. Thus, the statement:

REMOVE ('THE CAT SAT ON THE MAT', 'THE')

would return the string:

CAT SAT ON MAT

6.7. Produce a structured English design for a module called **TRIM** which will accept a single variable called **STRING** (of any length), and then remove all preceding spaces, all trailing spaces and reduce all internal spaces to a single space. Thus, the statement:

TRIM (' THE   CAT   SAT   ON   THE   MAT   ')

would return the string:

THE CAT SAT ON THE MAT

Interlude 2
The final stages

The systems analysis has been performed, and the new system has been designed and programmed, but there is still work to be done before it can be called a live system. Important amongst the remaining tasks are:

1. Testing: beyond the module and program testing of the programming phase, we must now face the combined testing of all the routines in the systems test and the acceptance test.
2. Implementation: we cannot simply switch to the new system overnight. This is true even for systems which have a definite start date, such as the start of the new tax year or 1st January. Plans must be made. We must ensure that all the data files are converted to the required format and all the other preparations are complete.
3. Documentation: there must be user manuals and technical manuals. Data preparation manuals and clerical procedures manuals may also be required. If the system involves radical changes – such as new invoices or new procedures – then it may also be necessary to write to the clients, suppliers and other people outside the organization, telling them about the changes.
4. Training: courses must be designed and the users must be fully trained in all operational aspects of the new system.

After all this has been done and the system has gone live, there is still work to be done:

5. Monitor and review: when the system is up and running, the duties of the analyst or the project leader continue with the monitoring of the system. For example, experience may show that the system is slower than expected or the files may not be able to cope with the volume of business which is coming in. You must identify such events, locate the causes and decide how they can be eliminated.
6. Maintenance: the final system is not a static unit, and parts of it will demand changes, corrections and enhancements in the long term.

We must also look for ways in which the system can be changed and extended to meet the continually changing requirements of a thriving business organization. As with any system, new sub-systems will need to be added, existing sub-systems will need to grow, shrink, change, or even die. When any such changes come to light, then we must review these and make arrangements to adapt the system to cater for our new needs. To do this, we go right back to the beginning.

Although these final stages are beyond the scope of the present discussion, the application of a structured methodology means that we no longer have to start from scratch every time. Instead, we can take the original documentation – the data flow diagrams, the data structure diagrams, the various maps and descriptions – and modify them appropriately. In this way, we can be sure that we produce systems which are consistent and systems which are easy to maintain when they next need to be changed.

7
Automated methods

In almost every DP department there are large backlogs of systems awaiting development. Furthermore, the systems analysts and programmers who are needed to release these backlogs and develop the necessary systems are expensive people, and good ones are rare. These factors have given rise to a number of solutions, a number of tools and techniques to smooth the design and development of an application, to make it more cost-effective. Some solutions even remove the analyst and programmer entirely from the development cycle, allowing the end-users to produce the solutions to their own requirements.

In this chapter, we shall look at some of these solutions.

7.1 DATA DICTIONARIES

We have acknowledged the use and value of CASE, CAD and diagramming tools in the development and production of the various diagrams and maps which the analyst will use during the analysis and design stages.

Possibly the most valuable tool, and certainly the one which is most widely applicable is the data dictionary.

A data dictionary holds a description of all the elements of the system which are related to the database. Those parts of the dictionary which refer to the data elements will contain information about:

1. the schemas and sub-schemas showing the data which are available
2. the data structures, including the relationships between the various pieces of data
3. the access authority – the departments or functional areas that are authorized to use each part of the database
4. the update authority – the departments or functional areas that are authorized to update each part of the database
5. the processes which use each part of the database
6. synonyms – the names by which each data item and each part of the database is known to the users

and for each attribute within the database:

7. the length of the attribute
8. the type of attribute – alphabetic, alphanumeric, numeric, integer, hexadecimal, binary and so on
9. whether the attribute is mandatory, or whether it holds optional information
10. the relationship between this attribute and other attributes in the database.

```
Description = 25 {character}

Product-code = 4 {digit}

Product-record = {Product-code} + {Description} + {Location}
     + {Quantity-in-stock} + {Product-price} + {Movement-
     date} + ITERATIONS OF {Supplier-code}

Movement-date = {date}

Invoice-record = {Invoice-number} + {Client-code} +
     ITERATIONS OF ( {Invoice-entry} + {Payment-flag} ) +
     {Date-ordered} + {Invoice-total}

Invoice-reference = {Invoice-number}

Location = {Bay-number} + "/" + {Shelf-number}

Charge-rate = {Product-price} OR {Special-price}
```

Figure 7.1 Data dictionary entry – 1.

Some simple data entries in a dictionary might look like those shown in Fig. 7.1.

If it is decided to make the dictionary more comprehensive, then a typical entry for a single field (or attribute) on a product information file (or entity) might look like that shown in Fig. 7.2.

In a moment, we shall see the use of such data dictionary entries in conjunction with a query language.

Despite the implications of the name, the data dictionary contains much more information than that relating simply to the data. It can also be used as a general repository to hold details of both the data model and the process model.

A typical data dictionary entry for a processing routine is shown in Fig. 7.3.

The data dictionary may even be the repository for the document flow, data flow and data structure diagrams. It can be used to record the way in which the conceptual models evolved into the logical models.

At the data analysis stage, the data dictionary can be used to record the sources of data, the forms and documents from which they are drawn, the stages of data normalization, the entities and their attributes, and the relationships between them.

At the functional analysis stage, the data dictionary can be used as a general repository to record the activities, events, processes and functions which are associated with the database. This enables the analyst to reconcile the process model with the data model and, by cross-referencing the functions with the data which they use, this will ensure that there are no omissions in the design. When the final programs are being produced, the dictionary can be used to record the names of the programs, the subroutines and the modules which make up the

DATA DICTIONARY ENTRY

DATA-ITEM:.............. QUANTITY

TYPE:................... ATTRIBUTE

DESIGNED:............... 10 APR 1988
LAST UPDATED:........... 10 APR 1988.

LOCATION:.............. LM34/V/9

RECORD:................ PRODUCT
ATTRIBUTE:.............. 3

PASSWORD:............... ABS445
UPDATE AUTHORITY:....... ADP

DESCRIPTION:

    THIS FIELD HOLDS THE CURRENT STOCKHOLDING OF THE ITEM.

FORMAT:

    NUMERIC
    INTEGER
    MAXIMUM VALUE:..9999999999
    NO LEADING ZEROES
    DISPLAYED:..RIGHT JUSTIFIED

SYNONYMS:

    QTY
    QUANTITY-IN-STOCK
    HOLDING
    STOCKHOLDING

THE DATA IS USED BY THE FOLLOWING PROCESSES:

    CREATED:................ PS.001

    READ:................... PS.003
                         PS.004
                         PS.7
                         VALN0001

    DELETED:................ PS.003
                         PS.002

Figure 7.2 Data dictionary entry – 2.

```
DATA_DICTIONARY_ENTRY

ROUTINE NAME: TCLPROCESS

LANGUAGE: BASIC

LAST UPDATED: 09:30:56   10 APR 1988

UPDATE AUTHORITY: ADP

DESCRIPTION:

        THIS FUNCTION  IS  USED  TO  INVOKE  THE
        GENERAL  PROCESSING ROUTINE FOR THE TEST
        CONTROL LOGIC SYSTEM.

THE ROUTINE IS CALLED BY:

        TCL001      TCL005

THE ROUTINE USES ONLY COMMON DATA.

THE ROUTINE CALLS:

        TCL05          TCL08          PROCESS00
        TCL06          TCL33          PROCESS01

THE ROUTINE USES THE FOLLOWING VARIABLES:

        ATTRNO         LAST.HEAD        PAGENO
        CLEAR.REST     LINES            VAR.END
        FILENO         LST.SUB.NO       VAR.LIST
        FILES          NUMERIC          VAR.NAME
        FUNC           NUMS             VARS
        HEADER         PAGE.LIMIT       ZERO.REC

THE ROUTINE USES THE FOLLOWING FILES:

        TERMINAL - OPEN / READ
        LOGIC - READ
        LOGIC2 - READ / WRITE
        LOGIC3 - READ / WRITE / DELETE
```

Figure 7.3 A typical data dictionary entry for a processing route.

processing system, and then cross-reference and reconcile these with the entities and sub-schemas which they use. It may even be decided to hold details of the source program code and the associated documentation.

When the data dictionary is applied to these extended areas, its value to the organization becomes immense. Moreover, its value spreads to the operational aspects of the system and well into – and beyond – the implementation and live running phases.

As an on-line resource, the data dictionary should be kept up-to-date so that it represents the true state of the system. It is advantageous if there is some way of checking that the situation reflected by the data dictionary is the same as that represented by the actual system. This may be achieved by software which derives the actual computer system from the model which the analyst and the programmer maintain on the data dictionary. There is also software which performs the reverse task, that is, which reduces the real system into a form which is similar to that held on the dictionary so that the two versions can be compared.

7.2   AUTOMATED PROGRAM DEVELOPMENT

Of the various manifestations of automated programming and the tools and techniques which are currently available, we shall consider the following:

- program generators
- application generators
- screen painters
- report generators
- query languages
- database management systems
- fourth generation languages
- prototyping
- expert systems

Some of these help the programmer to transfer all – or a part of – the analyst's design into the final coding. Others enable the programmer to handle the database in logical terms, as it was envisaged and designed by the analyst, removing much of the hindrance imposed by the physical and operational environment.

The most obvious encounters with automated programming tools are programming languages themselves: the first generation languages, where the binary code was entered or keyed in directly to the central processor, and which were largely dedicated to military and scientific systems; the second generation languages – the Assemblers which made commercial systems viable and paved the way for the familiar high-level third generation languages. About this time, during the late 1960s, the market saw the introduction of packages as a first attempt to speed up systems development.

The 1970s saw the emergence of a wide range of new methods and techniques: structured programming and GOTO-less programming, and productivity aids, such as program generators, report generators, and screen painters. These and similar systems were all designed to ease the programmer's tasks by generating a greater or lesser part of the required source or object programs. The concepts of databases and total systems also evolved at that time.

With the introduction and application of structured techniques, a number of new languages have been aligned in that direction. Notable amongst these are Pascal and the Unix language C.

In the 1980s, the fourth generation languages emerged as a response to the constraints and limitations of the earlier languages, and these were developed from ideas and experiences gained over many years in many different environments and in many different application areas.

Query languages are already with us, and in the future we can clearly see the prospect of fifth generation languages and expert systems. These will bring the users closer to producing the systems which they require, enabling them to develop their own programs without any intervention on the part of the systems analyst or the programmer. This is surely the ultimate stage of user involvement, enabling the user's own expertise – be it finance, accountancy, administration or whatever – to be applied directly to the systems design without any dilution of ideas, loss of definition or inability to respond, which may result when the user's intentions and requirements have to be interpreted by computer specialists who may not be completely conversant with the user's business.

7.3   PROGRAM GENERATORS

A **program generator** – or a **code generator** – is a software package that will accept the analyst's specifications and will produce a program to meet them. The advantage of using such facilities is that they remove much of the tedious part of program coding. Any typical commercial application contains a similar set of **OPEN, READ, WRITE** and **CLOSE** statements. A program generator will create these from the analyst's description and allow the programmer to concentrate upon the more complicated logic of the program. This speeds up program development. In most cases, the generated code may well be more efficient than equivalent coding produced by a programmer. This is particularly true if the programmer is inexperienced.

Some generators take just a part of the application – the screen formats or the file input–output – and produce a set of source language statements or an object language routine to perform that specific task. The programmer can then fill in the gaps to produce the required program.

As these generators become more elaborate and more powerful, and cater more to the needs of the final application program, they enter the grey area between simple utility software and fourth generation languages.

7.4   APPLICATION GENERATORS

The distinction between a program generator and an **application generator** is in terms of scope. We would probably use a program generator to produce a single program for, say, adding new records to a payroll file. An application generator, however, would probably be used to produce a program for adding new records to a payroll file, plus a program for deleting the records, plus a program for changing the records, plus a program for making enquiries about the records, and so on. Moreover, the application generator would link all these together for us and build an entire **application system**.

7.5   SCREEN PAINTERS

A **screen painter** may be an independent tool or it may be a component of one of the other tools. In the simplest case, a screen painter will allow the analyst to design screens by entering text, manipulating it and moving it about the screen until a satisfactory layout has been produced. This layout can then be printed off and used as a basis for the function description. The screen layouts shown in the solutions to the Case Study were produced by means of a screen painter.

7.6   REPORT GENERATORS

Report generators and **report program generators,** such as RPG and RPGII, were amongst the earliest utility software to appear. The earliest examples pre-date on-line systems, taking their data input from decks of punched cards. They came about because report production is arguably the most common requirement of a commercial application.

Report generators accept the analyst's specifications, and use these to produce a printed report. The parameters to be supplied normally include:

1. the name of the file, or files, which are the subject of the report
2. the location within the records of each of the fields that are to appear on the report
3. any selection criteria qualifying which records are to be used and which are to be ignored
4. any arithmetic operations which are to be performed on the data
5. any reformatting or conversion which is to be applied to the data
6. any control breaks which are to be made
7. any sub-totals and totals which are to be made
8. the page headings and footings, and column headings for the report.

These parameters may then be saved and submitted to the report generator whenever the report is required.

7.7   QUERY LANGUAGES

A query language can reduce much of the workload involved in the design and production of routine reports and on-line enquiries. If the language is sufficiently user-friendly and simple to use, it can even be offered to the end-users as a medium for generating *ad hoc* reports and for making one-off enquiries.

Several types of query language are available. Some take the form of simple statements such as:

LIST ALL OVERDUE INVOICES SHOWING NAME DATE-DUE TOTAL
    AMOUNT
PRINT THE NAME DATE AND BALANCE OF ACCOUNTS WITH DATE
    BEFORE "31/12/88"
DRAW A PIECHART OF THE SALES BY AREA
LIST STAFF-NAME AGE AND STAFF-ADDRESS

This last query might produce the report shown in Fig. 7.4.

Other languages take the form of a series of questions asked of the user by the

```
STAFF         EMPLOYEE                      EMPLOYEE
NUMBER....    NAME................   AGE    ADDRESS..........

0551          MCINTOSH, C            52     391, HIGH ST
1002          WILSON, L             33     92, BROWN RD
1166          BROWN, F              39     689, BROAD AVE
1922          SMITH, J.A            42     34, HIGH STREET
2298          GREEN, W              29     49, HIGH GROVE
2378          GREEN, A              27     49, HIGH GROVE
2437          GREEN, A              26     93, BROAD RD
2831          WILSON, C             23     276, BROAD RD
3351          GREEN, A              24     642, SMITH GROVE
3441          GREEN, C              59     42, GREEN CLOSE
4012          CALLAGHAN, W          38     411, BROWN AVE
4016          WILSON, W             25     19, BROWN AVE
4960          GREEN, N              34     87, GREEN CLOSE
5342          LIVINGSTONE, R        33     572, LONGMAN RD
5664          CALLAGHAN, I          24     45, WILSON AVE
6069          BROWN, P              37     45, SMITH AVE
6073          LIVINGSTONE, R        48     5, WILSON GROVE
6076          GREEN, F              40     59, LONGMAN ST
```

Figure 7.4 Query language report.

WHAT IS THE DATABASE CALLED: <u>STAFF</u>

WHICH FIELDS ARE TO BE DISPLAYED: <u>STAFF-NUMBER,</u> <u>STAFF-</u>
<u>NAME,</u> <u>STAFF-AGE,</u> <u>STAFF-ADDRESS</u>

Figure 7.5 Query language dialogue – 1.

language processor. For example, the above report might have been invoked by a sequence such as that shown in Fig. 7.5.

Alternatively, there might be a list of possible answers displayed, and the user will then make a selection from the available choices, as shown in Fig. 7.6.

Some form of data dictionary is used to define the various fields which are used in the enquiry sentences. Typical entries are shown in Fig. 7.1 and Fig. 7.2. Thus, in order to handle the sentence:

LIST STAFF-NAME AGE AND STAFF-ADDRESS

the dictionary must hold definitions for **STAFF-NAME**, **AGE** and **STAFF-ADDRESS**. Some query languages have a facility to learn the vocabulary which the users employ in their sentences, and even to modify their own data dictionary accordingly. For example, the user may type in a statement such as:

LIST NAME AND AGE

and the language processor may be unable to recognize the identifier **NAME**. The response by the query language may look like that shown in Fig. 7.7.

When the user has clarified his requirements and, possibly, indicated that he wishes to use the **STAFF-NAME**, the processor might then ask:

WHAT IS THE FILE CALLED?

    1)   CLIENTS
    2)   DEPOTS
    3)   PRICES
    4)   PRODUCTS
    5)   SALARIES
    6)   SALES
    7)   STAFF

ENTER YOUR SELECTION: <u>7</u>

WHICH FIELDS ARE TO BE DISPLAYED?

    1)   STAFF-ADDRESS
    2)   STAFF-AGE
    3)   STAFF-DATE-OF-BIRTH
    4)   STAFF-DATE-OF-JOINING
    5)   STAFF-LOCATION
    6)   STAFF-MANAGER
    7)   STAFF-NAME
    8)   STAFF-NUMBER
    9)   STAFF-REVIEW-DATE
 10)   STAFF-SALARY
 11)   STAFF-SALARY-HISTORY

ENTER YOUR SELECTION: <u>8 7 2 1</u>

Figure 7.6 Query language dialogue – 2.

It is not clear what you mean by NAME.

Is it one of the following?

    1)   PRODUCT-NAME
    2)   DEPOT-NAME
    3)   CLIENT-NAME
    4)   STAFF-NAME
    5)   SUPPLIER-NAME

Enter one of these names, or press <ESCAPE> to abandon:

Figure 7.7 Query language dialogue – 3.

Do you want me to identify **NAME** with **STAFF-NAME** in future? Enter **YES** or **NO**

In this manner, the query language processor builds up its vocabulary of file names, data names and the relationships between them.

Whatever the precise nature of the query language, in general, they offer a realistic and cost-effective way of producing reports and enquiries. Indeed, in some environments, the query language may be sufficiently powerful that an application programmer need never write a report program.

For any special requirements which cannot be handled by the language, it may be worth talking the user into accepting something which can be produced much more easily and more cheaply by the standard query language software.

So what are the pros and cons of query languages?

- they are simple to use;
- they provide a facility whereby the end-user may interrogate a database directly;
- they are flexible in the format and content of the report;
- they may be appropriate for both *ad hoc* enquiries and longer reports;
- they allow enquiries to be developed and made more quickly and without the long gestation period which is necessary when writing a standard program in, say, Cobol;
- they are easier to use than a third generation language, such as Cobol. A typical enquiry can often be specified in one line of typed input;
- if the user makes a mistake in the syntax or the logic of his enquiry, this will be detected and immediately rejected by the processor;
- they allow a process of trial and error in the enquiry; if a user finds that a particular query produces a large volume of output, then it may be reworded to reduce the size of the report.

On the other side of the argument:

- query languages are used only for making enquiries on the contents of the database – for data retrieval; standard programs still have to be provided to update and maintain the data;
- they may make considerable demands on the design of the database;
- they may demand that data be held in certain formats; for example, a date which is to be accessible by means of a query language may have to be held in a meaningful form such as 31/12/88 or 311288 instead of a more efficient internal or compacted form;
- they may require considerable support from the standard programs which are written to update the database, requiring the programs to establish and maintain entry points and other links within the database;
- if the users are unfamiliar with the structure of the data, they may make inappropriate demands with their enquiries, causing the query language to be inefficient when answering the enquiry, thereby wasting time and incurring expense;
- they may put the security of the data at risk or demand additional security checks to be provided and maintained as the data is accessed.

A query language may be used as a prototyping mechanism for developing a standard report program. The users can play around with the language until they have derived the sort of report which they want and then this can be rewritten as a – possibly more efficient – COBOL program.

7.8.   DATABASE MANAGEMENT SYSTEMS

We discussed the general concepts of databases in Chapter 4. A database management system (DBMS) is a collection of software which provides the database administrator with a range of facilities for monitoring and controlling the use of the database. The software allows the data to be redefined, restructured and reorganized without affecting any existing application programs that use the data. It also addresses the security of the database, ensuring that data are only accessed by authorized users, and the integrity of the data, taking care that any changes to the data are consistent with the overall picture of the database and its usage.

More importantly in our circumstances, the DBMS enables the application programmers to access, manipulate and use the contents of the database, permitting the data and all their complex relationships to be accessed by means of the standard programming languages. In order to allow the systems to take full advantage of the data relationships within the DBMS, most systems offer a data description language (DDL) to define the structure of the database, its entities and relationships, and a data manipulation language (DML) which extends the standard programming languages and allows the programmer to handle the data by means of the implied relationships.

The overall structure of the database, the schema, and the smaller views seen by the individual programmers, the sub-schemas, are specified in the DDL. There might be one sub-schema for the programmers working on the invoicing subsystem, and another schema for the team working on the stock control subsystem. Each team works with its own sub-schema, each sub-schema being a greater or smaller part of the total schema. The entire schema is probably only seen by the database administrator. Each sub-schema comprises a series of record and data descriptions which are needed by that team, although the actual parts of the sub-schema may be drawn from several physically distinct parts of the schema. The DBMS ensures that the data are accessible to the programmers when they need them – even though, from time to time, they may be physically reorganized by the database administrator. This feature of DBMS is known as **data independence** or **data transparency**.

There are many DBMSs available. Some of the most familiar include CICS, DB2, and IMS. The various DBMSs organize their files and their records in different ways, and are generally not compatible. They do, however, have a number of common features. Let us see how database management systems impact on the programmer and the programming task by looking at two types of DBMS – a CODASYL database and a relational DBMS.

7.8.1 Codasyl database

During the late 1960s, the Conference of Data Systems Languages (CODASYL), the committee which gave us COBOL, began to address the question of implementing logical data models, such as those represented by our data structure diagrams, on real computers. The Data Base Task Group (DBTG) which was set up within CODASYL, did this by specifying a DDL and a DML to define and then use a database which could be organized like the logical data models that we met earlier. The specifications, applied first to COBOL and then to FORTRAN indicate

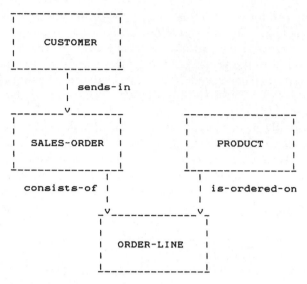

We could represent this as:

CLIENT (Client-number, Client-name, Client-address)

SALES-ORDER (Order-number, Order-date, Delivery-date, Order-
        value, Client-number)

PRODUCT (Product-code, Product-name, Product-price)

ORDER-LINE (Order-number, Product-number, Order-quantity,
        Line-value)

Figure 7.8 Data structures.

how the database would be handled in the respective languages. There was, however, no indication of how the requirements would be implemented in the physical environments. This was left up to the individual hardware and software suppliers. Like most committee work, the reports of the DBTG are continuing projects, and the brief summary offered here only indicates the general features of a CODASYL database.

The CODASYL data description language defines the schema and the sub-schemas, the entities or groups of entities (called areas or neighbourhoods), the records and the sets (or relationships) which are used by the program. To illustrate the DDL, let us look at the data model and the data structures shown in Fig. 7.8. These are concerned with just a part of the overall **ACCOUNTS** schema, and might be described in the CODASYL data description language by the statements shown in Fig. 7.9.

Anyone who is familiar with COBOL will recognize some of the style of that language here.

The DML augments standard Cobol with statements such as those in the

```
SCHEMA NAME IS ACCOUNTS.
AREA NAME IS ORDERING.
RECORD NAME IS CLIENT WITHIN ORDERING.
    01 CLIENT-NUMBER PICTURE "9999".
    01 CLIENT NAME TYPE IS CHARACTER 20.
    01 CLIENT-ADDRESS TYPE IS CHARACTER 80.
RECORD NAME IS SALES-ORDER WITHIN ORDERING.
    01 ORDER-NUMBER PICTURE "9999".
    01 ORDER-DATE.
        02 ORDER-DAY PICTURE "99".
        02 ORDER-MONTH PICTURE "99".
        02 ORDER-YEAR PICTURE "99".
    01 DELIVERY-DATE.
        02 DELIVERY-DAY PICTURE "99".
        02 DELIVERY-MONTH PICTURE "99".
        02 DELIVERY-YEAR PICTURE "99".
    01 ORDER-VALUE PICTURE "9999V99".
    01 CLIENT-NUMBER PICTURE "9999".
RECORD NAME IS PRODUCT WITHIN ORDERING.
    01 PRODUCT-CODE PICTURE "9999".
    01 PRODUCT-NAME TYPE IS CHARACTER 80.
    01 PRODUCT-PRICE PICTURE "999V99".
RECORD NAME IS ORDER-LINE WITHIN ORDERING.
    01 ORDER-LINE-NUMBER.
        02 ORDER-NUMBER PICTURE "9999".
        02 PRODUCT-NUMBER PICTURE "9999".
    01 ORDER-QUANTITY PICTURE "9999".
    01 LINE-VALUE PICTURE "99V99".
SET NAME IS SENDS-IN
    OWNER IS CUSTOMER
        ORDER IS NEXT
    MEMBER IS SALES-ORDER
        KEY IS ORDER-NUMBER.
SET NAME IS CONSISTS-OF
    OWNER IS SALES-ORDER
        ORDER IS SORTED
    MEMBER IS ORDER-LINE
        ASCENDING KEY IS ORDER-LINE-NUMBER.
SET NAME IS IS-ORDERED-ON
    OWNER IS PRODUCT
        ORDER IS SORTED
    MEMBER IS ORDER-LINE
        ASCENDING KEY IS ORDER-LINE-NUMBER.
```

Figure 7.9 Data description language.

sequence:

MOVE '1234' TO CLIENT-NUMBER
FIND ANY CLIENT
FIND FIRST SALES-ORDER RECORD WITHIN SENDS-IN

The processing would enter the DSD at the **CLIENT** file looking for client number 1234. If this were successful, then the third statement would descend the sends in relationship to find the first of the **SALES-ORDERS** which were linked to the **CLIENT**. The linking of records within relationships is accomplished by the **DBMS** when a member record is added to a relationship.

For languages other than COBOL, there are routines and subroutines available to provide the same facilities.

PRODUCT (P̲r̲o̲d̲u̲c̲t̲-̲c̲o̲d̲e̲, Product-name, Product-price)

```
PRODUCT
-------------------------------------
I          I          I          I
I PRODUCT  I PRODUCT  I PRODUCT  I
I  CODE    I  NAME    I  PRICE   I
I=========I_____I_____I
I          I          I          I
I  0500    I  DESK    I  40.00   I
I  0750    I  TABLE   I  50.00   I
I  1000    I  CHAIR   I  30.00   I
I  1250    I  STOOL   I   5.00   I
I  1500    I  LADDER  I  60.00   I
I=========I_____I_____I
```

Figure 7.10 PRODUCT relation.

7.8.2   Relational database management systems

If we consider that the CODASYL facilities deal with individual records within our database, then a **relational database management system (RDBMS)** deals with tables of data, or **relations**. Do not confuse this term with the **relationships** which we met earlier.

To illustrate the terminology of relations, let us imagine that we have a copy of a simple table like the one shown in Fig. 7.10.

Such a table of information is called a relation and comprises two main elements: the rows (also called tuples) shown in Fig. 7.11(a), and the columns (also called attributes) shown in Fig. 7.11(b). The column containing the key attribute is shown in Fig. 7.11(c).

```
       -----------------------------------
       I          I          I          I
       I  0750    I  TABLE   I  50.00   I
 (a)   I_____I_____I_____I
```

```
       -------------          -----------
       I          I          I          I
       I PRODUCT  I          I PRODUCT  I
       I  NAME    I          I  CODE    I
       I_____I          I=========I
       I          I          I          I
       I  DESK    I          I  0500    I
       I  TABLE   I          I  0750    I
       I  CHAIR   I          I  1000    I
       I  STOOL   I          I  1250    I
       I  LADDER  I          I  1500    I
 (b)   I_____I    (C)   I=========I
```

Figure 7.11 Rows and columns of a relation.

The properties of a relation are:

1. each relation has a name
2. no two rows can be the same
3. the order of the rows is not significant
4. each column must have a unique name
5. the order of the columns is not significant
6. at the intersection of any row and any column there is a single value
7. the values in any one column are all of the same type.

The number of columns in a table is a measure of the **degree** of the relation. A relation of degree 2 is called a pair. A relation of degree n is called an n-tuple. The above relation is of degree 3 that is, a 3-tuple. The number of rows in a table is a measure of the **cardinality** of the relation. The above relation has a cardinality of 5.

7.8.3 Relational calculus

The relational database concept was evolved by Codd and has a special set of operations for manipulating the tables. We can illustrate these if we consider the data model and the structures shown in Fig. 7.12. The situation is essentially the same as the one we saw earlier, except that we have included a further entity, CREDIT-LIMIT. This has a one-to-one relationship with the CLIENT entity. Occurrences of these relations are shown in Figs 7.13 – 7.16.

Relational calculus allows us to perform a range of operations on these relations. Typically, the operations allow us to:

SELECT – extract rows to form a new relation
PROJECT – extract columns to form a new relation
JOIN – add columns from one relation to another relation
UNION – join two relations to form a new relation
INTERSECT – form a new relation from two relations where the key values
    are the same
DIFFERENCE – form a new relation from the difference of two relations

and there are further operations to establish a new relation, to print a relation and to retain relations for future use.

Let us illustrate the action of these operations. As before, the key attributes are indicated.

SELECT will extract one or more rows from a relation according to specified conditions, using commands such as that shown in Fig. 7.17, producing the relation shown there.

PROJECT will extract one or more columns from a relation, using commands such as that shown in Fig. 7.18, producing the relation shown there.

We can also use the PROJECT operation to re-organize the columns of a relation that shown in Fig. 7.19, producing the relation shown there.

JOIN will add one relation to another, according to their key attributes, using

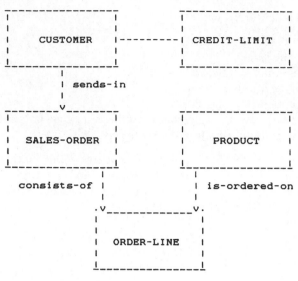

We can represent this data model as:

CLIENT (Client-number, Client-name, Client-address)

SALES-ORDER (Order-number, Order-date, Delivery-date, Value,
        Client-number)

PRODUCT (Product-code, Product-name, Product-price)

ORDER-LINE (Order-number, Product-number, Order-qty, Value)

CREDIT-LIMIT (Client-ref, Upper-limit)

Figure 7.12 Data model and entity structures.

CLIENT

CLIENT NUMBER	CLIENT NAME	CLIENT ADDRESS
===============	-------------	----------------
1000	JOHNSON AND CO	34 HIGH STREET
1100	SMITH AND SMITH	100 POLLARD HOUSE
1300	ANSTEE-SAYERS	108 MAIN STREET
1500	WILSON	200 MAIN STREET
1700	ALLINSON	DELSEY RISE
1900	SAYERS	HARVEY HOUSE
2100	WILSON	106 STATION CLOSE
2300	BROWN MATTHEWS	106 MAIN RD
2500	ATKINSON-POLLARD	110 STATION CLOSE

Figure 7.13 CLIENT relation.

SALES-ORDER

ORDER NUMBER	ORDER DATE	DELIVERY DATE	VALUE	CLIENT NUMBER
========	----------	----------	--------	--------
11004	02/02/87	02/03/87	350.00	2300
11006	02/02/87	02/03/87	15.00	1900
11007	02/02/87	02/03/87	60.00	1100
11010	03/02/87	03/02/87	240.00	1100
11045	04/02/87	10/03/87	135.00	1500
11055	05/02/87	05/03/87	40.00	1100
11066	06/02/87	06/03/87	180.00	1500
11087	06/02/87	04/03/87	90.00	1900

Figure 7.14 SALES-ORDER relation.

ORDER-LINE

ORDER NUMBER	PRODUCT NUMBER	ORDER QTY	VALUE
========	=========	-------	--------
11004	0750	1	50.00
11004	1500	5	300.00
11006	1250	3	15.00
11007	1000	2	60.00
11010	0750	2	100.00
11010	1250	4	20.00
11010	1500	2	120.00
11045	0500	3	120.00
11045	1250	3	15.00
11055	0500	1	40.00
11066	1500	3	180.00
11087	1000	3	90.00

Figure 7.15 ORDER-LINE relation.

CREDIT-LIMIT

CLIENT REF	UPPER LIMIT
========	--------
1000	1000.00
1100	1000.00
1300	2000.00
1500	1000.00
1700	500.00
1900	1000.00
2100	1500.00
2300	6000.00
2500	1000.00

Figure 7.16 Credit-limit relation.

HIGH-LIMIT = SELECT CREDIT-LIMIT UPPER-LIMIT > 1000.00

which would produce the new relation:

HIGH-LIMIT

CLIENT REF	UPPER LIMIT
===========	=============
1300	2000.00
2100	1500.00
2300	6000.00

Figure 7.17 Relational calculus – SELECT.

CURRENT = PROJECT SALES-ORDER(ORDER-NUMBER, DELIVERY-DATE, VALUE)

which would produce the new relation:

CURRENT

ORDER NUMBER	DELIVERY DATE	VALUE
============	=============	=========
11004	02/03/87	350.00
11006	02/03/87	15.00
11007	02/03/87	60.00
11010	03/02/87	240.00
11045	10/03/87	135.00
11055	05/03/87	40.00
11066	06/03/87	180.00
11087	04/03/87	90.00

Figure 7.18 Relational calculus – PROJECT.

SALES-REPORT = PROJECT SALES-ORDER (ORDER-NUMBER, CLIENT-NUMBER, ORDER-DATE, VALUE, DELIVERY-DATE)

SALES-REPORT

ORDER NUMBER	CLIENT NUMBER	ORDER DATE	VALUE	DELIVERY DATE
============	=============	============	=========	=============
11004	2300	02/02/87	350.00	02/03/87
11006	1900	02/02/87	15.00	02/03/87
11007	1100	02/02/87	60.00	02/03/87
11010	1100	03/02/87	240.00	03/02/87
11045	1500	04/02/87	135.00	10/03/87
11055	1100	05/02/87	40.00	05/03/87
11066	1500	06/02/87	180.00	06/03/87
11087	1900	06/02/87	90.00	04/03/87

Figure 7.19 Relational calculus – reorganisation with PROJECT.

```
STATISTICS = JOIN CLIENTS CREDIT-LIMIT
```

which would produce the new relation:

STATISTICS

CLIENT NUMBER	CLIENT NAME	CLIENT ADDRESS	UPPER LIMIT
1000	JOHNSON AND CO	34 HIGH STREET	1000.00
1100	SMITH AND SMITH	100 POLLARD HOUSE	1000.00
1300	ANSTEE-SAYERS	108 MAIN STREET	2000.00
1500	WILSON	200 MAIN STREET	1000.00
1700	ALLINSON	DELSEY RISE	500.00
1900	SAYERS	HARVEY HOUSE	1000.00
2100	WILSON	106 STATION CLOSE	1500.00
2300	BROWN MATTHEWS	106 MAIN RD	6000.00
2500	ATKINSON-POLLARD	110 STATION CLOSE	1000.00

Figure 7.20 Relational calculus – JOIN.

```
ORDER-DETAIL = JOIN ORDER-LINE(PRODUCT-NUMBER) PRODUCT
               (PRODUCT-CODE)
```

would produce the relation:

ORDER-DETAIL

ORDER NUMBER	PRODUCT NUMBER	ORDER QTY	VALUE	PRODUCT NAME	PRODUCT PRICE
11004	0750	1	50.00	TABLE	50.00
11004	1500	5	300.00	LADDER	60.00
11006	1250	3	15.00	STOOL	5.00
11007	1000	2	60.00	CHAIR	30.00
11010	0750	2	100.00	TABLE	50.00
11010	1250	4	20.00	STOOL	5.00
11010	1500	2	120.00	LADDER	60.00
11045	0500	3	120.00	DESK	40.00
11045	1250	3	15.00	STOOL	5.00
11055	0500	1	40.00	DESK	40.00
11066	1500	3	180.00	LADDER	60.00
11087	1000	3	90.00	CHAIR	30.00

Figure 7.21 Relational calculus – JOIN with non-key fields.

commands such as that shown in Fig. 7.20, producing the relation shown there.
    If the relations are to be linked by some field other than the key, then the corresponding fields will be specified. Thus, the command shown in Fig. 7.21 will produce the relation shown there.
    UNION and **INTERSECT** are used with their usual meaning in the theory of sets. Their use – together with that of the **DIFFERENCE** operation – is demonstrated by means of the series of commands which produces the relations shown in Figs 7.22–7.28.

```
ORDER-LINES-FOR-0750 = SELECT ORDER-LINE PRODUCT-NUMBER = 0750
```

would produce the new relation:

```
        ORDER-LINES-FOR-0750

    ----------------------------------------
    I          I          I        I        I
    I ORDER    I PRODUCT  I ORDER  I VALUE  I
    I NUMBER   I NUMBER   I QTY    I        I
    I ======== I ======== I _____I_____I
    I          I          I        I        I
    I 11004    I 0750     I   1    I  50.00 I
    I 11010    I 0750     I   2    I 100.00 I
    I ======== I ======== I _____I_____I
```

Figure 7.22 Relational calculus – 1.

```
ORDERS-FOR-0750 = PROJECT ORDER-LINES-FOR-0750 (ORDER-NUMBER)
```

would produce the new relation:

```
        ORDERS-FOR-0750

    ------------
    I          I
    I ORDER    I
    I NUMBER   I
    I ======== I
    I          I
    I 11004    I
    I 11010    I
    I ======== I
```

Figure 7.23 Relational calculus – 2.

```
ORDER-LINES-FOR-1500 = SELECT ORDER-LINE PRODUCT-NUMBER = 1500
```

would produce the new relation:

```
        ORDER-LINES-FOR-1500

    ----------------------------------------
    I          I          I        I        I
    I ORDER    I PRODUCT  I ORDER  I VALUE  I
    I NUMBER   I NUMBER   I QTY    I        I
    I ======== I ======== I _____I_____I
    I          I          I        I        I
    I 11004    I 1500     I   5    I 300.00 I
    I 11010    I 1500     I   2    I 120.00 I
    I 11066    I 1500     I   3    I 180.00 I
    I ======== I ======== I _____I_____I
```

Figure 7.24 Relational calculus – 3.

```
ORDERS-FOR-1500 = PROJECT ORDER-LINES-FOR-1500 (ORDER-NUMBER)

would produce the new relation:

           ORDERS-FOR-1500
           ----------
           I         I
           I  ORDER  I
           I NUMBER  I
           I=======I
           I         I
           I 11004   I
           I 11010   I
           I 11066   I
           I=======I
```
Figure 7.25 Relational calculus – 4.

```
ORDERS-FOR-0750-OR-1500 = UNION ORDERS-FOR-0750 ORDER-LINES-FOR-1500

would produce the new relation:

        ORDERS-FOR-0750-OR-1500
        ----------
        I         I
        I  ORDER  I
        I NUMBER  I
        I=======I
        I         I
        I 11004   I
        I 11010   I
        I 11066   I
        I=======I
```
Figure 7.26 Relational calculus – 5.

```
ORDERS-FOR-0750-AND-1500 = INTERSECT ORDERS-FOR-0750 ORDER-LINES-FOR-1500

to produce the new relation:

        ORDERS-FOR-0750-AND-1500
        ----------
        I         I
        I  ORDER  I
        I NUMBER  I
        I=======I
        I         I
        I 11004   I
        I 11010   I
        I=======I
```
Figure 7.27 Relational calculus – 6.

```
ORDERS-FOR-1500-NOT-0750 = DIFFERENCE ORDER-LINES-FOR-1500 ORDERS-FOR-0750

would produce the new relation:

        ORDERS-FOR-1500-NOT-0750
        ----------
        I          I
        I ORDER    I
        I NUMBER   I
        I========= I
        I          I
        I 11066    I
        I========= I
```

Figure 7.28 Relational calculus – 7.

These principles of relational calculus are embodied – implicitly or explicitly – in many query languages.

7.9 FOURTH GENERATION LANGUAGES

Fourth generation languages (4GLs) are of fairly recent origin. They were introduced to allow the user to develop computer systems without the chores usually associated with this task.

There is no formal definition of a 4GL. James Martin's requirements, that it should be easy to learn and offer a ten-fold improvement in efficiency, cannot be reconciled with the wide range of code generators, application generators, program generators and prototyping tools which currently fall within the *de facto* interpretation of the term. Some of these are listed in Fig. 7.29.

```
--------------------------------------------------------------------
I                                                                  I
I 4GL                GDX              Oracle                        I
I ABC                Gener/ol         Paradyme                      I
I Accolade/Imagine   Guest/IDT        Pro IV                        I
I Adabas             Ideal            Progress                      I
I ADS/O              Imagine          Ramis                         I
I All                InfoStar         RBase 5000                    I
I Cardbox+           Ingress          RPG III                       I
I CSP                Intelagen        SAS                           I
I Database           Keep It          SAS System                    I
I DataEase           Libra            Selcopy                       I
I Dataflex           Linc             Sensible Solution             I
I DataStar           M:SDT            Sourcemanager                 I
I Dbase II           Mantis           SQL/DS-QMF                    I
I Dbase III          Mapper           Superfile                     I
I Delta IV           Mark System      System W                      I
I Easytrieve Plus    Memphis          UFO                           I
I Elite              Natural          Unison                        I
I Focus              Netron/Cap       Visifile                      I
I Formula IV         Nomad                                          I
I Frontrunner        Open Access                                    I
I                                                                  I
I_____I
```

Figure 7.29 Fourth generation languages.

Of this wide – and widening – selection of 4GLs, some are only available for use in one particular environment, whilst others allow freedom of movement of systems from one computer to another, from one operating system to another. Some 4GLs are, indeed, easy to learn and to use, and they can be offered directly to end-users. Others, however, are sophisticated programming productivity tools which benefit from the application of trained programming skills. All 4GLs offer real reductions in the time-scale of the system development, the actual savings varying according to the tool that is being used: typical figures suggest that, using a 4GL, a program can be written in 25% of the time required to develop the same program in Cobol.

Some 4GLs utilize the programmers' input to generate source code or object code, some simply translating the user's high-level specification into a Cobol or Basic program. Others – such as PRO IV, described below – have a resident core of executive routines which access the parameters specifying the application as – and when – these are needed. In this case, a set of four programs which would traditionally occupy the computer memory in the manner shown in Fig. 7.30(a), can be held as a much smaller set of parameters, which are accessed and interpreted by the resident routines, as shown in Fig. 7.30(b). Clearly, the physical size of the programmer's coding makes it much easier to maintain, debug, and use.

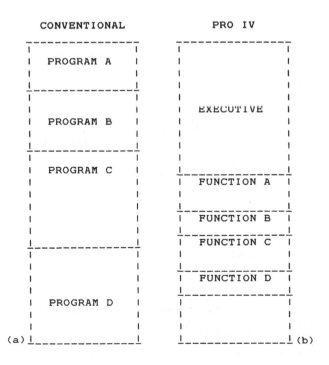

Figure 7.30 Programs/4GLs in memory.

7.9.1   Example of a fourth generation language

Let us take a brief look at PRO IV. This 4GL is available on most types of hardware, from mainframes to personal computers, and applications written in PRO IV are completely portable between hardware.

Our example presents a function which will allow us to add records to a file called **STOCK**. A function is the PRO IV equivalent of a program module. As with an ordinary program, its creation passes through several stages:

1. the programmer writes the function by filling in a series of screen forms to specify the requirements;
2. these specifications are filed away on disk; some of them are converted to an internal form for faster use at execution time;
3. when the function is invoked at execution time, the programmer's specifications are accessed and interpreted as required.

A structured English specification for the function is shown in Fig. 7.31.

```
* Function to add new records to the stock file
  Initialise message $$MSG
  clear screen
  display screen format
  accept stock number
  loop until stock number = "."
      pad stock number with leading zeroes
      re-display stock number
      if record with this stock number already exists
      then
          display error message
      else
          accept and re-display stock description
          accept and re-display bay code
          accept and re-display shelf number
          accept and re-display stock quantity
          accept and re-display minimum stock level
          obtain current date
          display current date
          accept and re-display stock price
          display message $$MSG to confirm addition
          accept user's response
          if response = "/"
          then
              ignore data
          else
              produce bay/shelf from bay code and shelf number
              build record
              write record to file
          endif
          clear screen
          display screen format
      endif
      accept stock number
  repeat
  return to main menu
```

Figure 7.31 Structured English function specification.

The information which is required to define the function is shown in Figs 7.32–7.37. For clarity and because they are not needed by this particular function, we have removed parts of the screen display – such as those relating to the security aspects of the system. The information shown is all that is required to produce the working function.

Fig. 7.32 shows the file definition. This is a global description of the file which we shall be using in the processing. It is not a part of our function specification but is created by the database administrator, one for each file in the database. The file

```
File Name : STOCK

----------------------- Field Definition ---------------------

                        Max
Fld  Type   Variable Name  Len

---  ----   ----------------  ---

001  K      STOCKNO         4
002  A      STOCKDESC      25
003  A      STOCKLOCN       8
004  N      STOCKQTY        8
005  N      STOCKMIN        8
006  N      STOCKDATE       6
007  N      STOCKPRICE      8
```

Figure 7.32 File definition.

```
Function Name: STOCK.ADD      Title: STOCK FILE MAINTENANCE SCREEN

            Type: S
                              Analyst: MBULL
                              Entry Date: 04/08/88
     Exit Link: STOCK.MENU    Reset On: 04/08/88    17:27:15
     Error Link: STOCK.MENU   By: MBULL

Ln#  ---------------------- D e s c r i p t i o n --------------

001  This function adds new records to the STOCK records file.
002  The function will ask for the STOCK NUMBER of the new part
003  then the DESCRIPTION, the BAY CODE, the SHELF NUMBER, the
004  CURRENT STOCK QUANTITY, and the MINIMUM STOCK LEVEL.  It will
005  then display the CURRENT DATE, and ask for the STOCK PRICE.
006
007  The new record will then be written away and the function
008  will repeat.
009
010  To stop the process, the user should type . When a new stock
011  number is requested or / at any other time
```

Figure 7.33 Function definition.

Figure 7.34 Screen format.

definition is made available whenever a function uses the file called **STOCK**, as indicated later in the screen characteristics of Fig. 7.36.

The file definition indicates the structure of the records on the file. The four-character field **STOCKNO** is the key, as indicated by the **K** in the **TYPE** column. Other fields in the **STOCK** records are Alphanumeric or Numeric.

Fig. 7.33 shows the **function definition**. In this example, we indicate that we are calling the function **STOCK.ADD**, and that it is a Screen type function, that is one which interacts with the user via a screen-based dialogue. Other possibilities are a Menu, a Report or a batch Update function. We have indicated that at execution time, when this routine is terminated by the user, or in the event of an error, control is to pass to a function called **STOCK.MENU**. Finally, there comes a text description of what the function does.

Fig. 7.34 shows the **screen format**. This is generated by painting the display which is to appear when we execute the function. We are only using one simple screen, but PRO IV offers the facility to have multiple, complex and paging screens, and windows.

Fig. 7.35 shows the **screen field definition**. This is probably the most important part of the specification and declares the fields which are to be displayed and entered, the row and column positions of the place on the screen at which they are to appear, and the length of input that is allowed.

If you compare the variable names with those on the file definition in Fig. 7.32, you will see that names such as **STOCKNO**, **STOCKDESC** and **STOCKDATE** are the same on both. Some names – **$BAY, $SHELF, $$MSG, $RESP** – do not appear on the file definition. These are local work variables.

The **Fld** number shows the sequence in which the fields on the screen are

```
Function Name: STOCK.ADD      Title: STOCK FILE MAINTENANCE SCREEN

                       Screen Field Definition
------------------------------------------------------------------

                                  Fill              M D Lgc
Fld  Variable Name Row  Col Len  Code  Display Code I O  ID

---  ------------- ---  --- --- ----  ------------- - - ---

001  STOCKNO         5   32   4  LFZ                 Y
     ENTER PART NUMBER FOR NEW STOCK ITEM

002  STOCKDESC       7   32  25                      Y
     ENTER DESCRIPTION

003  $BAY            9   32   5                      Y
     ENTER BAY CODE

004  $SHELF         11   32   5                      Y
     ENTER SHELF NUMBER

005  STOCKQTY       13   32   4       4.0            Y
     ENTER CURRENT STOCK QUANTITY

006  STOCKMIN       15   32   4       4.0            Y      3
     ENTER MINIMUM STOCK LEVEL

007  STOCKDATE      17   32  11       DATE             Y

008  STOCKPRICE     19   32   5       4.2-           Y
     ENTER PRICE FOR THIS STOCK ITEM

009  $$MSG          23    1  60                        Y

010  $RESP          23   45   1                        Y
```

Figure 7.35 Screen field definition.

processed, input or displayed. **STOCKNO**, therefore, is the first variable which is used in this function. Over on the right of the definition, a **Y** in the column headed **MI** (this means **mandatory input**) indicates that the user must enter a stock-number. The cursor will therefore move to row 5, column 32 and accept a field of up to four characters. If the user enters a number such as 35, then the system will re-display this according to the **FILL CODE LFZ** (left filled with zeroes). Thus, an input of 35 would be re-displayed as: 0035.

If the user enters a question marker? Instead of a number, then the run-time processor will display the message:

ENTER PART NUMBER FOR THE NEW STOCK ITEM

at the bottom of the screen. If the user enters a full stop or a slash instead of a number, then the run-time processor will abandon this function and return to the **STOCK.MENU**, as indicated on the function definition.

Since we are Adding a record to the **STOCK** file – as indicated on the file

```
Function Name: STOCK.ADD      Title: STOCK FILE MAINTENANCE SCREEN

                       Screen Characteristics

-------------------------------Screen Info----------------------

Logical Screen: 1
    Format ID: 1

Clear CRT: Y            Start Fld:    1
One Time: N             End Field:   10

Logic ID: 1

---------------------------File Information--------------------

File                       Rd  Err  Modes   Before  After-Read  Before
Access      File Name      Fld Rtn A C D L   Read    Error No-err Write
------    ---------------- --- --- -------  ------  ----- ------  ------

  01     STOCK               1      A                                    2
```

Figure 7.36 Screen characteristics.

information section of the screen characteristics in Fig. 7.36 – the run-time processor knows that, logically, the record we are adding must not already be present on the file. If we enter a stock number for a record which does exist, then a message will be displayed:

RECORD ALREADY EXISTS ON STOCK FILE

and we will be given another chance to enter the number. Similarly, if we were changing or deleting existing records, then the processor would expect the record to already be on file, and would generate suitable error messages if it were not. When the user has entered a valid stock number, the processing will proceed with field 2 (input **STOCKDESC**), field 3 (input **$BAY**), and field 4 (input **$SHELF**). When we process field 5 (input **STOCKQTY**), this will be re-displayed according to the code 4.0. That is four with no decimal places.

Having done this, we continue, processing field 6 (input **STOCKMIN**) and re-displaying the input data in the same manner. After we have handled this field, we go to logic routine number 3. Do you see the 3 over at the right-hand side? As we shall see when we look at the logic definition in Fig. 7.37, this puts today's date into the variable **STOCKDATE**. When we come to process field 7, **STOCKDATE** has a Y in the column headed **DO** (this means display only), and this field will be displayed according to the code **DATE**. Field 8 (input **STOCKPRICE**) accepts the price and the user's input data will be re-displayed according to the code 4.2-. That is four digits, a decimal point, two decimal places and an arithmetic sign.

Finally, we process field 9, displaying a work variable **$$MSG** which contains a message that we have put there in logic routine number 1 – this tells the user that the action is complete – and field 10 (input **$RESP**) accepts the user's response.

Fig. 7.36 shows the **screen characteristics**. This tells PRO IV that we have only one element to this function and that is the screen which we saw in Fig. 7.34. We indicate that the screen is to be cleared before the image is displayed, and the function is to be repeated until the user tells it to stop, by entering a full stop instead of a value for **STOCKNO**.

We also specify that when the function begins, logic routine number 1 is to be processed. This puts the message into variable **$$MSG** for use later. This is shown in Fig. 7.37, and is rather like setting up a constant in ordinary programming terms.

The **Start Fld** and the **End field** refer to the variables on the screen field definition in Fig. 7.35, and will allow nested screens and paging screens to be sectioned off.

The file information specifies that we wish to use only one file, **STOCK**. This ties in the file definition which we saw in Fig. 7.32. We also specify that we are Adding records to the file, using field number 1, **STOCKNO**, as the key. The field number is that shown in Fig. 7.35. The alternative actions may be any logical combination of A, C, D or L, indicating that this function is Changing an existing record, Deleting a record, or Looking at the contents of a record.

Over at the right-hand side, we indicate that we wish to perform logic routine number 2 before we write the records away. There are other slots for us to insert processing before reading the file (we may wish to rearrange the record key), after reading if the record is not found (we may wish to display our own messages), and after reading if the record is found (we may wish to reformat the incoming data).

Fig. 7.37 shows the **logic definition**. This is the second most important part of the specification and is the place where we specify any special pieces of coding which we may require. Obviously, the calculations, data manipulation and processing control can become very complicated, but in our case there are only three small routines:

1. logic routine number 1 is called when the function starts to execute – as indicated on the screen characteristics – and loads the text into the message **$$MSG**
2. logic routine number 2 is called before we write the new record away – as

```
Function Name: STOCK.ADD      Title: STOCK FILE MAINTENANCE SCREEN

                              Logic Definition

Lgc
ID   Ln# Step --------------------S t a t e m e n t-------------

001  001 *    Set up prompt for CONTINUE? Message
     002      $$MSG = "Press <RETURN> to add record or / to ignore"

002  001 *    Assemble stock location in BEFORE-WRITE logic
     002      STOCKLOCN = $BAY + "/" + $SHELF

003  001 *    Assign the current system date to STOCKDATE
     002      STOCKDATE = &DATE
```

Figure 7.37 Logic definition.

indicated on the file information section of the screen characteristics – and produces a string such as **AB/123** from the separate bay-code AB and the shelf-number 123

3. logic routine number 3 is called before we display the date – as indicated on the screen field definition – and loads the current date into the field **STOCKDATE** ready for display.

There are a few additional points to note about this simple illustration. Firstly, in addition to what is actually specified, the execution time standards and conventions of PRO IV allow the user to:

• Enter a ? to display a help message for any of the fields shown on the screen field definition
• Enter a / to cancel any input value and return to input a new STOCKNO
• Enter a . or a / instead of a STOCKNO to return to the exit-link routine – in our case – the calling menu STOCK.MENU.

Other conventions not illustrated by this example are:

> to tab forward through the fields on the screen,
< to tab backwards through the fields, and
to browse through the records in a file.

You will note that we have not moved the input data to the output record. We do not need to do this because we have used the same names on the screen field definition as those on the file definition: **STOCKNO, STOCKQTY**, and so on.

When we have processed the last field on the screen field definition, that is, entered the response into **$RESP**, the record will be automatically added to the file.

7.10 PROTOTYPING

The term **prototyping** describes a development cycle in which the outline requirements of the system are obtained and then re-worked and re-modelled until they meet the users' precise requirements. There is an exact analogy with the prototyping methods of mechanical engineering where a wooden model of a car, for example, may be constructed. This will then be honed and modified in the light of the reactions from drivers, from the motoring organizations, and indeed from all interested parties. When an acceptable level of satisfaction has been reached, this design can progress to the next stage where a steel version can be built.

When applying prototyping methods to the development of computer systems, the analyst first talks to the users to obtain a broad outline of their functional requirements – this may be quite detailed or it may be merely a rough outline – and a preliminary system is written to meet these requirements. There now starts an iterative process in which this prototype is demonstrated to the users, and modified in the light of their reaction and comments. The modify–demonstrate sequence is then repeated – adding more detail at each

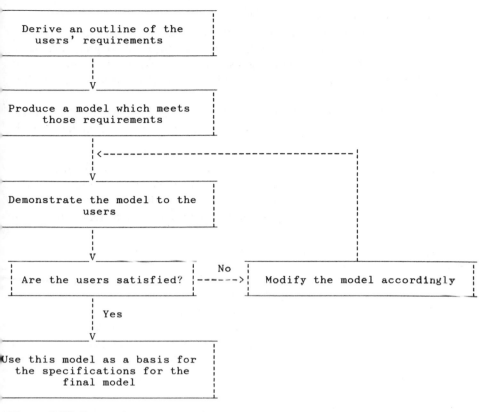

Figure 7.38 Prototyping.

pass – until the final system is acceptable to all the users. This is illustrated in Fig. 7.38.

Such a method has a number of advantages:

1. the system is modified specifically to the users' requirements as their requirements develop, by allowing the users to recognize, build up, and specify their own requirements after they have seen what can be done – users rarely know what they want, but they always know what they don't want;
2. the user is actively involved in design and development;
3. there is less room for confusion between what the user wants and what the user says;
4. there is a phased user-understanding because the user has 'grown up with the system' and therefore there are reduced user-training requirements;
5. there is a shorter development lead time; a prototype system can be produced within a few hours to give the users a flavour of what the final system will look like;
6. at this preliminary stage, the user may care to review the feasibility of the proposed system; this encourages the users and leads to an early commitment and involvement on their part;

7. the system is implemented quickly;

8. prototyping implies easy system modifications; since the system is originally developed by the modify–approve sequence, there is no great difference between the fixes and enhancements which take place during development and those which are required later, when the system has to be modified or upgraded;

9. this, in turn, leads to a longer life span for the system, since future modifications are implemented with the same ease and speed as those which made up the original system development.

The major disadvantage is that it demands considerable user-commitment. If the users are unable to accept these greater demands on their time, then the development cycle more closely follows that of the traditional methods, with the analyst or project leader accepting greater responsibility as the representative of the users.

Prototyping is entirely appropriate for developing the detail of the individual menus, screens, reports and, to a lesser extent, the processes of a system. The broad outline – the analysis and design – of the system, must still be derived in the ways we have discussed in the present book.

Although prototyping methods are not peculiar to 4GLs, the shorter development cycle offered by some 4GLs does mean that they are suitable for use as prototyping tools. Some 4GLs are such that it is perfectly feasible to use the final model as the final version of the program. In such instances, the final box on the diagram in Fig. 7.38, would be that shown in Fig. 7.39:

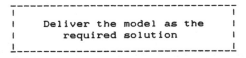

Figure 7.39 The final model.

Other 4GLs are such that when it has been produced, the model can be taken as the basis for the formal system specification which is then developed in other programming languages using standard programming methods. Other tools will take the model prescription derived by the prototyping tool and convert it automatically into a Cobol program.

7.11 EXPERT SYSTEMS

Data are letters, numbers and other characters that represent the resources used by an organization. By applying structure to these data, we derive information. If we now impose context and rules upon that information, then we obtain knowledge. We can illustrate this with a simple example. If I look at a document – a piece of paper or a piece of magnetic tape – I might encounter the characters

– 12345.

This is the raw data. I can give this structure which will enable me to interpret it as a sum of money:

£123.45 DR.

This gives me information. If I put this in the context of my bank account, and apply a simple rule of banking, I gain the knowledge that:

my bank account is overdrawn and I shall soon be getting a letter from my bank manager.

The ability to capture and apply rules such as:

if the balance of the account is less than the agreed credit limit, then the account is overdrawn and a letter should be sent to the customer

is the basis of computer software known as an **expert system**.

The rules which are appropriate for the specific task in hand are submitted to the expert system in much the same way that source program statements – in a language such as COBOL or BASIC are submitted to a compiler. The similarity between expert systems and other programming devices has led to the term fifth generation languages being used to describe such high-level media.

Unlike many programming languages, however, the features of an expert system can be applied both to conventional business situations and also to less numerate areas such as medical diagnosis and legal interpretation. This is possible because the rules

if the patient has a temperature of . . . and there is pain in the . . . accompanied by loss of . . . then . . .

or

if the defendant has admitted that . . . and the past record shows that . . . then . . .

can be provided by experts in the relevant subjects and disciplines. The expert system will first accept the experts' rules. It will then solicit the necessary information from the end-user – the facts of the case. A complex process of cross-referral and correlation of the input data with the various rules will then be performed, and the results will be displayed, together with an explanation of how and by which rules the final decision was reached.

Care must be taken with the compatibility of the rules. They must not conflict – or if they do, there must be some indication of the priority of one rule over another. If there are too many rules – one package suggests a maximum of fifty rules – then it may be impossible or time-consuming to make an interpretation.

7.12 SUMMARY

Modern commercial data processing is provided with a vast array of automated tools, techniques and utilities; some specific, some general. These are intended to facilitate the design, development and implementation of a computer solution.

For general applications, there are program generators, application generators, screen painters, report generators, query languages, fourth generation languages, and expert systems. To these we might also add database management systems which simplify the physical implementation of the logical data models produced by the analyst.

The technique of developing systems by prototyping methods illustrates how a heuristic – almost trial and error – approach to systems design and development can improve the user-satisfaction with the completed system.

8
Case Studies

CASE STUDY 1: ACME VIDEO LIBRARY

In this example we shall look at how one analyst applied the structured systems analysis and design techniques which have been encountered in the book. The pre-amble is as follows:

You have been called in by the management of the Acme Video Library in Lincoln. They run a number of shops hiring recorded video tapes to the public and they have asked you to look at the possible computerization of their member registration system and their tape library system.

We first give the background to the company, and this is followed by the transcripts of interviews with some of the people who are concerned with the system. There are also examples of the forms and documents which are used.

There are individual sections illustrating each of the steps taken during the systems analysis and the systems design stages. Because of the variety of languages which are available to the programmer, we have not pursued our methods through to the final coded modules and programs that might make up the system. However, the interested reader may wish to tranform some of the function descriptions and module descriptions into working versions by way of a chosen programming medium.

8.1 A NOTE ON THE SOLUTIONS

The reader should bear in mind that there is no definitive answer – no right or wrong solution – to systems development problems. In offering a worked case study, we are not implying that ours are the best possible answers – for in data processing, there are only solutions and better solutions and only our fictitious user could arbitrate here. But if we can stimulate the reader to find a better solution then we have achieved our objective – that of getting the analyst and programmer to use the structured techniques.

It should also be remembered that the various steps of our structured methodology are performed in parallel and each one benefits if its contents are compared with those of the other documents: the data structure diagram with the data flow diagram; the data flow diagram with the entity/function matrix, and so on. As a consequence of this, the solutions which we present only indicate our thinking at one point, and the contents of a solution which is offered at one stage will almost certainly be revised as the investigation, analysis and design proceed. For this reason, the solutions are necessarily incomplete and the reader is advised to continue the preparation and modification of the documents as would be done in practice: amending the solutions to earlier stages as more information comes to light.

8.2 BACKGROUND

The Acme Video Library is a small video tape hire company with eleven shops in and around the city of Lincoln. The company's business is the hire of video tapes to the public. You have been called in by Acme to look at their existing manual system with a view to transferring it to a computer.

You have conducted a number of interviews with the company's key personnel.

Mrs Ada Snowball is the managing director of the Acme Video Library:

> The system will link all eleven shops into a central computer here at our head office. We've more or less decided what machine we're having. Now we need you to write the software.
>
> There's a number of problems. We need to tighten up our accounting system. There's bits of paper floating about all over the place, and we never have accurate figures of what we've got at any moment.
>
> We also need more information, both for the managers at the shops and for us here at head office.
>
> In future, I'd like to look into the possibility of hiring video recorders. It would be nice if the system you write could expand to include this without too much fuss.

Mrs Caroline Steele is the manager of the Acme hire shop in Gainsborough:

> When a new member joins, they fill in a membership form so that I can get all the details and I make out a copy of this and send it to head office. This shows his name and address. We also need a deposit. This is a cheque for £50 and although we don't cash the cheque, we keep it just in case.
>
> Each member can borrow any number of tapes at one time. They borrow a tape for a day, a weekend, or for a week. Tapes have different rates: if they're new, then they're more expensive than the old ones. The rates are shown on the tape record card.
>
> When someone wants to borrow a tape, they tell us the title, then I go in the back and get the tape. They're held in order of title – although they're sometimes put back in the wrong place! I get out the tape record card and write the date and the borrower's name on it. Then, I get the member's record card out and write the title, today's date, the hire period and the charge on the card. Yes, it does take time. On a busy Saturday afternoon we can have quite a queue waiting while we try to find the tape record card and the member's record card. I shouldn't say it, but sometimes the staff do forget to write things on the cards.
>
> When a tape is returned, we look at the member's card to see when the tape was due back. If it's late, then we charge the overdue days at the daily rate. Even if it's, say, ten days late, we charge ten times the daily rate. Then I write this surcharge on the tape record card. Then, I write on the member's card to show that the tape's back in stock. I pay all the cash into the bank and then I send the bank slip to head office.

We need to know what tapes we have in stock at any one moment. Sometimes, we spend ages looking for a tape in the back when it's actually out on loan and somebody's forgotten to write it on the card.

I think there should be some system of keeping an eye on the tapes. When they've been used for more than 100 times, they get a bit dodgy. When a tape drops to bits, we send it to head office with a note explaining.

Mr Alfred Andrews is the manager of the Accounts Department at Acme head office:

When a new member joins us, he or she pays a £50 membership charge, in the form of a cheque. The member fills out a membership form and the shop sends me a copy together with the cheque. I keep the cheques here and the copy of the membership form. I always feel there's a loophole there – what if the member changes his bank and then runs off with some tapes? We can't cash the cheque. I don't know if your system can do anything about that.

I'd also like some way of finding the value of the stock at the shops – tapes depreciate at about 2% per month.

The money which the shops collect is paid into the bank, and I get a copy of the deposit slip sent here. There's no detailed breakdown of what the money represents; now I'm not saying that any of our staff would be dishonest, but some shops take on part-time staff to help over the busy periods, and, well, you never know. I'd really like to know the earnings from each tape – what are the best-selling categories: horror, spies, thrillers, comedy, or what?

I order the new tapes from a wholesaler and they are delivered straight to the shops. Usually each shop gets the same stock. In the future, I'd like to put this ordering and delivery on the computer, but not just yet. I'm also supposed to produce a catalogue and send this to the members. This shows the titles available at the shops, but quite honestly, I am a bit pushed in doing this.

8.2.1   The forms and documents

Examples of the following documents, which were collected during the investigation stage, are shown below:

- membership card (Fig. 8.1)
- video tape record card (Fig. 8.2)
- video tape catalogue (Fig. 8.3)

8.3   DOCUMENT FLOW MATRIX

We start by considering the external entities, the functional areas, the documents and the physical resources involved in the current system.

The **functional areas** within the Acme Video Library which receive or provide information are:

- Accounts Department
- cashier at the shops
- new members' registration

```
-------------------------------------------------------------------

NAME: Mrs C.Watkin,

ADDRESS: 14 Battinson St, Lincoln, LN1 2FG Lincolnshire

TELEPHONE: She hasn't got a phone

DATE JOINED: 20 December 1986

DEPOSIT PAID: Yes £50 on 20/12/86

TITLE                    BORROWED   PAID   RETURNED   FINE
                       |_____|_____|_____|_____|
                       |          |      |          |        |
The dogs of B-Gha      | 1/1/83   | 2.00 | 2/2/83   |        |
                       |          |      |          |        |
                       |          |      |          |        |
                       |          |      |          |        |
                       |          |      |          |        |
                       |          |      |          |        |
                       |          |      |          |        |
                       |          |      |          |        |
                       |          |      |          |        |
                       |          |      |          |        |
                       |          |      |          |        |
                       |          |      |          |        |
                       |          |      |          |        |
                       |_____|_____|_____|_____|

-------------------------------------------------------------------
```

Figure 8.1 Acme video library – Membership card.

- tape ordering
- tape borrowing
- tape returning.

You may have grouped some of these – tape borrowing, tape returning and cashier at the shops, for example – as one functional area, but since they perform separate tasks – or functions – they should be included as separate areas in our list even though they may be performed by the same person or the same office. By the same argument, you may have introduced a separate functional area – catalogue production. We have included this within the Accounts Department, so that you will see how this function – and any other unrecognized functions – will emerge as the analysis proceeds.

In case of any doubt, you should clarify with your user the exact scope of the proposed system: what will be included and what will be omitted? Can you think of any of the company's functional areas and activities which are not included within our system? Some absences are:

- payroll and wages
- premises rental – paying for the hire/purchase of the company's shops

```
TITLE:  THE DOGS OF BAMBIOOLA-GHA

DATE OBTAINED:  20/9/82

VHS / BETAMAX:  VHS
```

Date	Daily	Weekend	Weekly
20/9/82	2.50	3.00	12.50
11/11/83	2.00	2.50	10.00
1/1/84	1.80	2.00	8.00

Date	Borrower	Returned
23/9/82	Mrs Jellyby	29/9/82
2/10/82	Mr Jones	9/10/82
20/10/82		25/10/82
3/11/82	Peter Watson	5/11/82
11/11/82	Williams	
23/11/82	Mr Denton	23/11/82
30/11/82	John Williams	1/12/82
9/12/82		10/12/82
14/12/82	Mrs Watson	15/12/82
27/12/82	Mrs Watson	3/1/83
10/1/83	Jones	
25/1/83	Mrs J.Jenkins	29/1/83
1/2/83	Mrs Watkins	2/2/83

Figure 8.2 Acme video library – Video tape record card.

- personnel and recruitment
- advertising and marketing.

We have included the ordering and purchase of new video tapes in the above list, but you may have omitted it. As we shall soon see, our discussions with the users indicate that it will be considered outside the scope of our system.

The **external entities** which receive information from, or provide information to, the organization are:

- bank
- member
- wholesale video tape supplier

The **documents** which flow into, out of, and within the organization are:

- membership card
- membership card – copy

```
                ** ACME VIDEO LIBRARY **

    DATE: 1st September, 1984

    ADVENTURE: DOGS OF BAMBIOOLA-GHA
    ADVENTURE: HOUSE PARTY
    ADVENTURE: QUESTION OF A VICARAGE
    ADVENTURE: RAMBO XCIX
    ADVENTURE: SECRET OF THE DEAD
    ADVENTURE: SUNDAY II
    ADVENTURE: SUPERMAN 17

    CHILDREN: MYSTERY OF A FUNERAL
    CHILDREN: PARTY
    CHILDREN: SECRET OF A HAUNTED HOUSE
    CHILDREN: YES, SIR

    CLASSICS: ANNE OF GREEN GABLES
    CLASSICS: BLACK BEAUTY
    CLASSICS: HUNCHBACK OF NOTRE DAME
    CLASSICS: LES MISERABLES
    CLASSICS: LITTLE DORRIT
    CLASSICS: TALE OF TWO CITIES
    CLASSICS: TESS

    COMEDY: CARRY OUT
    COMEDY: HANKERING
    COMEDY: MYSTERY OF A HAUNTED HOUSE
    COMEDY: PROBLEM OF A WIDOW
    COMEDY: SALAD IN ROME
    COMEDY: THE THING

    DOCUMENTARY: A DAY IN THE LIFE ...
    DOCUMENTARY: MAKING OF FRIDAY 13TH
    DOCUMENTARY: WARS OF THE ROSES

    MYSTERY: AN AFFAIR AT A VICARAGE
    MYSTERY: BRITISH TELECOM
    MYSTERY: HOUSE
    MYSTERY: MYSTERY OF A WIDOW
    MYSTERY: MYSTERY OF EDWIN DROOD
    MYSTERY: PROBLEM OF A WIDOW'S LIVES
    MYSTERY: WATER MARGIN
    MYSTERY: WHISPERERS
    MYSTERY: ROMANCE
    MYSTERY: PROBLEM OF A FUNERAL

    THRILLER: FRIDAY 13TH 17
    THRILLER: HALLOWEEN 27TH
    THRILLER: SHINING
    THRILLER: TINY TIM'S DAY AT THE ZOO
```

Figure 8.3 Acme video library – Catalogue.

- tape catalogue
- bank deposit slip

The tape record card is used as a data store at the shop. It does not move about the organization and will therefore not appear on the document flow diagram.

The **physical resources and materials** which flow into, out of, and within the organization are:

- deposit cheques
- money – fees and fines
- tapes

Do you think that we should show the shelves where the tapes are stored between returning and re-issuing to members?

During the interviews, we noted a number of synonyms, that is where the same form or piece of data is known by different names.

1. the terms membership form, member's card, member's record card and membership card are used to indicate the same document;
2. the term surcharge used in Mrs Steele's interview is the same as the fine shown on the tape record card;
3. the terms deposit slip and bank slip are both used to indicate the same document.

We also noted at least one homonym, that is where different forms of pieces of data are called by the same name.

```
 ---------------------------------------------------------------
 | ACME VIDEO LIBRARY SYSTEM
 |------------------------------------------------------------
 | DOCUMENT FLOW MATRIX
 |------------------------------------------------------------
 |
 Accounts Department                                          | Y
                                                              |
 Cashier at the shops                                 |   | | Y
                                                      |   |
 New members' registration                        |  |   | | Y
                                                   |  |   |
 Tape ordering                                  |  |  |   | | N
                                                |  |  |   |
 Tape borrowing                             |   |  |  |   | | Y
                                            |   |  |  |   |
 Tape returning                        |    |   |  |  |   | | Y
                                       |    |   |  |  |   |
 Bank                             |    |    |   |  |  |   | | Y
                                  |    |    |   |  |  |   |
 Member                     |     |    |    |   |  |  |   | | Y
                            |     |    |    |   |  |  |   |
 Wholesale tape supplier |  |     |    |    |   |  |  |   | | N
                         |  |     |    |    |   |  |  |   |
 DOCUMENTS_and           |  |     |    |    |   |  |  |   |
 PHYSICAL_RESOURCES      |  |     |    |    |   |  |  |   |
                         |  |     |    |    |   |  |  |   |
 deposit cheques         |  | *>>>>>>>>>>>>>>>>>>* |  |   | | Y
 deposit cheques         |  |     |    |    |   | *>>>>>>>* | Y
 money - fees and fines  |  | *>>>>>>>>>>>>>>>>>>>>>* |   | | Y
 money - fees and fines  |  |   | *<<<<<<<<<<<<<<<<<<<* |   | | Y
 tapes - borrowed        |  | *<<<<<<<<<<<<* |  |  |   | | Y
 tapes - returned        |  | *>>>>>>>* |    |   |  |  |   | | Y
                         |  |   | |  |    |  |   |  |  |   | | Y
 bank deposit slip       |  |   | |  |    |  |   |  | *>>>* | Y
 membership card         |  | *>>>>>>>>>>>>>>>>>>* |  |   | | Y
 membership card - copy  |  |   | |  |    |  |   | *>>>>>>>* | Y
 tape catalogue          |  | *<<<<<<<<<<<<<<<<<<<<<<<<<<<<<<<* | Y
```

Figure 8.4 Acme video library – Document flow matrix.

The word *charge* is used by Mrs Steele to mean the normal rental fee, and by Mr Andrews to mean the membership deposit.

You should make a note of the synonyms and the homonyms which you encounter, and make some decision as to which term you will use.

Now that we have recorded the information about the functional areas, external entities, documents and the physical resources and materials, we can produce our document flow matrix. This is shown in Fig. 8.4.

You will see that we have only included the documents which were mentioned in the interviews. Thus, there are no documents or physical resources passing to or from the Tape Ordering functional area nor to or from the Wholesale Tape Supplier external entity. There must be some documents for such a sub-system – purchase orders and delivery notes, for example.

From discussions with Mr Andrews, we have learned that we need not consider the tape ordering system at this stage, and we have indicated this on the document flow matrix. We have also indicated those areas which are to consider.

8.4   DOCUMENT FLOW DIAGRAM

We can now produce the document flow diagram (Fig. 8.5) using the document flow matrix produced earlier. We have produced two possible diagrams: a simple

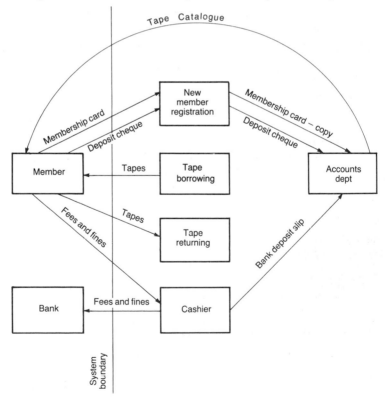

Figure 8.5 Acme video library – Document flow diagram.

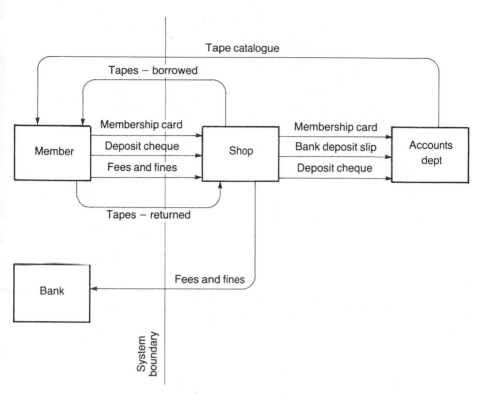

Figure 8.6 Acme video library – Document flow diagram – second version.

one (Fig. 8.5) which may have been produced by one analyst, and a more detailed one (Fig. 8.6) which may have been produced by another analyst.

Both are equally valid, and correctly identify all the entities and all the documents and resources which are flowing between the various entities, and we could have presented either as our solution. The major difference is that the separate functional areas were more clearly identified in the second DocFD than in the first. Nevertheless, our methodology would certainly resolve these into separate, more distinct functional areas as we proceed to derive the data flow diagram.

Only one document flow diagram will be produced for the current system. We shall continue the analysis using the second solution, that shown in Fig. 8.6.

In practice, you may prefer to produce the document flow diagram directly – omitting the document flow matrix – or you may prefer to use the document flow matrix alone – omitting the document flow diagram.

8.5 CURRENT DATA FLOW DIAGRAM

We can now produce the data flow diagram for the current system (Fig. 8.7) using the document flow diagram or the document flow matrix produced earlier.

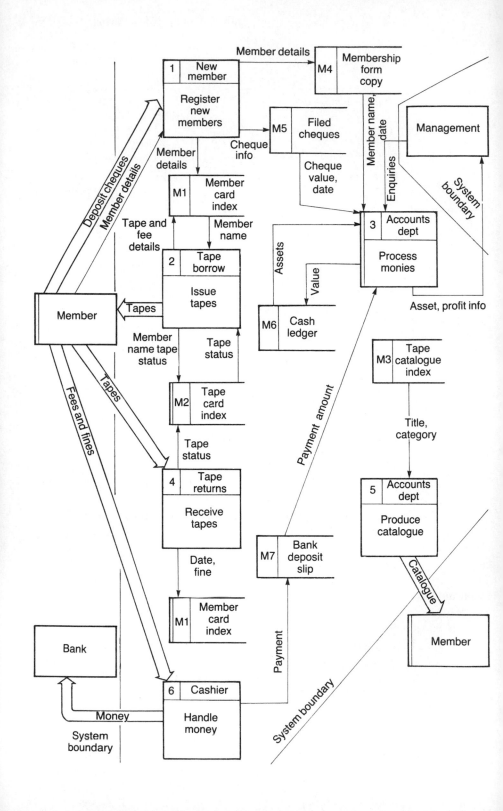

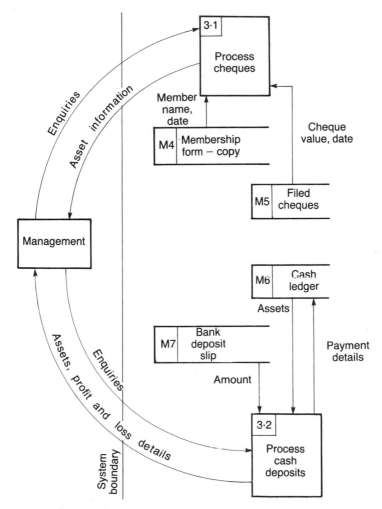

Figure 8.7 Acme video library – Current data flow diagrams.

8.6 CURRENT DATA STRUCTURE DIAGRAM

We can now produce the data structure diagram by considering the entities – the groups of data – held by Acme Video Library. The concepts about which the company holds data are:

1. members – the **MEMBER** entity on our data structure diagram
2. copy membership details – the **COPY-MEMBER** entity
3. tapes – the **TAPE** entity
4. cheques – the **CHEQUE** entity
5. payments – the **PAYMENT** entity
6. bank Deposit Slips – the **BANK-DEPOSIT** entity.

We have not had any indication that our system is to hold information about such concepts as:

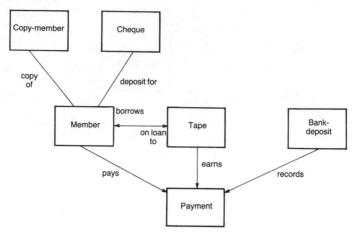

Figure 8.8. Acme video library – Current data structure diagram.

Shops: their addresses, staffing
Staff: their names, addresses, locations

We must go to the users and confirm that these are correct assumptions.

Our first data structure diagram looks like that shown in Fig. 8.8, with a many-to-many relationship between **MEMBER** and **TAPE**.

We then resolve the many-to-many relationship into two one-to-many

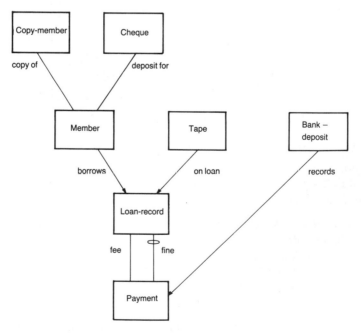

Figure 8.9 Acme video library – Current data structure diagram – 2.

relationships by introducing a new link entity, **LOAN-RECORD**, to produce the diagram shown in Fig. 8.9.

The following points about the relationships are of interest:

1. There is a one-to-one relationship called **Copy of** between **COPY-MEMBER** and **MEMBER**. We can write this as: **Copy of: COPY-MEMBER 1:1 MEMBER**.
2. **Deposit for: CHEQUE 1:1 MEMBER**
3. **Borrows: MEMBER 1:many LOAN-RECORD**
4. **On loan: TAPE 1:many LOAN-RECORD**
5. **Records: BANK-DEPOSIT 1:many PAYMENT**
6. Notice that we have shown two relationships between **LOAN-RECORD** and **PAYMENT**.
   (a) **Fee: LOAN-RECORD 1:1 PAYMENT**
   (b) **Fine: LOAN-RECORD 1:1 PAYMENT**
   The **Fine** relationship is optional because not all **LOAN-RECORDs** will involve a fine PAYMENT.

   It would have been perfectly acceptable to have two entities – FEE and FINE – instead of the single PAYMENT entity.

If we now compare this final data structure diagram with the data stores on our data flow diagram, we see that:

M1:MEMBER CARD INDEX

represents information which is contained in the **MEMBER** and **LOAN-RECORD** entities.

M2:TAPE CARD INDEX

represents information which is contained in the **TAPE** and **LOAN-RECORD** entities.

M3:TAPE CATALOGUE

is really the same as the **TAPE** entity. Or is it? This is only true if each shop holds a card index of its own tapes AND a separate tape catalogue is issued for each shop. Since we now know that we are not to consider information about the individual shops, we can assume that these assumptions are true.

M4:MEMBERSHIP FORM – COPY

is equivalent to the **COPY-MEMBER** entity.

M5:FILED CHEQUES

is equivalent to the **CHEQUE** entity.

M6:CASH LEDGER

is equivalent to the **PAYMENT** entity.

M7:BANK DEPOSIT SLIPS

is equivalent to the **BANK-DEPOSIT** entity.

By checking in this manner, to verify that our data structure diagram completely represents the contents of the data flow diagram – and vice versa – we can be sure that we have not missed anything. During the production and cross-checking of the two diagrams, we shall question many points relating to the business system, causing us, as analysts, to probe more deeply and thereby gain a thorough understanding of the current system.

If Mr Andrews had said that our system was to consider the individual shops, then there would have been another **SHOP** entity and this might have had relationships with **TAPE** (which tape is owned by which shop).

Owns: **SHOP 1:many TAPE**

and also with **MEMBER** (which member joined at which shop):

Joining: **SHOP 1:MEMBER.**

The current situation assumes that a member can only borrow tapes from the shop where he or she joined, and also that tapes must be returned to the shop from which they were borrowed. If Acme Video Library decided to offer these facilities to their members – borrow from anywhere, return to anywhere – then there would have to be two relationships between **TAPE** and **SHOP**, one as above showing which shop **Owns** which tapes, and another showing which shop currently **Holds** which tapes:

Holds: **SHOP 1:many TAPE**

8.7 PROBLEMS AND REQUIREMENTS LIST

The interviews have given us enough information to produce a problems and requirements list for the project.

In this section we have reproduced those parts of the transcripts which contained any sentences or remarks which suggest that there are faults in the present system, or where a requirement has been indicated. We also consider the impact of these problems on the company. The following describe the sort of impact which problems might have on an organization.

- deterioration of customer loyalty
- increase in costs
- inefficient use of resources
- lack of management information possibly leading to bad business decisions and loss of business
- loss of goodwill
- loss of income
- reduced profits
- time-wasting.

Finally, we indicate the action that our proposed system might take in order to overcome the problem or to meet the requirement.

During Mrs Ada Snowball's interview:

1. 'We need to tighten up our accounting system. There's bits of paper floating about all over the place...'
   Possible impact: wasted resources chasing the paperwork, and loss of management information.
   Action: the computer system will remove the need for paperwork.
2. '...and we never have accurate figures of how much we've got at any moment.'
   Possible impact: loss of management information.
   Action: produce a new report showing the cash currently held at the shops.
3. 'We also need more information. Both for the managers at the shops and for us here at head office.'
   Possible impact: loss of management information.
   Action: as for (2).
4. 'In future, I'd like to look into the possibility of hiring video recorders. It would be nice if the system you write could expand to include this without too much fuss.'
   This is less important that some of the other points, but should be borne in mind when you are designing the immediate system.
   Action: no action at present.

During Mrs Caroline Steele's interview:

5. '[The tapes are] held in order of title ... although they're sometimes put back in the wrong place!'
   Possible impact: wasted time and resources.
   Action: the computer system can do nothing about this. No action.
6. Too much clerical effort when issuing a tape: I get out the tape record card and write the date and the borrower's name on it.'
   Possible impact: wasted time and resources.
   Action: the computer system will amend the member and the tape records when tapes are borrowed.
7. 'Then, I get the member's record card out and write the title, today's date, the hire period and the amount paid on the card.'
   Possible impact: wasted time and resources.
   Action: as for (6).
8. 'Yes, it does take time. On a busy Saturday afternoon we can have quite a queue waiting while we try to find the tape record card and the member's record card.'
   Possible impact: loss of customer goodwill.
   Action: have an enquiry facility to locate member's records by name and to locate tapes by title.
9. 'I shouldn't say it, but sometimes the staff do forget to write things on the cards.'

Possible impact: loss of information.

Action: the computer system will improve this situation.

10. 'More clerical effort when the tape is returned: ... we look at the member's card to see when the tape was due back.'

    Possible impact: wasted time and resources.

    Action: when a tape is returned, the computer system will display the loan details together with the fine, if any.

11. 'We need to know what tapes we have in stock at any one moment. Sometimes, we spend ages looking for a tape in the back when it's actually out on loan and somebody's forgotten to write it on the card.'

    Possible impact: wasted time and resources.

    Action: a tape availability enquiry facility could be provided.

12. 'I think there should be some system of keeping an eye on the tapes. When they've been used for more than 100 times, they get a bit dodgy.'

    Possible impact: loss of customer goodwill if the tapes are damaged.

    Action: the computer system could retain a count of the number of times a tape has been borrowed and show this on enquiry.

During Mr Alfred Andrews's interview:

13. 'I always feel there's a loophole there – what if the member changes his bank and then runs off with some tapes? We can't cash the cheque. I don't know if your system can do anything about that.'

    Possible impact: possible loss of tapes and money.

    Action: we could produce a report showing the cheques which are held together with details of the bank account to which they refer. Some decision could then be taken by the Management in Acme Video Library to enquire at the member's bank or seek a renewed cheque. The status of the member could be held on the member's record and used to block any further borrowing in the event of a bounced cheque.

14. 'I'd also like some way of finding the value of the stock at the shops – tapes depreciate at about 2% per month.'

    Possible impact: lack of management information.

    Action: produce a report showing the cost price and the current value of the tapes.

15. 'There's no detailed breakdown of what the money represents ... now I'm not saying that any of our staff would be dishonest, but some shops take on part-time staff to help over the busy periods, and ... well, you never know.'

    Possible impact: loss of money.

    Action: produce and maintain a cash ledger for each shop. This could be used to prepare the bank cash deposit slip and as a covering letter when the bank deposit slip is sent to the Accounts department.

    There could also be an enquiry facility to display the cash in hand at each shop at any moment.

16. 'I'd really like to know the earnings from each tape ...'

    Possible impact: lack of management information.

Action: the record for each tape could retain a total of the income for that tape.

17. '...what are the best-selling categories?'

Possible impact: lack of management information and consequent loss of customer goodwill if popular tapes are not provided.

Action: a report could be produced showing the number of times which each tape has been borrowed and the category into which they fall.

18. 'In the future, I'd like to put this [tape] ordering on the computer, but not just yet.'

As with point (4), this should be borne in mind when you are designing the immediate system.

19. 'I'm also supposed to produce a catalogue and send this to the members. This shows the titles available at the shops, but quite honestly, I am a bit pushed in doing this.'

Possible impact: loss of customer goodwill, also loss of business if tapes are available but members do not know about them.

Action: a tape catalogue could be produced on demand.

8.8 PROPOSED SYSTEM

This section outlines the proposed system, and might be presented to the management at Acme Video Library before we go on to design the system.

The new system is intended to improve the service and performance of the Acme Video Library shops, and will utilize the computer system which will provide an on-line data processing service at the shops and at the Acme Video Library head office.

1. There will be two VDU keyboard terminals in each shop, and at least one such terminal for use in the Accounts Department at head office.
2. It will be possible to update the computer system if it is subsequently decided to input data at the shops via bar-code readers.
3. There will be at least one line-printer in the Accounts Department.

    It was originally suggested that there would be a printer in each shop and this would produce a cash deposit slip to accompany the cashier's deposit at the bank [see point (15) in the problems and requirements list]. However, because of the problems of maintaining and servicing these, it was decided to have line-printer facilities only at the head office. The shop will have a simple display facility to allow them to check the cash that has been paid in each day.
4. Each shop will have its own set of files and will be regarded as a separate user account.
5. The Accounts Department may log in to any of the shops' accounts.
6. In point (13) of the problems and requirements list, it was suggested that a report facility be provided to monitor the age of the deposit cheques and to chase these cheques with the member's bank. After some discussion, however, it was felt that this would put too great a burden on the Accounts Department. The proposed system will handle cheques as follows:

(a) On application to join the Acme Video Library, a member will complete a membership application form and hand over a deposit cheque to the value of £50 together with his or her bank cheque card. This is according to the current practice.

(b) All cheques will be held at the shop. They will not now be sent to Head Office.

(c) When a cheque is more than six months old, it is void and the bank will not honour it. This is standard banking procedure, and was a dangerous loophole in the old system. By monitoring the date on which the deposit was paid – or when it was renewed – the new system will be more secure than the current system which holds cheques indefinitely.

(d) A member of the tape library will not be allowed to borrow further tapes until the old cheque has been returned and a new one deposited.

7. There will be facilities for the shop assistant to change the name, address and/or telephone number of any member.

8. When a tape is borrowed, the member will ask for the tape by name or number and will also present his or her membership card. After checking that the tape is available, the computer system will ask about the required loan period. It will then calculate and display the fee which is due and the date when the tape is due back.

9. When a tape is returned, the system will calculate and display any fine that is due.

There will be an extensive range of management reporting facilities including the capacity to:

10. Produce a report of the cash held at a shop, and clear this down when the cash deposite slip has been submitted.

11. Add and change tape details.

12. Cancel and reinstate membership.

13. Produce a report of the income from tapes – this will be able to show the relative popularity of the various categories.

14. Produce letters asking the member to renew the deposit cheque in the event of a cheque being invalid or out-of-date – until this is done, the membership of that member may be cancelled.

15. Monitor the age of the tapes and the number-of-times used – this will be complemented by a facility to write-off tapes.

During the design of the system, the analyst may add further facilities where these will improve the effectiveness of the system.

8.9 DATA NORMALIZATION

We can now perform the data normalization using the documents gathered and the draft reports which we have suggested. We perform the steps described in Chapter 4.

1. List the raw data items, suggest a suitable key and indicate any repeating groups. You will see that, for practical reasons, we have chosen to identify members by a membership number and tapes by a tape number, rather than by the name and title. This pre-supposes the existence of entities:

   MEMBER (Membership-number, Name)
   TAPE (Tape-number, Title)

2. Remove any repeating groups and establish a new entity. Indicate a suitable key for the new entity.

3. For any entities with a compound key, remove any attributes which are not functionally dependent upon the entire key.

4. Remove any attributes which are dependent upon other attributes and establish a new entity.

Fig. 8.10 shows the process of data normalization for the membership card. This yields the entities: **MEMBER-2, LOAN-2, TAPE-1**.

Fig. 8.11 shows the process of data normalization for the video tape record card. This yields the entities: **TAPE-3, PRICE-CHANGE-1 and LOAN-3**.

Fig. 8.12 shows the process of data normalization for the video tape catalogue. This yields the entities: **CATALOGUE-2, CATALOGUE-ENTRY-2 and TITLE-1**.

In addition to the documents and reports – the data stores – of the existing system, we must also consider those which are to form a part of the proposed system. We do this by looking at our proposed data flow diagram and the problems and requirements list, together with the possible layouts of such documents and reports. The layouts and the possible normalized data structures are shown here.

The report of the cash held at the shop for management could be the same as the cash ledger/bank deposit slip produced for the shop cashier. A draft report is shown in Fig. 8.13.

```
 ----------------------------------------------------------------
| ACME VIDEO LIBRARY SYSTEM
|
|---------------------------------------------------------------
| MEMBERSHIP CARD - data normalization stages
|
|---------------------------------------------------------------

a) MEMBER-1 (Membership-number, Name, Address, Telephone,
            Date-joined, Deposit-indicator, (Tape-number, Title,
            Date-borrowed, Amount-paid, Date-returned, Fine-paid))

b) MEMBER-2 (Membership-number, Name, Address, Telephone,
            Date-joined, Deposit-indicator)

   LOAN-1 (Membership-number, Tape-number, Date-borrowed,
           Amount-paid, Date-returned, Fine-paid)

c) LOAN-2 (Membership-number, Tape-number, Date-borrowed,
           Date-returned, Fine-paid)

   TAPE-1 (Tape-number, Title, Amount-paid)
```

Figure 8.10 Acme video library – Membership card – data normalization.

```
 _____
| ACME VIDEO LIBRARY SYSTEM
|_____
| VIDEO TAPE RECORD CARD - data normalization stages
|_____
```

a) TAPE-2 (Tape-number, Title, Date-obtained, Tape-format,
         (Date-of-price-change, Daily-rate, Weekend-rate,
         Weekly-rate) (Date-borrowed, Membership-number, Name,
         Date-returned))

b) TAPE-3 (Tape-number, Title, Date-obtained, Tape-format)

   PRICE-CHANGE-1 (Tape-number, Sequence-number,
         Date-of-price-change, Daily-rate, Weekend-rate,
         Weekly-rate)

   LOAN-3 (Tape-number, Date-borrowed, Membership-number,
         Date-returned)

Figure 8.11 Acme video library – Video tape record card – data normalization

```
 _____
| ACME VIDEO LIBRARY SYSTEM
|_____
| VIDEO TAPE CATALOGUE - data normalization stages
|_____
```

a) CATALOGUE-1 (Date-produced, (Category, Tape-number, Title))

b) CATALOGUE-2 (Date-produced)

c) CATALOGUE-ENTRY-1 (Date-produced, Sequence-number, Category,
         Tape-number, Title)

d) CATALOGUE-ENTRY-2 (Date-produced, Sequence-number,
         Tape-number)

   TITLE-1 (Tape-number, Title, Category)

Figure 8.12 Acme video library – Video tape catalogue – data normalization.

```
 _____
| ACME VIDEO LIBRARY SYSTEM
|_____
| CASH HELD AT SHOP REPORT - draft format
|_____
```

Date	Member	Detail		Amount
01/01/88	Mrs Copley	Hire fee		2.50
01/01/88	Mr Johnson	Hire fee		2.50
01/01/88	Miss Leyton	Late fine		3.00
				=======
			TOTAL	£8.00

PAYMENT-1 (Payment-sequence-number, Date-paid, Member-name,
         Detail, Amount)

Figure 8.13 Acme video library – Cash held at shop report.

You will note that on this and the other financial reports, we have indicated totals. Because the totals are numerically dependent upon other attributes, they will be generated and printed when the report is produced and will not need to be held on the entities (the data files) as a separate value.

Find member's records by name and display details. If our **MEMBER** entity were to be organized by **Member-name**, then there would be no difficulty with this. But if the **MEMBER** is organized by **Member-number**, as we have decided, then we shall need an operational entity.

OP-NAME-1 (Name, Sequence-number, Membership-number)

```
-----------------------------------------------------
I ACME VIDEO LIBRARY SYSTEM
I
I CHEQUES HELD AT SHOP REPORT - draft format
I
-----------------------------------------------------

MEMBER NAME................ DATE JOINED CHEQUE NUMBER DATE RENEWED

2011    Mrs S.A. Henderson    01/01/88    123456789    01/01/88
2012    Mr J.A.Smith          01/01/88    234567890    01/07/88
```

CHEQUE-1 (Membership-number, Cheque-number, Date-joined, Date-renewed)

MEMBER-3 (Membership-number, Member-name)

Figure 8.14 Acme video library – Cheques held at shop report.

```
-----------------------------------------------------
I ACME VIDEO LIBRARY SYSTEM
I
I TAPE AGE REPORT - draft format
I
-----------------------------------------------------
                                  DATE    COST   CURRENT
        TAPE TITLE................ OBTAINED PRICE  VALUE

        1236 HUNCHBACK OF NOTRE DAME   01/01/88 35.00   11.55
        1263 RAMBO XCIX                01/01/88 35.00   11.55
        1290 QUESTION OF A VICARAGE    01/01/88 35.00   11.55
        1317 SECRET OF THE DEAD        01/01/88 35.00   11.55
        1344 ANNE OF GREEN GABLES      01/01/88 35.00   11.55
        1371 SUNDAY II                 01/01/88 35.00   11.55
        1398 BLACK BEAUTY              01/01/88 35.00   11.55
        1425 MYSTERY OF A FUNERAL      01/01/88 35.00   11.55
        1452 YES, SIR                  01/01/88 35.00   11.55
        1506 DOGS OF BAMBIOOLA-GHA     01/01/88 35.00   11.55
        1533 PARTY                     01/01/88 35.00   11.55
        1560 SUPERMAN 17               01/01/88 35.00   11.55
        1587 HOUSE PARTY               01/01/88 35.00   11.55

                                           =======
                        TOTAL              nnn.nn
                                           =======
```

TAPE-5 (Tape-number, Tape-title, Date-obtained, Cost-price, Current-value)

Figure 8.15 Acme video library – Tape age report.

```
 ┌──────────────────────────────────────────────────────────────
 │ ACME VIDEO LIBRARY SYSTEM
 │
 │ TAPE INCOME REPORT - draft format
 │
 └──────────────────────────────────────────────────────────────

                                        INCOME
         TAPE TITLE...................  TO DATE

         1236 HUNCHBACK OF NOTRE DAME    111.50
         1263 RAMBO XCIX                 111.50
         1290 QUESTION OF A VICARAGE     111.50
         1317 SECRET OF THE DEAD         111.50
         1344 ANNE OF GREEN GABLES       111.50
         1371 SUNDAY II                  111.50
         1398 BLACK BEAUTY               111.50
         1425 MYSTERY OF A FUNERAL       111.50
         1452 YES, SIR                   111.50
         1506 DOGS OF BAMBIOOLA-GHA      111.50
         1533 PARTY                      111.50
         1560 SUPERMAN 17                111.50
         1587 HOUSE PARTY                111.50
                                        =======
                              TOTAL     nnnn.nn
                                        =======

TAPE-5 (Tape-number, Tape-title, Income-to-date)
```

Figure 8.16 Acme video library – Tape income report.

```
 ┌──────────────────────────────────────────────────────────────
 │ ACME VIDEO LIBRARY SYSTEM
 │
 │ TAPE POPULARITY REPORT - draft format
 │
 └──────────────────────────────────────────────────────────────

TAPE CATEGORY.........  TITLE.....................  BORROWED

7114 MYSTERY          PROBLEM OF A FUNERAL          390
5717 DOCUMENTARY      WARS OF THE ROSES             387
6733 MYSTERY          WATER MARGIN                  383
7368 THRILLER         FRIDAY 13TH 17                383
5590 DOCUMENTARY      MAKING OF FRIDAY 13TH         382
6352 MYSTERY          MYSTERY OF A WIDOW            380
6479 MYSTERY          MYSTERY OF EDWIN DROOD        376
6225 MYSTERY          HOUSE                         372
6987 MYSTERY          THE CENTRAL LINE, 8 A.M.      363
7749 THRILLER         TINY TIM'S DAY AT THE 200     361
7622 THRILLER         SHINING                       353
5971 MYSTERY          AN AFFAIR AT A VICARAGE       352
7495 THRILLER         HALLOWEEN 27TH                345
5463 DOCUMENTARY      A DAY IN THE LIFE ...         343
6098 MYSTERY          BRITISH TELECOM               334
6606 MYSTERY          PROBLEM OF A WIDOW'S LIVES    333
6860 MYSTERY          WHISPERERS                    327

TAPE-6 (Tape-number, Category, Tape-title, Number-of-times-
       borrowed)
```

Figure 8.17 Acme video library – Tape popularity report.

Locate tapes by title and display details. If our **TAPE** entity were to be organized by Tape-title, then there would be no difficulty with this. But if the **TAPE** is organized by Tape-number, as we have decided, then we shall need an operational entity.

OP-TITLE-1 (Title, Sequence-number, Tape-number)

A draft layout of the *cheque report* is shown in Fig. 8.14.
Display cost price and current value of tape. A draft report is shown in Fig. 8.15.
Produce tape income report. A draft layout is shown in Fig. 8.16.
Display tape category and number of times borrowed. A draft report is shown in Fig. 8.17.

8.9.1 Consolidation

If we now consolidate the various entity structures, combining those entities which have identical keys, we arrive at those shown in Fig. 8.18. You will see that these structures allow any piece of data to be accessed, and they allow any of our documents and reports to be produced and any enquiries to be answered.

```
-----------------------------------------------------------------
| ACME VIDEO LIBRARY SYSTEM
|
|----------------------------------------------------------------
| CONSOLIDATED ENTITY STRUCTURES
|
|----------------------------------------------------------------

  LOAN (Membership-number, Tape-number, Date-borrowed, Date-
       returned, Fine-paid)

  MEMBER (Membership-number, Name, Address, Telephone, Date-
       joined, Deposit-indicator, Cheque-number, Date-
       renewed)

  OP-NAME (Name, Sequence-number, Membership-number)

  OP-TITLE (Title, Sequence-number, Tape-number)

  PAYMENT (Payment-sequence-number, Date-paid, Membership-
       number, Detail, Amount)

  PRICE-CHANGE (Tape-number, Sequence-number, Date-of-price-
       change, Daily-rate, Weekend-rate, Weekly-rate)

  TAPE (Tape-number, Title, Current-daily-rate, Current-
       weekend-rate, Current-weekly-rate, Date-obtained,
       Tape-format, Cost-price, Current-value, Income-to-
       date, Category, Number-of-times-borrowed)
```

Figure 8.18 Acme video library – Consolidated entity structures.

8.9.2 Asking questions

We then retrun to our users to ask some of the questions raised during the data normalization:

1. Do we need to hold the Deposit-indicator? Mr Andrews says that a member is only registered if and when the deposit has been paid. We can, therefore, remove this attribute from the **MEMBER** entity.
2. Is it necessary to hold a historical record of all the price changes? Mr Andrews said that this is not needed; the various charge rates were written down to avoid having to rub out the last figure. The **PRICE-CHANGE** entity can therefore be deleted.
3. Are standard rates charged for the hire of tapes? For example, do all those tapes which cost £2.50 for a day have the same weekend and weekly charge-rates? Mr Andrews said that this is so. There are about ten different charge rates according to the age and category of the tape. We therefore remove the daily, weekend and weekly charge-rates from the **TAPE** entity and replace this by a Charge-code, and then we establish a new **CHARGE-RATE** entity to hold the actual rates.
4. Mr Andrews also confirms that it is sensible to have a **CATEGORY-CODE** entity, instead of holding the text of each category on the **TAPE** entity.
5. The Fine-paid already appears on the **PAYMENT** entity, so we need not hold it on the **LOAN** entity. Mr Andrews tells us that the Date-returned is not needed, but we shall need the Date-due-back when our system is to calculate the fines to be paid.
6. How should we hold the member's name? As a single attribute:

   C. DICKENS

   or should we hold it as two attributes, initials and surname:

   C
   DICKENS

   or as first name and surname:

   CHARLES
   DICKENS

   Since the name will be used most frequently in its full form, and the surname will only be used when maintaining the **OP-NAME** entity, it was decided to hold the name as one attribute.

We also have to consider the demands of our database management system. Let us suppose that this does not automatically link master and detail records together. This requires us to do the following:

7. Add the Membership-number of the current borrower to the **TAPE** entity. Mr Andrews has indicated that when a tape is returned, he would like the identity of the last borrower to be retained on file, in case it is found to be damaged. For this reason, we have added a further Status attribute to the **TAPE** entity. This will show whether or not that tape has been returned.
8. Create a new **LOAN** entity which, with the changes shown above, now comprises:

```
---------------------------------------------------------
| ACME VIDEO LIBRARY SYSTEM
|
---------------------------------------------------------
| FINAL ENTITY STRUCTURES
|
---------------------------------------------------------
```

CATEGORY (Category-code, Category)

CHARGE-RATE (Charge-code, Daily-rate, Weekend-rate, Weekly-rate)

LOAN (Membership-number, Sequence-number, Tape-number, Date-borrowed, Date-due-back)

MEMBER (Membership-number, Name, Address, Telephone, Date-joined, Cheque-number, Date-renewed)

OP-NAME (Name, Sequence-number, Membership-number)

OP-TITLE (Title, Sequence-number, Tape-number)

PAYMENT (Payment-sequence-number, Date-paid, Membership-number, Detail, Amount)

TAPE (Tape-number, Title, Date-obtained, Charge-code, Tape-format, Cost-price, Current-value, Category-code)

TAPE-HISTORY (Tape-number, Income-to-date, Number-of-times-borrowed, Membership-number, Status)

Figure 8.19 Acme video library – Final entity structures.

LOAN (Membership-number, Sequence-number, Tape-number, Date-borrowed, Date-due-back)

Using these **TAPE** and **LOAN** entities, we are still able to find which member has borrowed any particular tape and which tapes are on loan to any particular member.

8.9.3   Dispersion

Finally, we decide to fragment the **TAPE** entity into a static and a volatile part, **TAPE** and **TAPE-HISTORY**. Applying all these points, we produce the entities shown in Fig. 8.19.

8.10   PROPOSED DATA STRUCTURE DIAGRAM

We can now produce the data structure diagram for our proposed system (Fig. 8.20) using the entities produced in Section 8.8.3. The following comments are offered:

1. The relationships have been named. This enables us to clarify the connection between the various entities and may be useful to the users and others who need to consult this document.

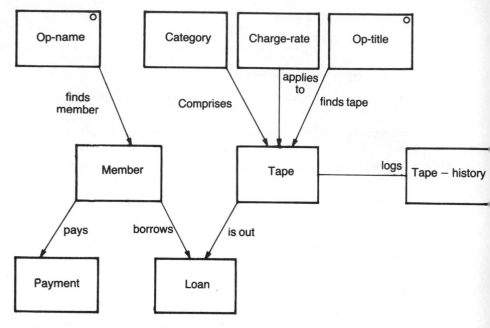

Figure 8.20 Acme video library – Data structure diagram – proposed.

2. The relationships themselves are not used, except in those database management systems, such as CODASYL, which use them to find and to link member and detail records.
3. There is a one-to-one relationship between **TAPE** and **TAPE-HISTORY**, there being one matching record one each entity for each tape. This is a consequence of our dispersing the attributes into a static (**TAPE**) part and a volatile (**TAPE-HISTORY**) part.
4. The 'is-out' relationship could be between **TAPE** and **LOAN**, as shown here, or it could be between **TAPE-HISTORY** and **LOAN**. If our physical environment means that we must hold the information to allow downward linkage in our relationships, then we would probably hold this pointer with the volatile **TAPE-HISTORY** data, and we could draw the relationship from **TAPE-HISTORY** to **LOAN**.

8.11 ENTITY DESCRIPTIONS

We can now produce the entity descriptions (Fig. 8.21) using the entity structures produced in Section 8.8.3. You will see that we have assigned entity reference numbers: D1, D2 and so on. We shall use these numbers for the data stores when they are used on the data flow diagrams later.

```
--------------------------------------------------------------------
| ACME VIDEO LIBRARY SYSTEM
|
|-------------------------------------------------------------------
| ENTITY DESCRIPTIONS
|
|-------------------------------------------------------------------


ENTITY REFERENCE: D1

ENTITY NAME: CATEGORY

ATTR  | ATTRIBUTE                    | FORMAT | COMMENTS
_____|_____|_____|_____
      |                              |        |
  K   | Category-code                | 1X     |
  1   | Category                     | 20X    |
_____|_____|_____|_____


ENTITY REFERENCE: D2

ENTITY NAME: CHARGE-RATE

ATTR  | ATTRIBUTE                    | FORMAT | COMMENTS
_____|_____|_____|_____
      |                              |        |
  K   | Charge-code                  | 1X     |
  1   | Daily-rate                   | 5N     | Pence
  2   | Weekend-rate                 | 5N     | Pence
  3   | Weekly-rate                  | 5N     | Pence
_____|_____|_____|_____


ENTITY REFERENCE: D3

ENTITY NAME: LOAN

ATTR  | ATTRIBUTE                    | FORMAT | COMMENTS
_____|_____|_____|_____
      |                              |        |
  K   | Membership-number            | 4N     | Leading zeroes
  K   | Sequence-number              | 4N     |
  1   | Tape-number                  | 4N     | Leading zeroes
  2   | Date-borrowed                | 6N     | DDMMYY
  3   | Date-due-back                | 6N     | DDMMYY
_____|_____|_____|_____


ENTITY REFERENCE: D4

ENTITY NAME: MEMBER

ATTR  | ATTRIBUTE                    | FORMAT | COMMENTS
_____|_____|_____|_____
      |                              |        |
  K   | Membership-number            | 4N     | Leading zeroes
  1   | Name                         | 20X    | Initials + Surname
  2   | Address                      | 50X    |
  3   | Telephone                    | 20X    |
  4   | Date-joined                  | 6N     | DDMMYY
  5   | Cheque-number                | 10N    |
  6   | Date-renewed                 | 6N     | DDMMYY
_____|_____|_____|_____
```

Figure 8.21 Acme video library – Entity descriptions (*continued*).

```
ENTITY REFERENCE: D5

ENTITY NAME: OP-NAME

ATTR | ATTRIBUTE                    | FORMAT | COMMENTS
_____|_____|_____|_____
     |                              |        |
  K  | Name                         | 20X    |
  K  | Sequence-number              | 4N     |
  1  | Membership-number            | 4N     | Leading zeroes
_____|_____|_____|_____

ENTITY REFERENCE: D6

ENTITY NAME: OP-TITLE

ATTR | ATTRIBUTE                    | FORMAT | COMMENTS
_____|_____|_____|_____
     |                              |        |
  K  | Title                        | 50X    |
  K  | Sequence-number              | 4N     |
  1  | Tape-number                  | 4N     | Leading zeroes
_____|_____|_____|_____

ENTITY REFERENCE: D7

ENTITY NAME: PAYMENT

ATTR | ATTRIBUTE                    | FORMAT | COMMENTS
_____|_____|_____|_____
     |                              |        |
  K  | Payment-sequence-number      | 4N     |
  1  | Date-paid                    | 6N     | DDMMYY
  2  | Membership-number            | 4N     | Leading zeroes
  3  | Detail                       | 50X    |
  4  | Amount                       | 5N     | Pence
_____|_____|_____|_____

ENTITY REFERENCE: D8

ENTITY NAME: TAPE

ATTR | ATTRIBUTE                    | FORMAT | COMMENTS
_____|_____|_____|_____
     |                              |        |
  K  | Tape-number                  | 4N     | Leading zeroes
  1  | Title                        | 50X    |
  2  | Date-obtained                | 6N     | DDMMYY
  3  | Charge-code                  | 1X     |
  4  | Tape-format                  | 1X     | V(HS) or B(etamax)
  5  | Cost-price                   | 5N     | Pence
  6  | Current-value                | 5N     | Pence
  7  | Category-code                | 1X     |
_____|_____|_____|_____
```

Figure 8.21 (*continued*)

```
ENTITY REFERENCE: D9

ENTITY NAME: TAPE-HISTORY

ATTR | ATTRIBUTE                | FORMAT | COMMENTS
_____|_____|_____|_____
     |                          |        |
  K  | Tape-number              | 4N     | Leading zeroes
  1  | Income-to-date           | 5N     | Pence
  2  | Number-of-times-borrowed | 4N     |
  3  | Membership-number        | 4N     | Leading zeroes
  4  | Status                   | 1X     | L(oan) or S(helf)
_____|_____|_____|_____
```

Figure 8.21 (*continued*)

8.12 EXAMPLES OF THE DATA

You may find it useful to document some examples of the attributes which are represented by the entity descriptions produced in Section 8.10. This will avoid any ambiguity about the meaning of the data. This is shown in Fig. 8.22.

You will notice that, because of the features of our database management system, we need only show leading zeroes where these are specified in the entity descriptions. All other fields are held as variable-length fields. In this case, the FORMAT shows the average length of the attributes.

8.13 PROPOSED DATA FLOW DIAGRAM

We can now produce the data flow diagrams for the proposed system (Fig. 8.23) using the problems and requirements list and the normalized data structures produced earlier.

You will notice that on the top-level data flow diagram in Fig. 8.23(a) we have not included the names of the data flows for those process boxes which are to be expanded at the lower level. This makes the picture less busy and does not affect the usefulness of the set of diagrams.

As the design proceeds, we may add further functions. We leave it to the reader to add any new functions to this data flow diagram.

8.14 FUNCTION CATALOGUE

We can now produce the function catalogue (Fig. 8.12) using the data flow diagram produced in section 8.13.

The **TYPE** indicates whether this is an On-line or a Batch function.

8.15 ENTITY/FUNCTION MATRIX

We can now develop the entity/function matrix (Fig. 8.25) using the entity descriptions and the function catalogue produced in Sections 8.11 and 8.14.

```
ACME VIDEO LIBRARY SYSTEM

SAMPLE ENTITY OCCURRENCES


ENTITY REFERENCE: D1          ENTITY NAME: CATEGORY

ATTR ¦ ATTRIBUTE              ¦ FORMAT ¦ EXAMPLE

  K  ¦ Category-code          ¦ 1X     ¦ A
  1  ¦ Category               ¦ 20X    ¦ ENTERTAINMENT


ENTITY REFERENCE: D2          ENTITY NAME: CHARGE-RATE

ATTR ¦ ATTRIBUTE              ¦ FORMAT ¦ EXAMPLE

  K  ¦ Charge-code            ¦ 1X     ¦ A
  1  ¦ Daily-rate             ¦ 5N     ¦ 200
  2  ¦ Weekend-rate           ¦ 5N     ¦ 300
  3  ¦ Weekly-rate            ¦ 5N     ¦ 1000


ENTITY REFERENCE: D3          ENTITY NAME: LOAN

ATTR ¦ ATTRIBUTE              ¦ FORMAT ¦ EXAMPLE

  K  ¦ Membership-number      ¦ 4N     ¦ 0001
  K  ¦ Sequence-number        ¦ 4N     ¦ 10
  1  ¦ Tape-number            ¦ 4N     ¦ 0002
  2  ¦ Date-borrowed          ¦ 6N     ¦ 251289
  3  ¦ Date-due-back          ¦ 6N     ¦ 261289


ENTITY REFERENCE: D4          ENTITY NAME: MEMBER

ATTR ¦ ATTRIBUTE              ¦ FORMAT ¦ EXAMPLE

  K  ¦ Membership-number      ¦ 4N     ¦ 0001
  1  ¦ Name                   ¦ 20X    ¦ W.S.CHURCHILL
  2  ¦ Address                ¦ 50X    ¦ 34 HIGH ST, WALFORD, E20
  3  ¦ Telephone              ¦ 20X    ¦ 01-999 999
  4  ¦ Date-joined            ¦ 6N     ¦ 010188
  5  ¦ Cheque-number          ¦ 10N    ¦ 1234567890
  6  ¦ Date-renewed           ¦ 6N     ¦ 010188
```

Figure 8.22 Acme video library – Sample entity occurrences (*continued*).

```
ENTITY REFERENCE: D5          ENTITY NAME: OP-NAME

ATTR │ ATTRIBUTE           /    │ FORMAT │ EXAMPLE
     │                          │        │
─────┼──────────────────────────┼────────┼──────────
  K  │ Name                     │ 20X    │ GLBRT
  K  │ Sequence-number          │ 4N     │ 1
  1  │ Membership-number        │ 4N     │ 0001
     │                          │        │


ENTITY REFERENCE: D6          ENTITY NAME: OP-TITLE

ATTR │ ATTRIBUTE                │ FORMAT │ EXAMPLE
     │                          │        │
─────┼──────────────────────────┼────────┼──────────
  K  │ Title                    │ 50X    │ RMB
  K  │ Sequence-number          │ 4N     │ 1
  1  │ Tape-number              │ 4N     │ 0002
     │                          │        │


ENTITY REFERENCE: D7          ENTITY NAME: PAYMENT

ATTR │ ATTRIBUTE                │ FORMAT │ EXAMPLE
     │                          │        │
─────┼──────────────────────────┼────────┼──────────────────────
  K  │ Payment-sequence-number  │ 4N     │ 123
  1  │ Date-paid                │ 6N     │ 010188
  2  │ Membership-number        │ 4N     │ 0001
  3  │ Detail                   │ 50X    │ TAPE HIRE FEE 0002
  4  │ Amount                   │ 5N     │ 200
     │                          │        │


ENTITY REFERENCE: D8          ENTITY NAME: TAPE

ATTR │ ATTRIBUTE                │ FORMAT │ EXAMPLE
     │                          │        │
─────┼──────────────────────────┼────────┼──────────
  K  │ Tape-number              │ 4N     │ 0002
  1  │ Title                    │ 50X    │ RAMBO
  2  │ Date-obtained            │ 6N     │ 010186
  3  │ Charge-code              │ 1X     │ A
  4  │ Tape-format              │ 1X     │ V
  5  │ Cost-price               │ 5N     │ 3500
  6  │ Current-value            │ 5N     │ 2400
  7  │ Category-code            │ 1X     │ A
     │                          │        │


ENTITY REFERENCE: D9          ENTITY NAME: TAPE-HISTORY

ATTR │ ATTRIBUTE                │ FORMAT │ EXAMPLE
     │                          │        │
─────┼──────────────────────────┼────────┼──────────
  K  │ Tape-number              │ 4N     │ 0002
  1  │ Income-to-date           │ 5N     │ 10000
  2  │ Number-of-times-borrowed │ 4N     │ 41
  3  │ Membership-number        │ 4N     │ 0005
  4  │ Status                   │ 1X     │ L
     │                          │        │
```

Figure 8.22 (*continued*)

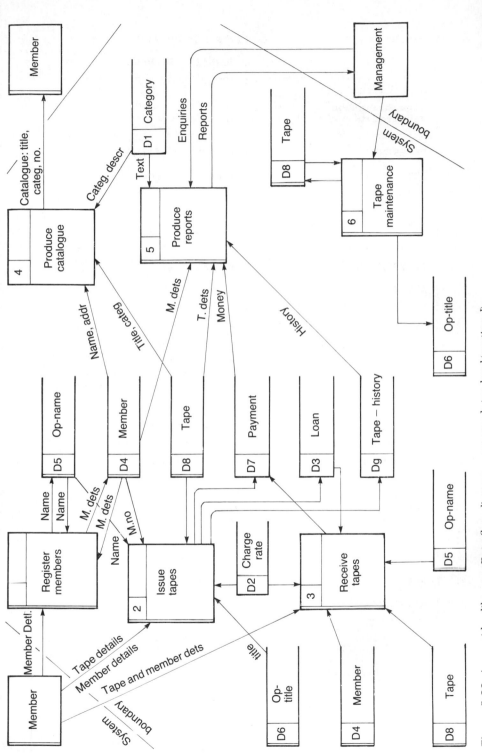

Figure 8.23 Acme video library – Data flow diagram – proposed: top level (*continued*).

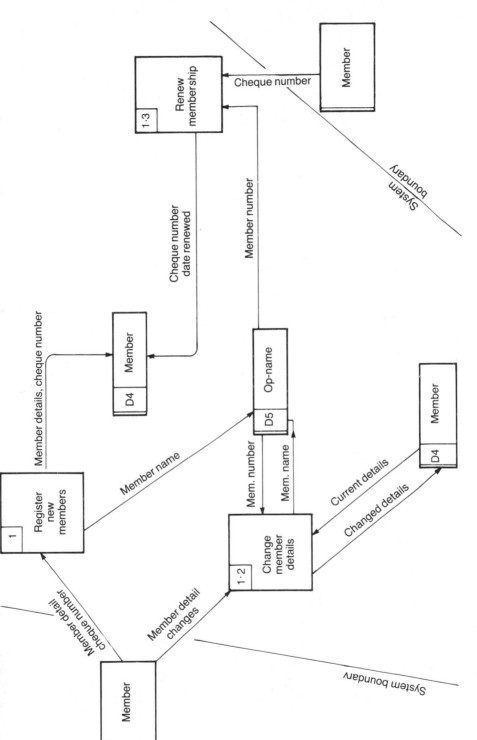

Figure 8.23 (continued)

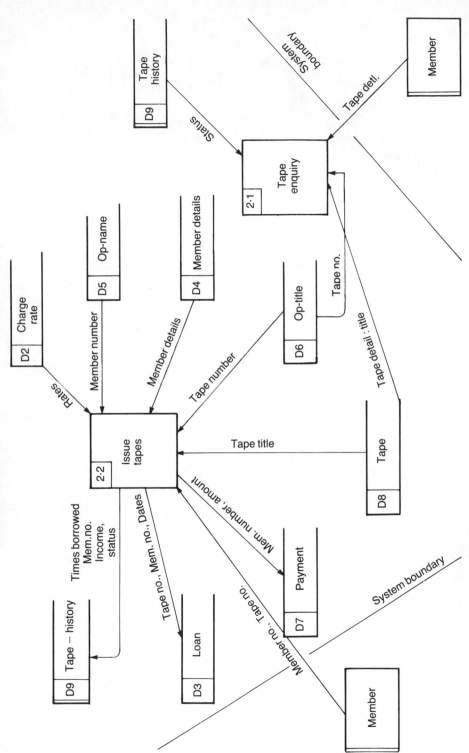

Figure 8.23 (continued)

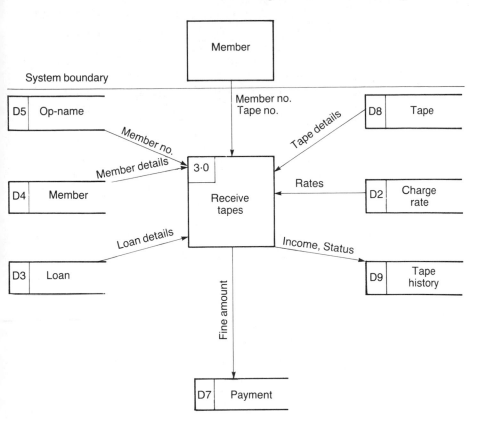

Figure 8.23 (*continued*)

If we look at each of the columns representing an entity, we can see that the processing of some entities is incomplete. Each entity should have an Insert event which creates the record on the file. You can see that there is no such facility for the **CATEGORY** and the **CHARGE-RATE** entities.

Each entity may also need a Delete event if the files are not to become too large.

The master or reference files, such as **CATEGORY**, may also need a facility to allow them to be Modified.

We discuss these with the users and add two new functions AVO019 and AVO020.

8.16 FUNCTION DESCRIPTIONS

We shall now produce the function descriptions for a few of our functions using the function catalogue produced in Section 8.14.

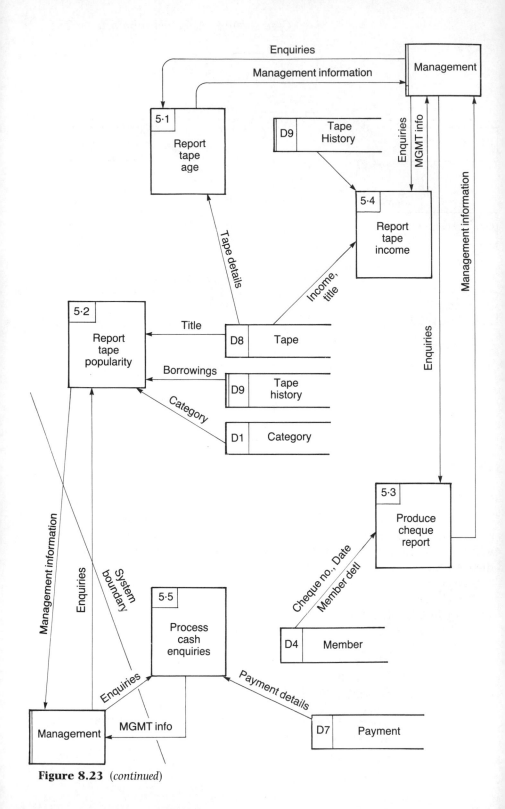

Figure 8.23 (*continued*)

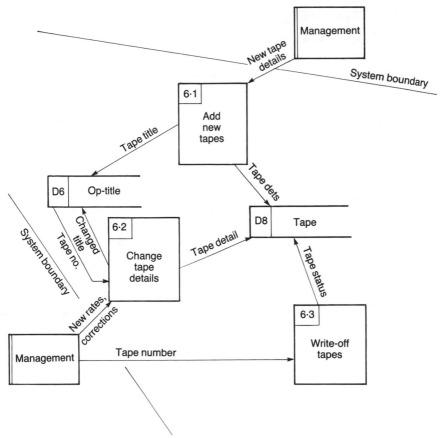

Figure 8.23 (*continued*)

We shall pre-empt the function maps which will be presented in Section 8.17 by including the main system menu function AV0000.

8.16.1 Function AV0000

Function reference: AV000M
Title: **MAIN SYSTEM MENU**
Data flow diagram reference: 1
Function type: On-line
Function description: This is the main system menu which will be presented when the users log their terminal on the computer.
Associated functions: This function calls AVS00M to vet the option.
Input specification: An option to select the required function.
Messages: None
Screen: See Fig. 8.26.

```
| ACME VIDEO LIBRARY SYSTEM
|
| FUNCTION CATALOGUE
|
```

FUNCTION REF	FUNCTION TITLE	DFD REF	TYPE	DESCRIPTION
AV0001	REGISTER NEW MEMBERS	1.1	O	Add details of new members
AV0002	CHANGE MEMBER DETAILS	1.2	O	Change details of existing members
AV0003	ISSUE TAPES	2.2	O	Issue tapes to member
AV0004	RECEIVE TAPES	3.0	O	Receive returned tape
AV0005	PRODUCE TAPE AGE REPORT	5.1	B	Produce report of tap ages
AV0006	PRODUCE TAPE POPULARITY REPORT	5.2	B	Produce report of tap popularity
AV0007	PRODUCE TAPE INCOME REPORT	5.4	B	Produce report of inc from tapes
AV0008	PRODUCE CATALOGUE	4	B	Produce catalogue of current titles
AV0009	PROCESS CASH ENQUIRIES	5.5	O	Produce a report of c in shop
AV0010	PRODUCE CHEQUE REPORT	5.3	B	Produce a report a cheques currently hel
AV0011	ADD NEW TAPES	6.1	O	Add a new tape to the library
AV0012	CHANGE TAPE DETAILS	6.2	O	Change the details of existing tape
AV0013	WRITE-OFF TAPES	6.3	O	Write-off old tapes
AV0014	RENEW MEMBERSHIP	1.3	O	Record that member ha deposited a new chequ
AV0018	TAPE ENQUIRY	2.1	O	Enquire about status a tape

Figure 8.24 Acme video library – Function catalogue.

Files: None
Processing: See Fig. 8.27.

8.16.2   Function AV0001

Function reference: AV0001
Title: **REGISTER NEW MEMBERS**
Data flow diagram reference: 1.1
Function type : On-line
Function description: Add details of new members
Usage: When a new member applies to join the library.
Associated functions: The member must first complete a membership application form.
Input specification: The function accepts the details from the membership application form. The cheque details are taken from the member's cheque.

```
 --------------------------------------------------------------
| ACME VIDEO LIBRARY SYSTEM
|
| -------------------------------------------------------------
| ENTITY / FUNCTION MATRIX
|
| -------------------------------------------------------------
                          E | C | C | L | M | O | O | P | T | T | D
                          N | A | H | O | E | P | P | A | A | A | F
                          T | T | A | A | M | - | - | Y | P | P | D
                          I | E | R | N | B | N | N | M | E | E |
                          T | G | G |   | E | A | I | I |   | - | R
                          I | O | E |   | R | M | T | N |   | H | E
                          E | R | - |   |   | E | L | T |   | I | F
                          S | Y | R |   |   |   | E |   |   | S |
                            |   | A |   |   |   | S |   |   | T |
                            |   | T |   |   |   |   |   |   | O |
U N C T I O N S             |   | E |   |   |   |   |   |   | R |
                            |   |   |   |   |   |   |   |   | Y |
'0001 | REGISTER NEW MEMBERS  |   |   |   | I | I |   |   |   |   |   | 1.1
'0002 | CHANGE MEMBER DETAILS |   |   |   | M | M |   |   |   |   |   | 1.2
'0003 | ISSUE TAPES           |   | L | I | L | L | L |   | I | L | M | 2.2
'0004 | RECEIVE TAPES         |   | L | M | L | L |   |   | I | L | M | 3.0
'0005 | TAPE AGE REPORT       |   |   |   |   |   |   |   |   | L |   | 5.1
'0006 | TAPE POPULARITY REPORT| L |   |   |   |   |   |   | L | L |   | 5.2
'0007 | TAPE INCOME REPORT    |   |   |   |   |   |   |   | L | L |   | 5.4
'0008 | PRODUCE CATALOGUE     |   |   |   |   | L |   |   |   | L |   | 4
'0009 | PROCESS CASH ENQUIRIES|   |   |   |   |   |   | L |   |   |   | 5.5
'0010 | CHEQUE REPORT         |   |   |   |   | L |   |   |   |   |   | 5.3
'0011 | ADD NEW TAPES         |   |   |   |   |   |   |   |   |   |   | 6.1
'0012 | CHANGE TAPE DETAILS   |   |   |   |   |   |   |   |   |   |   | 6.2
'0013 | WRITE-OFF TAPES       |   |   |   |   |   |   |   |   |   |   | 6.3
'0014 | RENEW MEMBERSHIP      |   |   |   |   |   |   |   |   |   |   | 1.3
'0018 | TAPE ENQUIRY          |   |   |   |   |   |   |   |   |   |   | 2.1
'0019 | MAINTAIN CATEGORY     |   |   |   |   |   |   |   |   |   |   |
 0020 | MAINTAIN CHARGE RATES |   |   |   |   |   |   |   |   |   |   |
 --------------------------------------------------------------
```

Figure 8.25 Acme video library – Entity/function matrix.

Messages: See Fig. 8.28.
Screen: See Fig. 8.29.
Files: D4, D5
Processing: See Fig. 8.30.

8.16.3   Function AV0002

Function reference: AV0002
Title: CHANGE MEMBER DETAILS
Data flow diagram reference: 1.2
Function type: On-line
Function description: Change details of existing members
Usage: When an existing member indicates that the name, address, or other details are to be changed.
Associated functions: None
Input specification: The function accepts details given verbally by the members.

```
       |  ACME VIDEO LIBRARY SYSTEM  |
       |                             |
       |  FUNCTION AV000M : SCREEN LAYOUT  |
       |                             |

           1         2         3         4         5         6         7         8
  1234567890123456789012345678901234567890123456789012345678901234567890123456789 0
  +++++++++++++++++++++++++++++++++++++++++++++++++++++++++++++++++++++++++++++++++++
01:AV0000           *** ACME VIDEO LIBRARY - MAIN MENU ***
02:
03:
04:
05:
06:
07:
08:               1       ISSUE TAPES
09:
10:               2       RECEIVE TAPES
11:
12:               3       MEMBERSHIP MAINTENANCE
13:
14:               ?       HELP ROUTINE
15:
16:               99      TERMINATE PROCESSING
17:
18:
19:
20:
21:
22:
23:
24:
  +++++++++++++++++++++++++++++++++++++++++++++++++++++++++++++++++++++++++++++++++++
  1234567890123456789012345678901234567890123456789012345678901234567890123456789 0
           1         2         3         4         5         6         7         8
```

Figure 8.26 Acme video library – Function AV000M: screen layout.

```
┌─────────────────────────────────────────────────────┐
│ ACME VIDEO LIBRARY SYSTEM                            │
│                                                      │
│ FUNCTION AV000M : PROCESSING DESCRIPTION             │
│                                                      │
└─────────────────────────────────────────────────────┘


*
*  main menu processing
*
1   loop
2         display menu screen
3         invoke module AVS00M to get option
4         case depending upon option
5              option = 1:
*  option 1 issue tapes
                invoke function AV0003
6              option = 2:
*  option 2 receive tapes
                invoke function AV0004
7              option = 3:
*  option 3 membership maintenance
                invoke function AV1000
8              option = ?:
*  option ? help routine
                invoke function AV000H
9              option = 99:
*  option 99 terminate processing
                invoke function AVSYS0
10            endcase
11  endloop
```

Figure 8.27 Acme video library – Function AV000M: processing description.

```
┌─────────────────────────────────────────────────────────────┐
│ ACME VIDEO LIBRARY SYSTEM                                    │
│                                                              │
│ FUNCTION AV0001 : MESSAGES                                   │
│                                                              │
└─────────────────────────────────────────────────────────────┘

┌─────────────┬───────────────────────────────────────────────┐
│ REFERENCE   │ TEXT                                           │
├─────────────┼───────────────────────────────────────────────┤
│             │                                                │
│ AVM0001     │ DO YOU WISH TO ENROLL A NEW MEMBER? YES/NO?    │
│ AVM0002     │ MEMBERSHIP NUMBER: nnnn                        │
│ AVM0003     │ ENTER MEMBER'S NAME                            │
│ AVM0004     │ ENTER MEMBER'S ADDRESS                         │
│ AVM0005     │ ENTER MEMBER'S TELEPHONE NUMBER, IF ANY        │
│ AVM0006     │ ENTER MEMBER'S CHEQUE NUMBER                   │
│ AVM0007     │ WRITE CHEQUE CARD NO. AND MEMBERSHIP NO. ON BACK OF THE CHEQU│
│ AVM0008     │ DO YOU WISH TO PROCEED? YES/NO?                │
│ AVM0009     │ NOW GIVE THE MEMBER A MEMBERSHIP CARD WITH THE NUMBER nnnn│
│ AVM0010     │ RETURN THE CHEQUE CARD TO THE MEMBER           │
│ AVM0011     │ DATA IGNORED_ PLEASE RE-ENTER FROM BEGINNING   │
│ AVM0012     │ DO YOU WISH TO ENROL MORE MEMBERS? YES/NO?     │
└─────────────┴───────────────────────────────────────────────┘
```

Figure 8.28 Acme video library – Function AV0001: messages.

```
| ACME VIDEO LIBRARY SYSTEM ------------------------------------------
|_____
| FUNCTION AVOOO1 : SCREEN LAYOUT ------------------------------------
|_____

         1         2         3         4         5         6         7         8
 1234567890123456789012345678901234567890123456789012345678901234567890123456789 0
 +++++++++++++++++++++++++++++++++++++++++++++++++++++++++++++++++++++++++++++++++
01:                                ** ADD A NEW MEMBER **
02:
03: Membership number ..: NNNN
04: Name ..............: XXXXXXXXXXXXXXXXXXXX
05: Address ...........: XXXXXXXXXXXXXXXXXXXXXXXXXXXXXXXXXXXXXXXXXXXXXXXXXXXXX
06: Telephone .........: XXXXXXXXXXXXXXXXXXXX
07:
08:
09:
10:                                ** CHEQUE DETAILS **
11:
12: Cheque number ......: XXXXXXXXXX
13:
14:
15:
16:
17:
18:
19:
20:
21:
22:
23:
24:XXXXX MESSAGES XXXXX
 +++++++++++++++++++++++++++++++++++++++++++++++++++++++++++++++++++++++++++++++++
 1234567890123456789012345678901234567890123456789012345678901234567890123456789 0
         1         2         3         4         5         6         7         8
```

Figure 8.29 Acme video library – Function AV0001: screen layout.

Messages: See Fig. 8.31.
Screen: See Fig. 8.32.
Output specification:
Report format: None
Files: D4, D5
Processing: See Fig. 8.33.

8.16.4   Function AV0003

Function reference: AV0003
Title: **ISSUE TAPES**
Data flow diagram reference: 2.2
Function type: On-line
Function description: Issue tapes to members
Usage: When a member applies to borrow a tape.
Associated functions: Shop assistant finds tape from library and issues it to member, and collects fee.
Input specification:
Messages: See Fig. 8.34.
Screen: See Fig. 8.35.
Output specification:

```
---------------------------------------------------------------
I ACME VIDEO LIBRARY SYSTEM
I
I_____
I FUNCTION AVOOO1 : PROCESSING DESCRIPTION
I
I_____

 1    ask if member is to be added: AVMOOO1
 2    accept reply
 3    loop until reply = no
 4        generate unique memno: AVMOOO2
 5        ask for and accept member name: AVMOOO3
 6        ask for and accept address: AVMOOO4
 7        ask for and accept telephone number: AVMOOO5
 8        ask for and accept cheque-number: AVMOOO6
 9        display message reminding assistant to write
          cheque card number and membership-number on
          back of check: AVMOOO7
10        ask if this correct: AVMOOO8
11        accept reply
12        if reply = yes
13        then
14            create new member record
15            display message reminding assistant to issue
              membership card: AVMOOO9
16            establish entry on op-name entity using
              member's surname
17            create new cheque record
18            display message reminding assistant to
              return cheque card: AVMOO10
19            create new payment record
20        else
21            display message asking to re-enter data: AVMOO11
22        endif
23        ask if more new members to be added: AVMOO12
24        accept reply
25    endloop
```

Figure 8.30 Acme video library – Function AV0001: processing description.

```
---------------------------------------------------------------
I ACME VIDEO LIBRARY SYSTEM
I
I_____
I FUNCTION AVOOO2 : MESSAGES
I
I_____

              I
REFERENCE  I TEXT
_____I_____
              I
 AVM1001  I DO YOU WISH TO CHANGE MEMBER'S DETAILS? YES/NO?
 AVM1002  I ENTER MEMBERSHIP NUMBER. ENTER ? IF NUMBER IS NOT KNOWN
 AVM1003  I ENTER NEW NAME. <RETURN> IF NO CHANGE
 AVM1004  I ENTER NEW ADDRESS. <RETURN> IF NO CHANGE
 AVM1005  I ENTER NEW TELEPHONE NUMBER. <RETURN> IF NO CHANGE
 AVM1006  I DO YOU WISH TO CHANGE MORE MEMBER DETAILS? YES/NO?
_____I_____
```

Figure 8.31 Acme video library – Function AV0002: messages.

Figure 8.32 Acme video library – Function AV0002: screen layout.

Report format: None
Files: D2, D3, D4, D5, D6, D7, D8, D9
Processing: See Fig. 8.36.

8.16.5   Function AV0008

Function reference: AV0008
Title: **PRODUCE CATALOGUE**
Data flow diagram reference: 4
Function type: Batch
Function description: Produce catalogue of current titles
Usage: An *ad hoc* function invoked according to Management's requirements.
Associated functions: The printed catalogue will be sent to the print room and then distributed to the shops.
Input specification: The user will enter the date and the heading which are to be shown on the Catalogue.
Messages: See Fig. 8.37.
Screen: See Fig. 8.38.
Output specification
Report format: The printout is to be A4 format. The report will show all the

```
| ACME VIDEO LIBRARY SYSTEM
|
| FUNCTION AV0002 : PROCESSING DESCRIPTION
|
```

```
1    ask if member details are to be changed: AVM1001
2    accept reply
3    loop until reply = NO
4         ask for and accept member number: AVM1002
5         if member number = ?
6         Then
7              call module to display all users with specific
               name
8              ask for and accept member number: AVM1002
9         endif
10        display member's current record
11        ask for and accept new member name: AVM1003
12        if member name is not null
13        then
14             amend member name
15        endif
16        ask for and accept new address: AVM1004
17        if address is not null
18        then
19             amend address
20        endif
21        ask for and accept new telephone number: AVM1005
22        if telephone number is not null
23        then
24             amend telephone number
25        endif
26        ask if this correct: AVM0010
27        accept reply
28        if reply = YES
29        then
30             amend member record
31             if surname has been changed
32             then
33                  modify entry on op-name entity using member's
                    old surname
34                  establish entry on op-name entity using
                    member's new surname
35             endif
36        else
37             display message asking to re-enter data: AVM0013
38        endif
39        ask if more members to be changed: AVM1006
40        accept reply
41   endloop
```

Figure 8.33 Acme video library – Function AV0002: processing description.

tapes which are held at the shop. The report will be sorted into title within alphabetic category. The categories and the titles are to be printed in upper- and lower-case with capitals: the titles on the file are all in upper-case. See Fig. 8.39.

Files: D4, D8

Processing: See Fig. 8.40.

```
| ACME VIDEO LIBRARY SYSTEM
|
| FUNCTION AVOOO3 : MESSAGES
|
```

```
-------------------------------------------------------------------------
              |
REFERENCE     | TEXT
--------------|----------------------------------------------------------
              |
   AVM3001    | DO YOU WISH TO ISSUE TAPES? YES/NO?
   AVM3002    | THIS MEMBER'S DEPOSIT CHEQUE MUST BE RENEWED
   AVM3003    | IS THIS THE CORRECT MEMBER? YES/NO?
   AVM3004    | ENTER TAPE NUMBER. ENTER ? IF NUMBER NOT KNOWN.
   AVM3005    | IS THIS THE CORRECT TAPE? YES/NO?
   AVM3006    | TRANSACTION IGNORED.
   AVM3007    | ENTER LOAN PERIOD 1˜ (=DAY) 2 (=WEEKEND) 3 (=WEEK)
   AVM3008    | ARE MORE TAPES TO BE LOANED TO THIS MEMBER? YES/NO?
   AVM3009    | DO YOU WISH TO LOAN MORE TAPES TO OTHER MEMBERS? YES/NO?
--------------|----------------------------------------------------------
```

Figure 8.34 Acme video library – Function AV0003: messages.

```
| ACME VIDEO LIBRARY SYSTEM
|
| FUNCTION AVOOO3 : SCREEN LAYOUT
|
```

```
              1         2         3         4         5         6         7         8
     12345678901234567890123456789012345678901234567890123456789012345678901234567890
     ++++++++++++++++++++++++++++++++++++++++++++++++++++++++++++++++++++++++++++++++++
01:                                  ** ISSUE TAPES **
02:
03: Membership number  ....: NNNN
04:
05:    Name: XXXXXXXXXXXXXXXXXXXX
06:    Address: XXXXXXXXXXXXXXXXXXXXXXXXXXXXXXXXXXXXXXXXXXXXXXXXXX
07:
08: Tape number  .........: NNNN
09:
10:    Title: XXXXXXXXXXXXXXXXXXXXXXXXXXXXXXXXXXXXXXXXXXXXXXXXXX
11:
12:    Category: XXXXXXXXXXXXXXXXXXX
13:
14:    1) Daily-rate: #NNN.NN
15:    2) Weekend-rate: #NNN.NN
16:    3) Weekly-rate: #NNN.NN
17:
18: Loan Period: X
19:
20:    Amount due: #NNN.NN
21:
22:    Date due-back: DD/MM/YY
23:
24: XXXXX MESSAGES XXXXX
     ++++++++++++++++++++++++++++++++++++++++++++++++++++++++++++++++++++++++++++++++++
     12345678901234567890123456789012345678901234567890123456789012345678901234567890
              1         2         3         4         5         6         7         8
```

Figure 8.35 Acme video library – Function AV0003: screen layout.

```
 _____
| ACME VIDEO LIBRARY SYSTEM
|_____
| FUNCTION AVOOO3 : PROCESSING DESCRIPTION
|_____

1   ask if tapes are to be issued: AVM3001
2   accept reply
3   loop until reply = no
4     ask for and accept member number: AVM1002
5     if member number = ?
6     then
7        call module to display all users with specific name
8        ask for and accept member number: AVM1002
9     endif
10    display member's name and address
11    if deposit cheque is more than six months old
12    then
13       display warning message: AVM3002
14       pass to function AVO0014: renew deposit cheque
15    else
16       ask if this is the correct member?: AVM3003
17       accept reply
18       loop until reply = no
19         ask for and accept tape number: AVM3004
20         if tape number = ?
21         then
22            call module to display all tapes with specific title
23            ask for and accept tape number: AVM3004
24         endif
25         display tape's title, category and charge rates
26         ask if this is the correct tape?: AVM3005
27         accept reply
28         if reply = no
29         then
30            display message showing tape ignored: AVM3006
31         else
32            ask for and accept loan period: AVM3007
33            loop until loan period = 1 or 2 or 3
34               ask for and accept loan period: AVM3007
35            endloop
36            display amount due
37            calculate and display date due back
38            ask if this is correct: AVM0010
39            accept reply
40            if reply = yes
41            then
42               update member record
43               update loan record
44               update tape-loan record
45               update payment record
46            else
47               display message showing loan cancelled: AVM3006
48            endif
49         endif
50         ask if more tapes are to be issued to this member: AVM3008
51         accept reply
52       endloop
53    endif
54    ask if more tapes are to be issued to other members: AVM3009
55    accept reply
56  endloop
```

Figure 8.36 Acme video library – Function AVO003: processing description.

```
| ACME VIDEO LIBRARY SYSTEM
|
| FUNCTION AV0008 : MESSAGES
|


              |
  REFERENCE   | TEXT
              |
--------------|
              |
  AVM8001     | DO YOU WANT TO PRODUCE A TAPE CATALOGUE? YES/NO?
  AVM8002     | ENTER THE DATE FOR THE CATALOGUE. <RETURN>
              | ASSUMES TODAY'S DATE
  AVM8003     | ENTER UP TO FOUR LINES OF HEADING FOR THE
              | CATALOGUE
  AVM8004     | CATALOGUE HAS BEEN SENT TO THE PRINTER
  AVM8005     | DO YOU WANT TO PRODUCE ANY MORE CATALOGUES?
              | YES/NO?
              |
```

Figure 8.37 Acme video library – Function AV0008: messages.

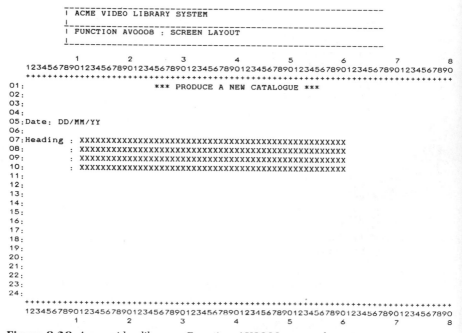

Figure 8.38 Acme video library – Function AV0008: screen layout.

```
 ----------------------------------------------------------
 | ACME VIDEO LIBRARY SYSTEM
 |---------------------------------------------------------
 | FUNCTION AVOOO8 : REPORT LAYOUT
 |_____

     ACME VIDEO LIBRARY CATALOGUE - Dated: 29 July 1999
 ...................................................

                    Acme Video Library
         134 Main Street, Gainsborough, Lincolnshire
                        LN2 2ZZ
               Telephone: Gainsborough 999 999

 Category....... Title.....................................

 Adventure       Dogs of Bambioola-Gha
 Adventure       House Party
 Adventure       Question of a Vicarage
 Adventure       Rambo XCIX
 Adventure       Secret of the Dead
 Adventure       Sunday II
 Adventure       Superman 17

 Children        Mystery of a Funeral
 Children        Party
 Children        Secret of a Haunted House
 Children        Yes, Sir

 Classics        Anne of Green Gables
 Classics        Black Beauty
 Classics        Hunchback of Notre Dame
 Classics        Les Miserables
 Classics        Little Dorrit
 Classics        Tale of Two Cities
 Classics        Tess

 Comedy          Carry Out
 Comedy          Hankering
 Comedy          Mystery of a Haunted House
 Comedy          Problem of a Widow
 Comedy          Salad in Rome
 ...................................................
                         Page n
```

Figure 8.39 Acme video library – Function AV0008: report layout.

8.17 FUNCTION MAPS

We can now produce the function map (Fig. 8.41) using the function catalogue produced in Section 8.14.

You will notice that we have added Help and Exit routines for each menu, and we have shown the Option Codes on this map.

The functions **AV0009 PRODUCE CASH REPORT** and **AV0010 PRODUCE CHEQUE REPORT** are accessible from several places. Why do you think this is so? Why do they have different Option Codes when they are accessed from the various places?

```
I ACME VIDEO LIBRARY SYSTEM
I
I FUNCTION AVO008 : PROCESSING DESCRIPTION
I

1    ask if user wants to print a catalogue: AVM8001
2    accept reply
3    loop until reply = no
4        ask for and accept and validate the date: AVM8002
5        if date = null
6        then
7             use today's date
8        else
9             loop until valid date
10                ask for and accept and validate the
                  date: AVM8002
11                if date = null
12                then
13                     use today's date
14                endif
15            endloop
16        endif
17        for four lines of heading
18            ask for and accept a heading line: AVM8003
19        endfor
20        produce catalogue
21        display message showing action complete: AVM8004
22        ask if user wants to print any more
             catalogues: AVM8005
23        accept reply
24   endloop
```

Figure 8.40 Acme video library – Function AV0008: processing description.

Notice also that function **AV0014 RENEW DEPOSIT CHEQUE** is accessible from function **AV0003 ISSUE TAPES**. Why is this?

8.18   MODULE CATALOGUE

The function descriptions offered in Section 8.16 are not really sufficient to identify many common areas, other than those of the general type mentioned in the main text:

- display a menu and ask for option: AVS00M
- display the MEMBER detail screen blank: AVS0002
- read a MEMBER record from disk: AVS0003
- amend a field on the MEMBER record: AVS0004
- Convert an entire record to upper-case characters before writing to disk: AVS0005
- write a MEMBER record to disk: AVS0006
- calculate the fine due on an overdue tape: AVS0007
- calculate tape value depreciation: AVS0008
- clear the message line and display a new message: AVS0009
- convert an upper-case string to capitals and lower-case letters: AVS0010

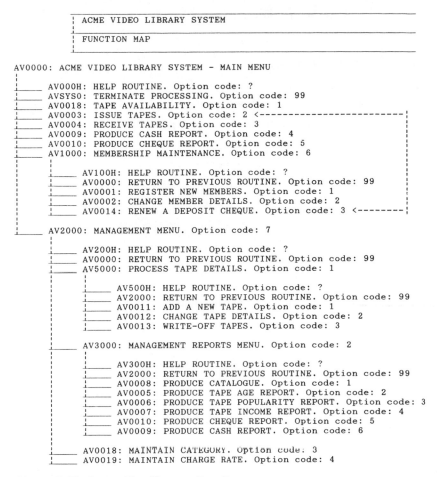

Figure 8.41 Acme video library – Function map.

There are, however, some particularly interesting routines:

- find a MEMBER record using the surname: AVSO001
- find a TAPE record using the title: AVSO011
- modify a surname or a title for use with these routines: AVSO012
- maintain the surname index: AVSO013
- maintain the title index: AVSO014
- renew a member's deposit cheque: AVSO015; this must be a module since we need to call it as a part of the main AVO014 RENEW A DEPOSIT CHEQUE function, and we also need to be able to access it from the AVO003 ISSUE TAPES routine

A partial extract from the module catalogue is shown in Fig. 8.42.

We give a description of modules AVSO00M, AVSO001 and AVSO012 in the following sections.

268   *Case studies*

```
| ACME VIDEO LIBRARY SYSTEM
|
| MODULE CATALOGUE
|
| MODULE   |  MODULE DESCRIPTION                             | Used in
| REF      |                                                |
|_____|_____|_____
|          |                                                |
| AVS0001  | find a MEMBER record using the surname         | AV0001
|          |                                                | AV0002
| AVS0002  | display the MEMBER detail screen blank         | AV0001
|          |                                                | AV0002
| AVS0003  | read a MEMBER record from disk                 | AV0001
|          |                                                | AV0002
| AVS0004  | amend a field on the MEMBER record             | AV0001
|          |                                                | AV0002
| AVS0005  | convert a record to upper-case characters      | AV0001
|          |                                                | AV0002
| AVS0006  | write a MEMBER record to disk                  | AV0001
|          |                                                | AV0002
| AVS0009  | clear the message line and display a message   | AV0001
|          |                                                | AV0002
| AVS0012  | modify a surname or a title                    | AV0001
|          |                                                | AV0002
| AVS0013  | maintain the surname index                     | AV0001
|          |                                                | AV0002
|_____|_____|_____
```

Figure 8.42 Acme video library – Module catalogue.

8.19   MODULE MAP

We can now produce the module maps using the function maps and the module catalogue produced earlier.

For clarity, we shall restrict the map in Fig. 8.43 to those modules which we have shown in the module catalogue in Section 8.18 as they apply to the **MEMBERSHIP MAINTENANCE** sub-system.

8.20   MODULE DESCRIPTIONS

Only three modules are described here. We leave the reader to develop the remainder.

8.20.1   Module AVS000M

Module reference: AVS000M
Title: REQUEST AND VALIDATE AN OPTION CODE
Module description: This module requests an option in the range Start-option to End-option, or ? or 99. A warning message is invoked if the response is invalid.
Entry parameters: Start-option, End-option,
Return parameters: Return-option.
Input specification: An option on line 3.
Messages: See Fig. 8.44.
Processing: See Fig. 8.45.

```
| ACME VIDEO LIBRARY SYSTEM
|_____
: MODULE MAP : AV1000 MEMBERSHIP MAINTENANCE
|_____


AV1000: MEMBERSHIP MAINTENANCE
|      | |
|      | |____  display a menu and ask for option: AVSOOM.
|
|____  AV100H: HELP ROUTINE
|
|____  AVOOOO: RETURN TO PREVIOUS ROUTINE
|
|____  AVO0O1: REGISTER NEW MEMBERS
|      | |
|      | |____  display the MEMBER detail screen blank: AVS0002
|      | |____  read a MEMBER record from disk: AVS0003
|      | |____  amend a field on the MEMBER record: AVS0004
|      | |____  convert a record to upper-case characters: AVS0005
|      | |____  write a MEMBER record to disk: AVS0006
|      | |____  clear the message line and display a message: AVS0009
|      | |____  find a MEMBER record using the surname: AVS0001
|      | |____  modify a surname or a title: AVS0012
|      | |____  maintain the surname index: AVS0013
|
|____  AVO0O2: CHANGE MEMBER DETAILS
       | |
       | |____  display the MEMBER detail screen blank: AVS0002
       | |____  read a MEMBER record from disk: AVS0003
       | |____  amend a field on the MEMBER record: AVS0004
       | |____  convert a record to upper-case characters: AVS0005
       | |____  write a MEMBER record to disk: AVS0006
       | |____  clear the message line and display a message: AVS0009
       | |____  find a MEMBER record using the surname: AVS0001
       | |____  modify a surname or a title: AVS0012
       | |____  maintain the surname index: AVS0013
```

Figure 8.43 Acme video library – Module map: AV1000 membership maintenance.

```
| ACME VIDEO LIBRARY SYSTEM
|_____
: MODULE AVSOOM : MESSAGES
|_____


            |
REFERENCE   | TEXT
_____|_____
            |
AVSO1M      | ENTER AN OPTION IN THE RANGE Start-option TO End-option
_____|_____
```

Figure 8.44 Acme video library – Module AVSOOM: messages.

8.20.2   Module AVS0001

Module reference: AVS0001
Title: DISPLAY MEMBERS WITH A GIVEN SURNAME
Module description: This module allows the user to locate the membership-number by means of the member's surname. The OP-NAMES entity contains

```
| ACME VIDEO LIBRARY SYSTEM ----------------------------------------
|
| MODULE AVSOOM : PROCESSING DESCRIPTION ----------------------------
|------------------------------------------------------------------

*
* module description
*
* to accept and validate a menu option as being in a
* specific range.
*
* Entry parameters: Start-option, End-option
*
* Return parameters:  Return-option.
*
1    set option-switch to invalid
2    loop until option-switch is valid
3        ask for and accept user's option
4        if user's option is in range start-option to
         end-option, or ? or 99
5        then
6            set option-switch to valid
7        else
8            display error message AVSO1M
9        endif
10   endloop
11   set return-option to user's option
12   return to calling routine
```

Figure 8.45 Acme video library – Module AVSOOM: processing description.

```
| ACME VIDEO LIBRARY SYSTEM ----------------------------------------
|
| MODULE AVSOOO1 : MESSAGES ----------------------------------------
|------------------------------------------------------------------

----------------------------------------------------------------
            |
REFERENCE   | TEXT
----------------------------------------------------------------
            |
AVSMOO1     | ENTER THE MEMBER'S SURNAME
AVSMOO2     | RECORD CANNOT BE FOUND FOR MEMBER NAME xxxxxxxxxx
----------------------------------------------------------------
```

Figure 8.46 Acme video library – Module AVSOOO1: messages.

records which use the modified member-surname as their key. The modification routine AVSOO12 is described separately.

Input specification: the module requires the surname of the member.

Messages: See Fig. 8.46.

Processing: See Fig. 8.47.

8.20.3 Module AVSOO12

Module reference: AVSOO12

Title: **MODIFY A SURNAME OR A TITLE.**

```
--------------------------------------------------------
| ACME VIDEO LIBRARY SYSTEM
|_____
| MODULE AVS0001 : PROCESSING DESCRIPTION
|_____

* module description
*
* to display all members with a specific surname
*
* no data input or output from this routine

1    ask for and accept surname: AVSM001
2    convert surname to modified form: AVS0012
3    read entry on op-names file
4    if no record
5    then
6         display message saying that name cannot be
          found: AVSM002
7    else
8         for all entries on record
9             find member-ship number in entry
10            read record from member file: AVS003
11            display name and address
12        endfor
13        pause to allow user to select required name
14   endif
15   return to calling function
```

Figure 8.47 Acme video library – Module AVS0001: processing description.

Module description: see Fig. 8.48.
Messages: None.
Processing: A partial design is given in Fig. 8.49. We leave the reader to refine this. Which do you think is the more precise definition of the requirements, the narrative shown above, or the structured English design? What differences are there?

8.21   FURTHER WORK: ACME VIDEO LIBRARY

Complete the following tasks, using the results which were provided to the Acme Video Library system.

1. On average, each Acme Video Library shops stocks about 700 tapes and serves about 400 members. Each member takes out one or two tapes at a time. Seventy per cent of the loans are for weekends, 25% for single days during the week, and 5% for weekly periods. Using this information, add the sizing details to the data structure diagram.
2. Amend the function descriptions for AV0001 and AV0002 so that they indicate which attributes (fields) of each entity are affected when a record is created or amended. For example:

   Update tape-loan record (Income-to-date; Number-of-times-borrowed; Membership-number; Status)

```
---------------------------------------------------------------
I ACME VIDEO LIBRARY SYSTEM
I
---------------------------------------------------------------
I MODULE AVS0012 : MODULE DESCRIPTION
I
---------------------------------------------------------------
```

This module converts a text-string, representing either a
member's surname or a tape-title, into a modifed form for
use with the indexing files OP-NAME and OP-TITLE.

The modified test consists of only the significant
consonants with the vowels, non-initial W, and Y removed.
Double letters are reduced to single letters.

All spaces are removed from the text string.

It is assumed that the text string is in upper-case
characters.

In the case of titles, the following words are removed:

    THE
    A
    AN

Certain consonant combinations are replaced as follows:

    MAC is replaced by 1
    MC is replaced by 1
    NG is replaced by 2
    PH is replaced by F
    SH is replaced by 3
    TH is replaced by 4
    WH is replaced by W

Input parameters the module requires a single text string,
Instring.

Output parameters the module returns the modified text as a
single text string, Outstring.

Figure 8.48 Acme video library – Module AVS0012: module description.

3. Write a complete function description for AV0018 (**MAINTAIN CATEGORY**).

4. Write a complete function description for AV0017 (Print a cheque renewal letter) so that it will utilize a word-processing package which is available on the computer system.

5. Write a module description for AVS008 (**MODIFY A STRING**) which can be used to convert a member's surname to the modified form, and to convert a tape title to the modified form. Pay particular attention to the structured English processing description.

6. Check the integrity of the processing of the entities according to the life cycles shown on the entity/function matrix. Add any necessary functions to maintain the integrity.

```
  _____
| ACME VIDEO LIBRARY SYSTEM
|_____
| MODULE AVS0012 : PROCESSING DESCRIPTION
|_____

   *
   * module avs0012
   *
   * modify an uppercase text string: surname or title
   *
   * input parameter: Instring
   *
   * output parameter: Outstring
   *
   1     set Outstring to null
   * remove preceding spaces
   2        loop until first character is not a space
   3           remove first character from Instring
   4        endloop
   5        if this is a title
   6        then
   7           remove standard words from Outstring
   8        endif
   9        case depending upon first letter
  10              first letter = W : set Outstring to W
  11              first letter = Y : set Outstring to Y
  12        endcase
  13        replace all special consonant combinations in Instring
  14        remove all H from Instring
  15        remove all W from Instring
  16        remove all Y from Instring
  17        remove all vowels from Instring
  18        remove all spaces from Instring
  19        append Instring to end of Outstring
  20        return to calling routine
```

Figure 8.49 Acme video library -- Module AVS0012: processing description.

7. Ensure that all the documentation is consistent.

8. Mr Andrews wishes to change function AV0008 (**PRODUCE CATALOGUE**) so that he can enter either:
   (a) four lines of heading, as at present, or
   (b) A Shop-code. This code will be used to retrieve the address and telephone number of the appropriate shop and incorporate this into the heading for the catalogue.
   Modify the function description, the entity descriptions and the data structure diagram as necessary.

9. Mr Andrews has asked if function AV2000, the management menu, can be protected from use by the shop assistants by requesting a password whenever Option 2 of the Main Menu is selected. Modify the function description for AV0000 to do this.

10. Mr Andrews later asks if it would be possible for him to change this password from time to time. How would you achieve this?

11. A request has been made to modify the Acme Video Library system as follows:

> If a tape is out on loan, a member may place a reservation on the tape. When the tape is next returned, a message will be displayed instructing the shop assistant to place that tape in a reserved stack.

> What additional entities will be required? Which of the existing functions will need to be changed? What additional functions will be needed? Modify function AV0004 to display the reserved message.

12. Complete any missing parts of the documentation for the Acme Video Library system.

13. If you are going to be responsible for writing programs, you should produce coding for the functions and the modules derived for the Acme Video Library system. Choose the language – or languages – which you are most likely to use. If you will have other software facilities available, such as word-processing, query languages, report generators, and so on, then you should incorporate these into your system.

CASE STUDY 2: ACME VIDEO LIBRARY

The management of the Acme Video Library have called you back to discuss a major enhancement to the video tape library system which you produced earlier. Mrs Ada Snowball, the managing director of the Acme Video Library, tells you about the new system:

> We are most satisfied with the system you put into the shops. There were a few hiccoughs, mostly operational, but we got round them and it's working very well now. Now we'd like to go ahead with the video recorder hire service I mentioned to you before. This is what we want.
>
> There are two sorts of video recorder, or should I say VCR. There's VHS and there's Betamax, like the tapes. We plan to make these available on hire at our shops. The member can hire these for a weekend, a week, a month or longer. We are also going to hire out video cameras, videocams, on the same basis.
>
> If a member wants to hire out either piece of equipment, then they must pay a £100 deposit. If they're already a member, then they only need to pay the extra £50. The deposit will be handled exactly like it is at present. That idea of yours to hold the cheques at the shops and then renew them every six months was very good. When the member returns the equipment, and it's in good condition, then we work out – or your computer system works out – how much is owing. If it's not in good condition, then we hold the deposit until one of Mr Andrews' people has made a decision as to how much is owing. Then we deduct the deposit from this and charge them the difference, or refund the difference. Doesn't that sound a bit complicated? Perhaps not.
>
> Our sales and marketing people have decided on these charge rates: £40 for a weekend, that's Friday or Saturday until Monday; £60 for a week, that's Monday to Monday or Thursday to Thursday, for example; and £199 for a month, that's a complete calendar month or, say, the 17th of one month to the 17th of the next. If

they borrow equipment for an odd period, then we want to calculate the hire charge as so many complete months, so many complete weeks, and so many days at £20 a day.

We want the same sort of information about the equipment as we currently have about the tapes: equipment income report; number of times a piece of equipment has been out on hire. The current cash reports will include the equipment charges together with the tape fees and fines.

We also want to be sure that each piece of equipment is serviced regularly. The manufacturers recommend that we service them after every 100 days use. We're not sure about that, so we might want to change that so they're serviced more frequently or less frequently, depending on our experience. That should be one of the parameters about the system we can change.

If any piece of equipment is damaged or unusable, then we'd like the shop to be able to key in the identity of the equipment. Mr Andrews can then produce a report of these items and arrange to have them serviced and put back into circulation, or to have them written off. We were thinking about having a way of selling them off cheap if they're damaged or if they're more than three years old. So that's something else your system could do.

We'd also like to have a similar facility for notifying Mr Andrews of any damaged tapes so that he can have them collected, probably by a messenger service, and then write them off. At present the shop has to tell Mr Andrews about any damaged tapes in a letter or in a telephone call.

The equipment will be identified by a code number, like the tapes are. But for our servicing calls we need to know the supplier, the manufacturer and the individual maker's identity number of the machine.

Well, that's all that I can think of at the moment. If there's anything else you want to know, then feel free to give me a ring or I'll arrange for Mr Andrews to expect you. Can you help us?

1. Can you satisfy all these new requirements? Justify your answers.
2. Write an outline of the proposed system.
3. Design the new reports.
4. Design the new entities.
5. Produce the new entity descriptions, and modify the existing descriptions if required.
6. Modify the existing data structure diagram to incorporate the new entities.
7. Modify the existing data flow diagram to accommodate the new processing.
8. Modify the entity/function matrix. Check the integrity of the matrix and add any new processes to the data flow diagram.

CASE STUDY 3: ACME MAIL ORDER COMPANY

You have been called in by the management of the Acme Mail Order Company in York. They have asked you to look at their agent registration and agent ordering systems. This is the part of the activities which deals with the agents, their customers and the orders for goods which they send in to the company. Later, you might be required to look into their purchase orders system which buys goods from outside suppliers.

We first give the background to the company, and then there follow the transcripts of interviews with some of the people who are concerned with the system: Mrs Copley, an Acme Mail Order Company agent; Mr Lawson, the Manager of Acme Mail Order Company's Accounts Department; Mrs Davies, the head of Agent Recruitment and Advertising; Mrs Swaby, the Manager of the Acme Mail Order Company Warehouse. There are also some examples of the forms and documents which are used.

8.22   THE BACKGROUND

The Acme Mail Order Company is a small organization based in York. The company's business is retailing of domestic goods – clothes, household electrical appliances, furniture, toys and garden equipment. The goods are sold through agents who are recruited via advertisements in the national press. Typically, the agents are housewives selling Acme Mail Order Company's goods to their friends and neighbours.

You have been called in by the Acme Mail Order Company to look at their existing manual system with a view to transferring it to a computer.

Mrs Christine Copley is an Acme Mail Order Company agent in Lincoln:

I saw the Acme advertisement in the *TV Times*; that was in 1984. They were giving a free clock or one of those slow-cooker things with your first order. I've seen their adverts a lot; they're giving a £15 voucher away if you join now. I use my slow-cooker a lot – when I finally got it!

You have to fill in an application form when you start – then they'll send you the catalogue – but there's not too much form-filling

It's quite easy to get customers round here. Mrs Wood next door, she was my first. Then her sister joined . . . and, of course, I buy things myself for the kids.

When I get a new one – customer, that is – I write their details down in my Customer Book. Then I give them a customer code and write it on the Club Card that I give them. As an agent, my number is LM043 and my own customer code is LM04300. Mrs Wood's number is LM04301, and it goes on like that.

I can send in the orders at any time, but I usually send them when I send off the payment money. When somebody gives me an order, they fill in a customer order form and give it to me, then I send it off, although the goods are delivered to their home address. Acme send them a statement of their account when every time the customer places an order.

When somebody buys something, they can pay it all at once, or they can pay in installments. Sometimes it's spread over 26 weeks and for some things – usually larger and more expensive things – it's over 52 weeks. It's the same price whether they pay all at once or on the never-never. Round here, they pay me every Friday and I mark it on their Club Card. Then I send the money off, usually first thing on Saturday morning. I send in a Money form to the company with the money.

If you don't like something you've ordered, then I just fill in a Returned Goods form and send it back to Acme with the goods you don't want.

I like Acme because, for every sale I make – even the things I buy for myself – they credit me with 5%. I get the money back on the anniversary of the day I became an agent.

They sometime send out a new price list, you know, price changes, special offers, cancelled lines, that sort of thing. Then I have to make sure that I use the correct price if I order any of these things.

Mr Geoffrey Lawson is the Manager of the Accounts Department at the Acme Mail Order Company's Head Office:

At present, we use accounting machines to keep all the accounts up to date. It's not very efficient, and pieces of paper – record cards orders, letters and so on – they often get lost.

When I receive an order from an agent, I give the order an internal reference number and then check the details of the order – agent's details, product code and prices – to see that they are correct, and if the customer is new, I add their details to a new customer account card in the files. Then I pass the order on to the Warehouse. If any of the order lines is wrong – a non-existent product, for example – then I highlight it on the order and send a copy of it back to the agent with a Invalid Order Letter.

When money comes in, I check it against the Cash Dispatch Form and credit it on the customer's account card, and I also credit the agent's fee to the agent's own account – that's 5% of all they sell. We send them a letter when we have credited the 5%. It's done once a year. If they want the money in cash, then they return a form – it's actually the bottom half of the letter – and we send them a cheque and debit their agent account.

Mary, my assistant, keeps an eye on the customer's accounts. If they haven't paid anything for over four weeks, then we send them a letter – that's a Customer Reminder Letter – and if they still haven't sent anything in another four weeks, then we get a debt recovery agent to get it for us. If that happens, we write off 20% of the debt to the recovery agent as his fee, but I don't think you'll be dealing with that just yet, and anyway we're usually so rushed that we don't get round to it as often as we might.

When a customer returns goods, I get the covering form from Warehouse, then I credit the customer's account and debit the commission from the agent.

From time to time, we have price changes. When this happens, I amend the price on the catalogue details, then I send details of the new prices to Mrs Davies and she tells the agents. I'll give you a copy of the last one we did.

We are also responsible for buying in goods. When I receive a Stock Reorder Form from Warehouse, I look through the list of Suppliers and telephone them to see if they can deliver within two weeks. I usually start with the one who gives us the biggest discount or the best price, but if he can't help, then I have to try the others. This takes quite some time. When I've found one – and agreed a price – I complete a Purchase Order and send a cheque for the goods – that's one of Mr Fotheringham's strong points – he's our founder – he always sent the money with the order. When I receive the goods inward delivery note from Warehouse, I mark it off on the Supplier's record card.

We have a few problems in other areas. I never really know what we have in stock. When the board want figures about sales or about stock, it takes me and Mary a long time to provide the information they want. Then it's usually out of date. I've been thinking about the sort of information that would be most useful – a sort of stock report, and a stock sales report – and I've drafted the sort of report that I'd like. I'll get Mary to give you a copy.

Mrs Ethel Davies is in charge of the agent recruitment and advertising at the Acme Mail Order Company's Head Office:

I put the advertisements in the papers, and sometimes we do direct mail shots. Then when someone returns the coupon to say they're interested in becoming an agent, I send them an Agent Detail Form. If they return that, and it seems alright, then they become an agent – I allocate an agent reference number, make out an Agent Record Card – and then I send them a catalogue, and a supply of stationery, you know, customer book, order forms, blank customer cards to record their payments, that sort of thing. They get a free gift with the first order from them or from one of their customers. I watch their account and then when they send in their first order, I send a free gift requisition to the warehouse, that also lets me see how well they are making their payments. Although at present, the free gift often gets forgotten until the agent writes to say we haven't sent it.

Every six month's I get a new catalogue printed. Geoffrey, that's Mr Lawson, gives me the details. I'm also responsible for sending new catalogues to the agents. We have these printed every six months.

Mrs Sonia Swaby is the Manager of the Warehouse at the Acme Mail Order Company's Head Office:

When we receive an order from Accounts, we check the details about the goods. If the goods are in stock, then I make out a Delivery Note – one for each item – and I make up an Order Picking List form. I also amend the Stock Record Card.

If the terms are not in stock, then I make out an Unfilled Items Letter and a Stock Reorder Form. The Item Delivery Note and the Order Picking List – we call it a bundle – then go to the stores and they make up the order. The goods and the bundle are carried in a basket – or a trolley if it's a large order – and these then go on to Packing who parcel the goods and send them off with their own Delivery Notes. I send the Unfilled Items Letters to the customer. They have to re-order it again if they still want it. We use the Post Office, British Rail and private carriers to deliver the goods. If a customer sends goods back – either because they're damaged, or they don't want them, we receive them here with a returned goods form. I check the goods and the form and pass it on the Accounts. We also receive goods inward – when Accounts have ordered the goods and they've been delivered. I send the delivery notes to Mr Lawson. We don't do any chasing of purchase orders.

8.23   THE FORMS AND DOCUMENTS

Examples of the following documents, which were collected during the investigation stage, are shown.

- an AGENT CREDIT LETTER (Fig. 8.50)
- an AGENT RECORD CARD (Fig. 8.51)
- a CATALOGUE DETAILS REPORT (Fig. 8.52)
- a CUSTOMER ACCOUNT CARD (Fig. 8.53)
- a CUSTOMER ORDER FORM (Fig. 8.54)
- a CUSTOMER REMINDER LETTER (Fig. 8.55)
- a CUSTOMER STATEMENT (Fig. 8.56)

AGENT CREDIT LETTER

Agent Number: LM043

Mrs C. Copley,
14 Battinson St,
Lincoln,
Lincolnshire
LN1 2FG.

Dear Mrs Copley,

You will be pleased to know that on 16th June 1985 your
account was credited with the sum of #5.70 which represented
an agent's fee of 5% of the total sales of #114.00 which you
made during the last 12 months.

As you know, you may use the money to make purchases from
the Acme Mail Order Company catalogue, or you may obtain the
cash sum by signing the bottom half of this letter and
returning it to me.

We at Acme Mail Order Company are delighted with the
contribution which you are making to the Company's
successful sales record, and we look forward to a continued
happy relationship with you.

Thank you again,

I remain,

Yours sincerely,

Geoffrey Lawson
Manager
Accounts Department,
Acme Mail Order Company

================== CASH SETTLEMENT FORM ===================

Agent Number: LM043

Mrs C. Copley,
14 Battinson St,
Lincoln,
Lincolnshire
LN1 2FG

I wish to receive my agent's fee as a cash sum of #5.70

Signed: Christine Copley

Figure 8.50 Acme mail order – Agent credit letter.

```
                    AGENT  RECORD  CARD
                                                . . . . . . . . . . . .
TITLE:.........MRS........................    :                      :
                                              :                      :
SURNAME:.......COPLEY.....................    :    LM043             :
                                              :                      :
INITIALS:......C..........................    :                      :
                                              :. . . . . . . . . . . :

ADDRESS:.......14 BATTINSON STREET.........................

:.............LINCOLN...................................

:.............LN1 2FG...................................

:.............LINCOLNSHIRE..............................


TELEPHONE: NO



BANK ACCOUNT NUMBER: NO

BANK SORT CODE:......................................

:..................................... BANK LIMITED

ADDRESS:............................................

:...................................................

:...................................................

:...................................................


CREDIT CARDS:  NO

ACCESS .............................................

BARCLAYCARD ........................................

AMERICAN EXPRESS ...................................

DINERS CLUB ........................................
```

Figure 8.51 Acme mail order – Agent record card.

CATALOGUE DETAILS REPORT

PRODUCT	PAGE	DESCRIPTION
AM/12300	23	ELECTRIC TOASTER

Colour: WHITE or CHROME

Price: £15.99 (69p per week over 26 weeks)

Crisp toast with your breakfast is
guaranteed with this smart toaster that
would grace any kitchen.

PRODUCT	PAGE	DESCRIPTION
AM/11302	23	ELECTRIC UNDER BLANKET

Colour: BEIGE or BLUE or PINK or WHITE

Price: SINGLE #49.99 (£1.99 over 26 weeks), DOUBLE £52.99
(£2.11 over 26 weeks, £1.07 over 52 weeks), KING SIZE £55.99
(£2.23 over 26 weeks, £1.13 over 52 weeks)

A delightful way to make sure that you
sleep well during those cold winter
nights.

PRODUCT	PAGE	DESCRIPTION
PE/13445	50	VINYL CASSETTE HOLDER

Colour: RED or BLACK or WHITE

Price: £10.99 (49p over 26 weeks)

Music anywhere ... anytime with the
smart, waterproof cassette holder to
carry up to 25 compact cassettes

PRODUCT	PAGE	DESCRIPTION
QW/0244	36	GIRLS' FASHION SKIRT

Colour: BLACK or BLUE or BROWN or WHITE

Size: SMALL or MEDIUM

Price: £15.99 (69p per week over 26 weeks)

Be the envy of your friends with this
smart - yet stylish - addition to your
playtime wardrobe

Figure 8.52 Acme mail order – Catalogue details report.

```
                      CUSTOMER ACCOUNT CARD

AGENT NUMBER ......LM043..............................

CUSTOMER NUMBER ...LM04300...........................

I DATE    I VOUCHER NUMBER   I DEBIT  I CREDIT I BALANCE I
I_____I_____I_____I_____I_____I
I26/7/88 I Order D799        I 47.98  I        I 47.98   I
I_____I_____I_____I_____I_____I
I31/7/87 I MD 920            I        I 5.00   I 42.98   I
I_____I_____I_____I_____I_____I
I         I                  I        I        I         I
I_____I_____I_____I_____I_____I
I         I                  I        I        I         I
I_____I_____I_____I_____I_____I
I         I                  I        I        I         I
I_____I_____I_____I_____I_____I
I         I                  I        I        I         I
I_____I_____I_____I_____I_____I
I         I                  I        I        I         I
I_____I_____I_____I_____I_____I
I         I                  I        I        I         I
I_____I_____I_____I_____I_____I
I         I                  I        I        I         I
I_____I_____I_____I_____I_____I
```

Figure 8.53 Acme mail order – Customer account card.

- a DELIVERY NOTE (Fig. 8.57)
- an INVALID ORDER LETTER (Fig. 8.58)
- an ITEM DELIVERY NOTE (Fig. 8.59)
- a MONEY DISPATCH FORM (Fig. 8.60)
- a ORDER PICKING LIST (Fig. 8.61)
- a PRICE CHANGE NOTIFICATION (Fig. 8.62)
- a PURCHASE ORDER (Fig. 8.63)
- a RETURNED GOODS VOUCHER (Fig. 8.64)
- a STOCK RECORD CARD (Fig. 8.65)
- a STOCK REORDER FORM (Fig. 8.66)
- a STOCK REPORT (Fig. 8.67)
- a STOCK SALES REPORT (Fig. 8.68)
- a SUPPLIER RECORD CARD (Fig. 8.69)
- an UNFILLED ITEMS FORM (Fig. 8.70)

CUSTOMER ORDER FORM

```
                                              ---------------
                                              | ORDER NO    |
AGENT NUMBER  :........LMO43.................  |             |
                                              |             |
CUSTOMER NUMBER  :.....LMO4301...............  |             |
                                              |   D 799     |
CUSTOMER NAME  :.......MRS R WOOD............  |             |
                                              |             |
DATE:.......24 JULY 1987...................   |_____|
```

Please deliver the undermentioned goods to my home address

:.........16 BATTINSON STREET................................

:.........LINCOLN...

:.........LN1 2FG...

CATALOGUE NUMBER	SIZE	COLOUR	QUANTITY	PRICE	TOTAL
AM 12300		WHITE	1	15.99	15.99
DESCRIPTION ELECTRIC TOASTER					
VS 4865	SMALL	BLUE	1	31.99	31.99
DESCRIPTION MEN'S FASHION COAT					
DESCRIPTION					
DESCRIPTION					
DESCRIPTION					
DESCRIPTION					

```
                           TOTAL VALUE OF THIS ORDER | 47.98 |
                                                     |_____|
SIGNED .......MRS R WOOD.................................
```

Figure 8.54 Acme mail order – Customer order form.

```
                    CUSTOMER REMINDER LETTER

Customer Number: AW03309

Mrs Watson,
123 Henderson Villas,
Devenish,
DV5 5RT.

12Th February 1984

Dear Mrs Watson,

        Our records show that you have made no payments on your
Acme Mail Order Company account since  10th October, 1983.
We feel sure that this is an oversight on your part.

        We look forward to receiving your payments within the
next seven days.

        If this is not received, then we shall have no
alternative but to take swift and forceful action to recover
the debt.

        If you have made any payments since the date of this
letter, then please ignore this reminder.

        I remain,

        Yours sincerely,




GEOFFREY LAWSON
Manager
Accounts Department,
Acme Mail Order Company
```

Figure 8.55 Acme mail order – Customer reminder letter.

                        CUSTOMER STATEMENT

AGENT NUMBER: LM043

CUSTOMER NUMBER: LM 04301

Mrs R.Wood
16 Battinson Street,
Lincoln,
Lincolnshire,
LN1 2FG.

28 July 1987

Dear Mrs Wood,

We thank you for your recent valued order, and have pleasure
in sending you details of your account to date.

DATE	NEW ORDER VALUE	BALANCE
		O
26/7/87	47.98	47.98

We thank you again for your support and your interest in the
ACME MAIL ORDER COMPANY, and its products.

I remain,

Yours sincerely,

Geoffrey Lawson
Manager
Accounts Department,
Acme Mail Order Company

Figure 8.56 Acme mail order – Customer statement.

PACKING DELIVERY NOTE

CUSTOMER NUMBER _____

CUSTOMER NAME _____

```
    ----------------
    I  D.N. NO  I
    I           I
    I           I
    I           I
    I_____I
```

DELIVERY ADDRESS _____

_____

_____

_____

CATALOGUE NUMBER	DESCRIPTION	QUANTITY	PRICE	TOTAL

CARRIER _____

Figure 8.57 Acme mail order – Packing delivery note.

INVALID ORDER LETTER

Customer Number: .....number.....

M.....name.....,
.....street.....,
.....town.....,
.....county.....,
.....post code.....

.....Date.....

Dear .....name.....,

I enclose a copy of your recent valued order.

You will note that certain items cannot be supplied for the
reasons stated there. The Acme Mail Order Company has
credited your account with the value of the item(s)
concerned.

I remain,

Yours sincerely,

GEOFFREY LAWSON
Manager
Accounts Department,
Acme Mail Order Company

Figure 8.58 Acme mail order – Invalid order letter.

ITEM DELIVERY NOTE

IDN NUMBER :_____

CUSTOMER NUMBER :_____

CUSTOMER NAME :_____

ADDRESS:_____

_____

_____

_____

ORDER NUMBER :_____

DATED:_____

PRODUCT NUMBER   DESCRIPTION   QUANTITY

PARCEL NUMBER :_____

Figure 8.59 Acme mail order – Item delivery note.

MONEY DISPATCH FORM

```
                              ┌─────────────────────┐
                              │                     │
                              │      MD 920         │
                              └─────────────────────┘

AGENT NUMBER  .....LM043.............................

AGENT NAME  .......MRS C COPLEY......................

│ CUSTOMER │ CUSTOMER NAME        │ AMOUNT RECEIVED │
│ NUMBER   │                      │                 │
│──────────│──────────────────────│─────────────────│
│ LM04301  │ MRS R WOOD           │      5.00       │
│──────────│──────────────────────│─────────────────│
│          │                      │                 │
│──────────│──────────────────────│─────────────────│
│          │                      │                 │
│──────────│──────────────────────│─────────────────│
│          │                      │                 │
│──────────│──────────────────────│─────────────────│
│          │                      │                 │
│──────────│──────────────────────│─────────────────│
│          │                      │                 │
│──────────│──────────────────────│─────────────────│
│          │                      │                 │
│──────────│──────────────────────│─────────────────│
│          │                      │                 │
│──────────│──────────────────────│─────────────────│
│          │                      │                 │
│──────────│──────────────────────│─────────────────│
│          │                      │                 │
│──────────│──────────────────────│─────────────────│
│          │                      │                 │
│──────────│──────────────────────│─────────────────│
                                  │                 │
DATE  ....31/7/87........   TOTAL │      5.00       │
                                  └─────────────────┘
```

Figure 8.60 Acme mail order – Money dispatch form.

```
                        ORDER PICKING LIST

     ORDER NUMBER    ......................................

     CUSTOMER NUMBER  .....................................

     CUSTOMER NAME    ......................................

     DATE  ................................................

     I ITEM NUMBER I DESCRIPTION  I BAY  I RACK  I QTY I
     I_____I_____I_____I_____I_____I
     I             I            I     I      I      I     I
     I_____I_____I_____I_____I_____I
     I             I            I     I      I      I     I
     I_____I_____I_____I_____I_____I
     I             I            I     I      I      I     I
     I_____I_____I_____I_____I_____I
     I             I            I     I      I      I     I
     I_____I_____I_____I_____I_____I
     I             I            I     I      I      I     I
     I_____I_____I_____I_____I_____I
     I             I            I     I      I      I     I
     I_____I_____I_____I_____I_____I
     I             I            I     I      I      I     I
     I_____I_____I_____I_____I_____I
     I             I            I     I      I      I     I
     I_____I_____I_____I_____I_____I
     I             I            I     I      I      I     I
     I_____I_____I_____I_____I_____I
     I             I            I     I      I      I     I
     I_____I_____I_____I_____I_____I
     I             I            I     I      I      I     I
     I_____I_____I_____I_____I_____I
```

Figure 8.61 Acme mail order – Order picking list.

                        PRICE CHANGE NOTIFICATION

     Dear Agent,

     The following prices will be effective as from 1st March
     next. Please be sure to use the new prices for all order
     placed on or after that date.

     Please let your customers know the good news.

PRODUCT	PAGE	DESCRIPTION	OLD PRICE	NEW PRICE
AM/12300	23	WHITE ELECTRIC TOASTER	15.00	13.50
AM/12301	23	ELECTRIC UNDER BLANKET	49.00	48.00
AM/12302	23	ELECTRIC OVER BLANKET	50.00	56.00
PE/13445	50	VINYL CASSETTE HOLDER	10.00	9.00
PE/32211	51	VIDEO CASSETTE CARRIER	7.00	6.50

     Yours faithfully,

     GEOFFREY LAWSON

     ACME MAIL ORDER COMPANY

Figure 8.62 Acme mail order – Price change notification.

```
                    PURCHASE ORDER

FROM: ACME MAIL ORDER COMPANY

OUR REFERENCE NUMBER : PO NUMBER.....................

TO :...............................................

.......................................................

.......................................................

.......................................................

YOUR REFERENCE NUMBER :.............................

Pleae supply the following items as agreed in our recent
telephone conversation.  Payment is enclosed.

I PRODUCT I DESCRIPTION            I QTY I PRICE I COST I
I NUMBER  I                        I     I       I      I
```

Figure 8.63 Acme mail order – Purchase order.

RETURNED GOODS VOUCHER

```
CUSTOMER NUMBER  . . . . . . . . . . . . . . . . . . . . . . . |   RGV  NO  |
                                                              |            |
CUSTOMER NAME  . . . . . . . . . . . . . . . . . . . . . . . |            |
                                                              |            |
ADDRESS. . . . . . . . . . . . . . . . . . . . . . . . . . . |            |
                                                              |            |
 . . . . . . . . . . . . . . . . . . . . . . . . . . . . . . |_____|

 . . . . . . . . . . . . . . . . . . . . . . . . . . . . . . . . . . . . . .

 . . . . . . . . . . . . . . . . . . . . . . . . . . . . . . . . . . . . . .

ORDER NUMBER  . . . . . . . . . . . . . . . . . . . . . . . . . . . . . . . .

DATED. . . . . . . . . . . . . . . . . . . . . . . . . . . . . . . . . . . .

PRODUCT NUMBER      DESCRIPTION              QUANTITY
```

Figure 8.64 Acme mail order – Returned goods voucher.

```
                    STOCK RECORD CARD
  PRODUCT CODE .......................................

  DESCRIPTION ........................................

  SIZE .............................................

  COLOUR ...........................................

  RE-ORDER LEVEL ....................................

  RE-ORDER QUANTITY .................................

  BAY ..................... RACK ...................

  I DATE   I ORDER NUMBER   I QUANTITY   I QUANTITY IN I
  I        I               I            I STOCK        I
  I_____I_____I_____I_____I
  I        I               I            I              I
  I_____I_____I_____I_____I
  I        I               I            I              I
  I_____I_____I_____I_____I
  I        I               I            I              I
  I_____I_____I_____I_____I
  I        I               I            I              I
  I_____I_____I_____I_____I
  I        I               I            I              I
  I_____I_____I_____I_____I
  I        I               I            I              I
  I_____I_____I_____I_____I
  I        I               I            I              I
  I_____I_____I_____I_____I
  I        I               I            I              I
  I_____I_____I_____I_____I
  I        I               I            I              I
  I_____I_____I_____I_____I
```

Figure 8.65 Acme mail order – Stock record card.

```
                    STOCK RE-ORDER FORM

  TO: ACCOUNT DEPARTMENT

  FROM: WAREHOUSE

  Please re-order the following item:

  PRODUCT NUMBER :_____

  PRODUCT NAME :_____

  RE-ORDER QUANTITY :_____

  SIGNED :_____
```

Figure 8.66 Acme mail order – Stock re-order form.

STOCK REPORT

CODE....	DESCRIPTION.........	COLOUR	SIZE......	MIN LEVEL	ORDER QTY	BAY	RACK	VALUE	STOCK	PRICE	26 WKS	52 WKS	
AM/12300	ELECTRIC TOASTER	SILVER		150	200	L21	71	4205.37	263	15.99	0.69		
AM/12300	ELECTRIC TOASTER	WHITE		150	200	L21	53	5124.17	383	15.99	0.69		
								10329.54					
AM/12301	ELECTRIC UNDER BLANKET	BEIGE	DOUBLE	70	100	A2	51	9432.22	178	52.99	2.11	1.07	
AM/12301	ELECTRIC UNDER BLANKET	BEIGE	KING SIZE	70	100	B39	28	8790.43	157	55.99	2.23	1.13	
AM/12301	ELECTRIC UNDER BLANKET	BEIGE	SINGLE	70	100	B74	46	9748.05	195	49.99	1.99		
AM/12301	ELECTRIC UNDER BLANKET	BLUE	DOUBLE	70	100	E76	32	10280.06	194	52.99	2.11	1.07	
AM/12301	ELECTRIC UNDER BLANKET	BLUE	KING SIZE	70	100	E99	32	7614.64	136	55.99	2.23	1.13	
AM/12301	ELECTRIC UNDER BLANKET	BLUE	SINGLE	70	100	A47	13	4699.06	94	49.99	1.99		
AM/12301	ELECTRIC UNDER BLANKET	PINK	DOUBLE	70	100	D17	86	3020.43	57	52.99	2.11	1.07	
AM/12301	ELECTRIC UNDER BLANKET	PINK	KING SIZE	70	100	D94	58	9182.36	164	55.99	2.23	1.13	
AM/12301	ELECTRIC UNDER BLANKET	PINK	SINGLE	70	100	C35	7	7998.40	160	49.99	1.99		BELOW STOCK
AM/12301	ELECTRIC UNDER BLANKET	WHITE	DOUBLE	70	100	C37	45	5669.93	107	52.99	2.11	1.07	
AM/12301	ELECTRIC UNDER BLANKET	WHITE	KING SIZE	70	100	E21	77	7446.67	133	55.99	2.23	1.13	
AM/12301	ELECTRIC UNDER BLANKET	WHITE	SINGLE	70	100	A19	54	5598.88	112	49.99	1.99		
								89481.13					
VS/4865	MEN'S FASHION COAT	BLACK	EXTRALARGE	70	100	B42	96	4894.47	153	31.99	1.30		
VS/4865	MEN'S FASHION COAT	BLACK	LARGE	70	100	C3	2	5566.26	174	31.99	1.30		BELOW STOCK
VS/4865	MEN'S FASHION COAT	BLACK	MEDIUM	70	100	D98	53	5790.19	181	31.99	1.30		
VS/4865	MEN'S FASHION COAT	BLACK	SMALL	70	100	E20	14	2079.35	65	31.99	1.30		
VS/4865	MEN'S FASHION COAT	BLUE	EXTRALARGE	70	100	A38	22	4766.51	149	31.99	1.30		
VS/4865	MEN'S FASHION COAT	BLUE	LARGE	70	100	C25	6	3390.94	106	31.99	1.30		
VS/4865	MEN'S FASHION COAT	BLUE	MEDIUM	70	100	A99	78	4158.70	130	31.99	1.30		
VS/4865	MEN'S FASHION COAT	BLUE	SMALL	70	100	B56	35	6366.01	199	31.99	1.30		
VS/4865	MEN'S FASHION COAT	BROWN	EXTRALARGE	70	100	C26	75	2367.26	74	31.99	1.30		
VS/4865	MEN'S FASHION COAT	BROWN	LARGE	70	100	A71	20	3934.77	123	31.99	1.30		
VS/4865	MEN'S FASHION COAT	BROWN	MEDIUM	70	100	A76	91	2975.07	93	31.99	1.30		
VS/4865	MEN'S FASHION COAT	BROWN	SMALL	70	100	B37	51	2655.17	83	31.99	1.30		
VS/4865	MEN'S FASHION COAT	WHITE	EXTRALARGE	70	100	E1	45	4382.63	137	31.99	1.30		
VS/4865	MEN'S FASHION COAT	WHITE	LARGE	70	100	D15	16	2015.37	63	31.99	1.30		BELOW STOCK
VS/4865	MEN'S FASHION COAT	WHITE	MEDIUM	70	100	A13	36	6142.08	192	31.99	1.30		
VS/4865	MEN'S FASHION COAT	WHITE	SMALL	70	100	B86	27	6046.11	189	31.99	1.30		
								67530.89					
								167341.56					

Figure 8.67 Acme mail order – Stock report.

```
                          STOCK REPORT

CODE.... DESCRIPTION..........  COLOUR SIZE......  LAST  THIS  DIFF    VALUE.
                                                   WEEK  WEEK          THIS WK

AM/12300 ELECTRIC TOASTER       SILVER              62    49   <13>    783.51
AM/12300 ELECTRIC TOASTER       WHITE               61    66    5     1055.34
                                                   ----  ----        ---------
                                                   123   115         1838.85
                                                   ----  ----        ---------

AM/12301 ELECTRIC UNDER BLANKET BEIGE  DOUBLE       18    17   <1>     900.83
AM/12301 ELECTRIC UNDER BLANKET BEIGE  SINGLE       15    19    4      949.81
AM/12301 ELECTRIC UNDER BLANKET BEIGE  KING SIZE    13    13    0      727.87
AM/12301 ELECTRIC UNDER BLANKET BLUE   DOUBLE       14    19    5     1006.81
AM/12301 ELECTRIC UNDER BLANKET BLUE   SINGLE       15    17    2      849.83
AM/12301 ELECTRIC UNDER BLANKET BLUE   KING SIZE    13    15    2      839.85
AM/12301 ELECTRIC UNDER BLANKET PINK   DOUBLE       13    13    0      688.87
AM/12301 ELECTRIC UNDER BLANKET PINK   SINGLE       20    14   <6>     699.86
AM/12301 ELECTRIC UNDER BLANKET PINK   KING SIZE    16    16    0      895.84
AM/12301 ELECTRIC UNDER BLANKET WHITE  DOUBLE       15    13   <2>     688.87
AM/12301 ELECTRIC UNDER BLANKET WHITE  SINGLE       19    12   <7>     599.88
AM/12301 ELECTRIC UNDER BLANKET WHITE  KING SIZE    15    12   <3>     671.88
                                                   ----  ----        ---------
                                                   186   180         ?520.20
                                                   ----  ----        ---------

VS/4865  MEN'S FASHION COAT     BLACK  LARGE        28    22   <6>     703.78
VS/4865  MEN'S FASHION COAT     BLACK  MEDIUM       31    28   <3>     895.72
VS/4865  MEN'S FASHION COAT     BLACK  SMALL        29    26   <3>     831.74
VS/4865  MEN'S FASHION COAT     BLACK  EXTRALARGE   29     0  <29>       0.00
VS/4865  MEN'S FASHION COAT     BLUE   LARGE        30    23   <7>     735.77
VS/4865  MEN'S FASHION COAT     BLUE   MEDIUM       30    27   <3>     863.73
VS/4865  MEN'S FASHION COAT     BLUE   SMALL        31    27   <4>     863.73
VS/4865  MEN'S FASHION COAT     BLUE   EXTRALARGE   26    22   <4>     703.78
VS/4865  MEN'S FASHION COAT     BROWN  LARGE        27    25   <2>     799.75
VS/4865  MEN'S FASHION COAT     BROWN  MEDIUM       28    28    0      895.72
VS/4865  MEN'S FASHION COAT     BROWN  SMALL        31    36    5     1151.64
VS/4865  MEN'S FASHION COAT     BROWN  EXTRALARGE   31    25   <6>     799.75
VS/4865  MEN'S FASHION COAT     WHITE  LARGE        31    27   <4>     863.73
VS/4865  MEN'S FASHION COAT     WHITE  MEDIUM       26    22   <4>     703.78
VS/4865  MEN'S FASHION COAT     WHITE  SMALL        30    20  <10>     639.80
VS/4865  MEN'S FASHION COAT     WHITE  EXTRALARGE   29    28   <1>     895.72
                                                   ----  ----        ---------
                                                   467   386        12348.14
                                                   ----  ----        ---------

                                                   ====  ====        =========
                                                   776   681        23707.19
                                                   ====  ====        =========
```

Figure 8.68 Acme mail order – Stock sales report.

SUPPLIER RECORD CARD

SUPPLIER CODE _____

NAME _____

ADDRESS _____

_____

PRODUCT NUMBER	PRICE		PRODUCT NUMBER	PRICE

DATE ORDERED	P.O.NUMBER	QUANTITY	DATE RECEIVED

Figure 8.69 Acme mail order – Supplier record card.

```
                    UNFILLED ITEMS LETTER

Customer Number: AC055

Mr W.Watkins,
109, Main Avenue,
Halifax,
HX99 9RX
West Yorkshire,

23 July, 1988

Dear Mr Watkins,

We thank you for your recent valued order, but we regret
that the undermentioned items are not available in our
Warehouse.

We expect to have a further stock of these within the next
four weeks, and we hope that you will care to submit an
order then.  In the meantime, the ACME MAIL ORDER COMPANY
has credited your account with the value of the item(s)
concerned.

Yours sincerely,

GEOFFREY LAWSON

ACME MAIL ORDER COMPANY

================== ITEMS OUT OF STOCK ==================

I PRODUCT CODE I DESCRIPTION                                I
I_____I_____I
I              I                                           I
I  AM/12301    I  BEIGE ELECTRIC UNDER BLANKET             I
I_____I_____I
I              I                                           I
I_____I_____I
I              I                                           I
I_____I_____I
I              I                                           I
I_____I_____I
I              I                                           I
I_____I_____I
```

Figure 8.70 Acme mail order – Unfilled items letter.

CASE STUDY 4: ACME DISCOUNT WAREHOUSE

You have been called in by the management of the Acme Mail Order Company in York. They have asked you to design a computer system to support a new series of trade outlets – to be known as the Acme Discount Warehouses – which they are planning.

They already offer a mail order service, as we saw in the previous case study. Now they intend to open a number of discount warehouses from which they will sell their products direct to the public.

8.24   THE BACKGROUND

Mr Geoffrey Lawson is manager of the Accounts Department at the Acme Mail Order Company's Head Office:

The products which we shall sell at the discount warehouses are identical to those available by mail order. The only difference is that they are only sold for cash – or credit card. The customers cannot pay by installments as they can with goods bought from the catalogue.

We plan to open six warehouses at first. Each will be independent, and each will have its own mini-computer to handle the stock. The minis won't link up to the large system which handles the mail order.

What will happen is this: a customer goes to the warehouse – it's a big store really – music, café, somewhere to put the kids – and chooses the product she wants to buy. Then she goes to a customer terminal to check the availability and the price. This is a VDU with a simple numeric keypad – this means we shall have to re-code the product-codes which we use on the main computer system because they've got letters and numbers. If that's OK, then the customer completes a simple order form – I'd like you to design that: something simple, just the code for the goods, the price, and the quantity. We'd also like to get hold of their address so that we can send them a one of our catalogues in future. The customer then goes to a cashier at a cash-register, well it's actually a point-of-sales terminal linked into the mini, and they give the cashier their order form and pay for the goods. They can pay by cash, cheque, or by credit card. The computer displays the status of the goods to allow the cashier to check that the goods are available and the prices are correct. The order form, with the customer's name and address goes downstairs where a clerk types them in – in batches, I imagine – and they are added to the name and address file if they're not already there. If a customer goes to more than one of our shops, she'll probably get a catalogue from each of them, at least that's the way it looks to me. Can you do anything about this? While the customer is paying for the goods, the computer system will send a message down to the stores. This will tell the stores clerks what goods to send upstairs. The goods are then put on a conveyor belt and sent to the floor where the customer collects them. Can you think of any way, other than bits of paper, to make sure that the right goods go to the right customer at the delivery desk? If not, then the cashier could give the customer a receipt and the delivery clerk could stamp it when they hand over the goods.

We don't want any sophisticated stock control system. When a delivery of goods arrives, the clerks will add the goods into stock and inform the computer system. As

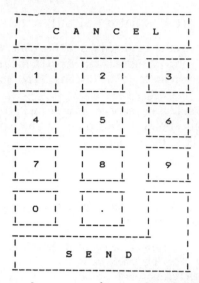

Figure 8.71 Acme discount warehouse – Customer terminal keypad.

goods are sold, the computer will keep a record. If stock levels are low, then the computer will produce an end-of-day report for the clerks, and they will contact my department who will do the re-ordering.

Can you help us?

8.25   TECHNICAL NOTE

The numeric keypad which is used by the customers when they are enquiring about the stock of goods looks like that shown in Fig. 8.71. There are ten numeric keys and a decimal point, together with a **SEND** and a **CANCEL** key. The screen can display up to twenty lines of forty alphanumeric characters and will be supported by **QCOMMS** communications software.

The cashiers' terminals have input similar to that of the customers' keypad – thirteen keys. The display is just one line of forty alphanumeric characters of text.

Appendix A: Further reading

There are a great many books on the structured topics which we have covered. The following are valuable.

DAHL, O.J., DIJKSTRA, A.W. and HOARE, C.A.R. (1972) *Structured Programming*, Academic Press, New York.

DE MARCO, T. (1978) *Structured Analysis and System Specification*. Yourdon, London.

GANE, C. and SARSON, T. (1977) *Structured Systems Analysis: Tools and Techniques*, IST Databooks, New York.

JACKSON, M.A. (1975) *Principles of Program Design*, Academic Press, New York.

MARTIN, J. (1982) *Applications Development without Programmers*, Prentice-Hall, Englewood Cliffs, NJ.

MARTIN, J. and McCLURE, C. (1985) *Structured Techniques for Computing*, Prentice-Hall, Englewood Cliffs, NJ.

ORR, K. (1977) *Structured Systems Development*, Yourdon, London.

PAGE-JONES, M. (1980) *Practical Guide to Structured Systems Design*, Yourdon, London.

YOURDON, E. and CONSTANTINE, L. (1979) *Structured Design*, Prentice-Hall, Englewood Cliffs, NJ.

Appendix B: Glossary

In this Appendix, we define some of the terms which you may encounter in the present book and elsewhere in the literature of software engineering and structured techniques. The INDEX gives the meaning of acronyms which are used.

ACTIVITY: a task which consumes time and resources and which is necessary to proceed from one event to another.

ATTRIBUTE: a property or quality of an **entity** about which there is a need to record and hold data. The term is synonymous with the term **field** as used in other areas of data processing. A number of attributes represent an **item**.

COMPUTER BASED INFORMATION SYSTEM: an information system in which the computer forms an integral part of the system and provides for the flow and storage of information.

CONCEPTUAL MODELLING: the first stage of design which identifies the information which is used by the organization. Until the later **logical model** and **physical model**, no attempt is made to represent the information and data physically.

DATA: any collection of letters, numbers and other symbols which represents the **information** resources that are held by or that refer to any organization or its activities.

DATA ANALYSIS: the analysis and structuring of information in order to produce a global data model representing the information needs of an organization.

DATA ITEM: one of the units of data, such as a field, a key or an attribute, that make up an entity.

DATA ITEM TYPE: a class of **data items**. Examples are name, age, address, price.

DATA MODEL: a logical representation of the data requirements of an organization – the global data model – or those of a specific functional area within an organization – a local data model.

DATA TYPE: the format or nature of the data which is held within an **attribute**. Examples are integer, alphanumeric string, integer less than 100.

DATABASE: a collection of stored data, organized in such a way that it satisfies all the data requirements of an organization. In general, there is only one copy of each item of data within the database.

ENTITY: an object or a concept which is meaningful to an organization and about which there is a need to record and hold data. The term is also used to denote the groups of data which are held about such objects or concepts, and for this reason, an entity corresponds to a file at a physical level. See also EXTERNAL ENTITY.

EVENT: the receipt of information, often corresponding to the termination of one or more activities. An occurrence in the outside world which triggers a **process**.

EXTERNAL ENTITY: a source or recipient of data which lies outside the boundary of a specific system. In a general case, examples might be Customer and Supplier. If a Stock Control System is under consideration, then the Wages Department might be an external entity. See also ENTITY.

FACILITY: the basic unit of functionality. A single facility performs the processing associated with a single event within the application (real-time facilities) or with the triggering of a batch run. Usually each facility will be called up by making a menu option.

FIFTH GENERATION LANGUAGE: very high-level end-user-oriented problem-solving tools, which accept a set of rules relating to a certain situation and then make decisions and produce results by interpreting these rules. The term is used as a synonym for **expert systems.**

FIRST GENERATION LANGUAGE: low-level machine-oriented language which includes the switch setting and machine code by which the first electronic computers were controlled.

FIRST NORMAL FORM: of data during DATA NORMALIZATION is produced by removing repeating data groups from the entity.

FOURTH GENERATION LANGUAGE: very high-level application-oriented tools for systems design and development. Examples are FOCUS and PRO IV.

FUNCTIONAL ANALYSIS: the analysis of the data and the ways in which they are associated, and of the processing requirements of functional areas, disregarding any physical constraints or limitations.

FUNCTIONAL AREA: that part of an organization which performs a separately identifiable function. In a small organization, these may have names such as **ACCOUNTS** or **WAGES**, but in a larger organization they may be further subdivided. **NEW ACCOUNTS, CUSTOMER QUERIES, SALES ORDERS OR PURCHASING.**

GLOBAL DATA MODEL: a logical representation of the total data requirements of an organization. It represents the combined **local data models** for the several **functional areas** of the organization.

INFORMATION: any form of communication which provides understandable and useful knowledge for the person receiving it, and is derived by placing a structure upon the **data** to which that person has access.

INFORMATION ENGINEERING: the application of techniques for analysing the data requirements of the organization, for designing the files that hold those data, and for providing means by which they can be made accessible to programs and end-users alike.

INFORMATION SYSTEM: a means of catering for the flow and storage of information, so as to satisfy the requirements of all users.

ITEM: synonymous with the term **record** as used in other areas of data processing. A file is made up of one or more **items.** Each item may comprise one or more attributes.

KNOWLEDGE: the benefit which a person or organization derives by placing an interpretation or a set of rules upon the **information** to which it has access.

LOCAL DATA MODEL: a logical representation of the data requirements of a specific functional area within an organization. The several local data models are combined to produce the **global data model** for the organization.

LOGICAL: as contrasted with physical, indicates the effect rather than the operation or the method of implementation.

MANAGEMENT INFORMATION: that information which is used to control and monitor the performance of an organization.

NORMALIZATION: a step-by-step procedure for analysing data into their constituent entities and attributes.

OPERATIONAL INFORMATION: that information which is required for the regular operation of the activities of an organization.

PHYSICAL: as contrasted with logical, indicates the method of implementation or the actual use rather than the pure effect.

PLANNING INFORMATION: that information which is used to help plan and decide the future activities of an organization.

PROCESS: any operation which logically changes the contents of a data store or of a data flow, or which validates the contents of an input data flow. A process is triggered by an **event**.

ROUTINE: a single piece of computer executable code.

SECOND GENERATION LANGUAGE: low-level machine-oriented languages including Assembler, Usercode, and Autocoder.

SECOND NORMAL FORM: of data during DATA NORMALIZATION is produced by removing – from any entities which have a compound key – any attributes which are not functionally dependent upon the entire key.

SOFTWARE ENGINEERING: the application of rigorous methods and structured techniques to the production of reliable and maintainable software.

SUB-SYSTEM: a system which is one of several similar components of a larger system, and the largest unit of functionality that interacts with other parts of the system. In systems development, this term is usually applied when an application is being developed separately from others with which it will interact.

SYSTEM: an organized collection of parts – sub-systems – which are linked together so as to function as a unit with a common purpose or objective.

THIRD GENERATION LANGUAGE: high-level problem-oriented languages which include **BASIC, COBOL, FORTRAN, PL/1**, and **PASCAL**.

THIRD NORMAL FORM: of data during DATA NORMALIZATION is produced by removing from an entity any attributes which are functionally dependent upon other attributes.

TRANSACTION: the data that are received when an event occurs and which must be handled by the appropriate facility.

USER: a user of an information system is any individual or group of people who have requirements for providing input to the system or for receiving output from the system.

Index